AN AMERICAN ODYSSEY

Patricia A. Etter
Little Rock, Arkansas
August 3, 1983

Robert Brownlee, prior to 1876. *Courtesy, the Bancroft Library.*

An American Odyssey

THE AUTOBIOGRAPHY OF A 19TH-CENTURY SCOTSMAN, ROBERT BROWNLEE, AT THE REQUEST OF HIS CHILDREN.

NAPA COUNTY, CALIFORNIA

OCTOBER 1892

Edited by Patricia A. Etter

The University of Arkansas Press
Fayetteville   1986

Copyright © 1986 by The Board of Trustees of the University of Arkansas
The University of Arkansas Press, Fayetteville, Arkansas 72701
Library of Congress Catalog Card Number 85-8633
All Rights Reserved
Manufactured in the United States of America

Designer: Patricia Douglas Crowder
Typeface: Linotron 202 Janson
Typesetter: G & S Typesetters, Inc.
Printer: Thomson-Shore, Inc.
Binder: John H. Dekker & Sons, Inc.

This project is funded in part by a grant from the Arkansas Endowment for the Humanities.

The paper used in this publication meets the minimum requirements of the American National Standard for Permanence of Paper for Printed Library Materials Z39.48-1984. ∞

LIBRARY OF CONGRESS CATALOGING-IN-PUBLICATION DATA

Brownlee, Robert.
  An American odyssey.
  Bibliography: p.
  Includes index.
  1. Brownlee, Robert. 2. Scottish Americans—Biography. 3. Overland journeys to the Pacific. 4. Pioneers—California—Biography. 5. California—Biography. 6. California—History—1850–1950. 7. Little Rock (Ark.)—Biography. I. Etter, Patricia A., 1932– . II. Title.
E184.S3B76 · 1986   978'.0049163024   85-8633
ISBN 0-938626-53-1

To all Brownlee descendants, wherever they may be.

Contents

	Illustrations	ix
	Preface	xiii
CHAPTER I	Life in a Lowland Village	1
CHAPTER II	A Greenhorn in America	16
CHAPTER III	An Arkansas Traveler	28
CHAPTER IV	To See the Elephant	51
CHAPTER V	Ho! California!	90
CHAPTER VI	All That Glitters . . .	107
CHAPTER VII	Sentimental Journey	149
CHAPTER VIII	Forty Years in Napa Valley	165
APPENDIX I	Arkansas Emigrants	197
APPENDIX II	Southern Route Journals	207
	References Cited	221
	Index	233

List of Illustrations

Unless otherwise noted, photographs and illustrations are by the author.

FRONTICEPIECE	Robert Brownlee prior to 1876.
CENTER SECTION	Row Houses, Bonkle, Scotland.
	Alcath Cottage, Bonkle, Scotland.
	Whitebank, Allanton Road, Bonkle, Scotland.
	Old State House, Little Rock, Arkansas.
	The Brownlee House at Arkansas Territorial Restoration, Little Rock.
	Capped Rock, Guadalupe Canyon, New Mexico.
	Agua Fria Valley.
	The Brownlee family home, Sunnyside Farm.
	Annie Brownlee.
	Sunnyside Farm (1959).
	The Robert Brownlee Family.
MAPS	Route of the Little Rock Company, page 50.
	California Trail map, page 90.
	The Southern, Gila and Apache Pass trails, page 206.

AN AMERICAN ODYSSEY

Preface

On a March day in 1836, Robert Brownlee impulsively set aside his stonecutting tools and said, "I'm going to America." The young man from the Scottish Lowlands was as good as his word and, by May 11, was hard at work in New York.

Brownlee was one among thousands of immigrants who set foot expectantly on American shores in the 1830s and then worked to build and settle the country while new frontiers opened during an era of expansion. He neither achieved fame nor acquired great wealth, but he did leave a colorful story that recounts the major events in a long and diversified life.

Brownlee certainly knew how to turn a phrase, and through his words the American experience comes alive. At the same time, he serves as a lens through which we can observe the life and activities of a fast-growing nation. He is a classic example of an immigrant frontiersman who had to cope and adapt his skills through changing times. His recollections of travel on the Southern Trail in 1849 and subsequent sojourn in the California mines reflects his experiences, and also becomes the story of countless others.

We can be grateful that his daughters encouraged him to record these memoirs which he wrote in 1892. One of his daughters typed at least two copies of the autobiography (the volume I have worked from appears to be a carbon copy), and had them leather-bound for safekeeping. In the late 1930s or early 1940s, a Brownlee granddaughter, Mrs. Bessie Leitch of Sacramento, allowed the Bancroft Library to make a typescript of her volume of the memoirs (I have not been able to locate the Leitch copy). My grandmother, the late Margaret Russell Ross of Winnipeg, Canada, and a Brownlee great-niece, gave her copy of the autobiography to my brother, Alex Waugh, in 1952 (we do not know how it came into her possession). Appreciation, therefore, must be extended to Brownlee descendants who preserved or gave family memorabilia and documents to the California Historical Society, the Bancroft Library, Sacramento Area Parks, and the California State Library.

I have altered the original text but little as the manuscript was retyped. Obvious typos and spelling errors were corrected and punctuation was changed for readability. The text was then divided into chapters and a few paragraphs were moved into proper sequence. Brownlee often referred to individuals by surname only. In these cases, I have bracketed initials or Christian names if identification was possible.

Research shows that Brownlee was amazingly accurate in recalling dates, names, and places, even though he wrote some forty years after the fact. Moreover, he tended to downplay his adventures. Wherever possible, I have drawn upon writings of his contemporaries, especially for the overland journey, when I was able to find manuscripts or published books written by men who were on the trail at approximately the same time.

Brownlee's is the first known history of the trip by the Little Rock (Arkansas) Company to the California goldfields in 1849. It is also one of a small number of journals and reminiscences that document travel to California on the Southern Trail, which took emigrants through Mexico, New Mexico, Arizona, and Southern California. Arkansas newspapers published many of the letters that Robert Brownlee and members of his company wrote home. Excerpts from some of these letters (including those written by Brownlee) have been previously published in several works illustrating the Southern Route by Ralph Bieber (1937), Owen Coy (1929), and Grant Foreman (1939). These texts, however, give little information about individual immigrants, whereas Brownlee's memoirs identify a number of Forty Niners and give them personalities as well.

Having decided that panning for gold was not the easiest way to earn a living, Brownlee opened a store and gambling house in the hamlet of Agua Fria, California, a town created overnight by the sudden influx of hundreds of newly-arrived gold-seekers. He offers some interesting vignettes on life in the now extinct mining town, as well as providing new information on the lives and personalities of James Savage, leader of the Mariposa Battalion, and Sheriff James Burney of Mariposa County. Mrs. Bertha Schroeder, a historian in Mariposa County, assisted my documentation and contributed many hours of archival research at the historic county courthouse. She also drove me through the countryside to point out sites mentioned by Brownlee in his memoirs.

As a California pioneer, Brownlee witnessed early days in Vallejo and Benicia when the two towns were vying to replace San Jose as state capital, and when squatters on the Soscol Ranch challenged his right to own property in Napa County in 1867. Mrs. Thelma Bachelor bought Brownlee's property from his descendants in 1945 and, in an interview, described the old Brownlee home in detail, adding reminiscences about family life on the ranch. She also supplied a photograph of the house as it appeared in 1959 before being destroyed by fire.

Brownlee's details about his birthplace raised many questions, and I am grateful to Janet and Nicholas Bull, who contacted residents in Bonkle, Scotland, and spent hours delving into Scottish archives. I visited the site in 1981, where long-time residents, Henry and Elsie Archibald, welcomed me into their 150-year-old home (built by Elsie's ancestors, the town joiners). They enthusiastically introduced me to present-day life in the former feudal village. Residents of Bonkle researched their deeds and opened their Brownlee-built homes to me. Mr. Peter Wilson and Mrs. Margaret Whitlock invited me to their apartments in former Brownlee row houses. Mrs. Margaret Russell and Mrs. Margaret Cringean gave me tea and allowed me to tour their homes, Alcath Cottage and Whitebank, which were also Brownlee-built. Betty Marshall of Wishaw came forward with copies of the Murdestoun School Bible. Townsmen welcomed me at Bonkle Church, which the Brownlee family had attended since 1818. The generous hospitality of these Scotsmen and their interest in the project of a stranger from California will never be forgotten.

As good fortune would have it, the house that Brownlee built in Little Rock, Arkansas, is now restored as a museum, and some of his stone and brickwork is still standing. Bill Worthen, director of the

Arkansas Territorial Restoration, Dr. Priscilla McArthur, Project Director, and Swannee Bennett, Research Curator, opened up their files to share their Brownlee research and to relate historical anecdotes on early Little Rock. In a sense, Robert Brownlee has returned to Little Rock, for my brother and I have sent our copy of his autobiography to Arkansas Territorial Restoration for permanent housing. I was also shown through Ten Mile House, Little Rock, and roamed the kitchen that Brownlee built for his friend, John McHenry, some time in the 1840s.

As I tried to learn more about an elusive part of the old emigrant trail, Guadalupe Pass, Rex McDonald and Marvin Follet of Douglas, Arizona, shared their knowledge of the area with me. I am particularly indebted to Diana Hadley, also of Douglas and owner of one of the ranches crossed by the trail. She extended western hospitality to me and my friend, Dr. Jane Rosenthal, helped saddle our horses, and guided us over an incredibly beautiful, but wild and rugged terrain to search for remains of the old trail between Guadalupe Canyon and the Animas Valley. As far as we know, we have been the first researchers to study the trail "on site," and the trip enabled me to redefine the emigrant trail over Guadalupe Pass, which has often been incorrectly traced on many published maps.

Ranger Donna Wells pointed out little seen portions of the emigrant trail still existing in Anza Borrego Desert State Park, California, and shared stories by our campfire about the trials and travails that emigrants must have suffered in that part of the California desert during the summer of '49.

Frances Bejan of New York devoted many hours of archival research to Brownlee's New York sojourn. Christine Hagan of Ancaster, Ontario, and Elisabeth Pace, London, Ontario, Canada, visited graveyards and archives to help identify Brownlee's Canadian kin. Juanita Knox at the California State University Library, Long Beach, found no request too difficult and was able to gather pertinent books and manuscripts from all over the country. David Robrock, Special Collections Librarian at the University of Arizona was an enormous help in locating rare materials. Anne Ross of Santa Monica and Dr. Jane Rosenthal of Long Beach read the copy for content and errors. Dr. Stephen Williams of Los Angeles analyzed and identified the rocks from Guadalupe Pass. Jess Doud of the Napa County Historical Society,

Estelle Rebec of the Bancroft Library, M. K. Swingle of the California Historical Society, and the staff of Sacramento Area Parks all helped locate Brownlee materials. The title for this book was suggested by my mentor and dear friend, Professor William S. Evans, Jr., of Santa Monica College, California.

I am no less grateful to Dr. Jeanne Muñoz of Long Beach, who first suggested that annotation of the manuscript would be a valuable addition to history; to Dr. Glenn S. Dumke, Chancellor Emeritus, California State University system, and author of *Mexican Gold Trail*, who shared information from his own research on the Southern Trail; and to Dr. Nicholas Hardeman, Professor of History, California State University, Long Beach, who has not only shown interest in the manuscript but has given valuable suggestions and consistent encouragement in the continuation of the work.

My husband, Paul, has shared my enthusiasm for this project and joined me in retracing Brownlee's travels. Over a period of years, he has driven thousands of miles, from Little Rock to Albuquerque, and into the back country of southwestern New Mexico, Arizona, and California, as we searched for vestiges of the old emigrant trail. We often pitched camp and hiked over considerable portions of the terrain.

The University of Arkansas Press and my patient editor, Katharine Villard, have provided constant encouragement and valuable editorial suggestions as the manuscript was being prepared for publication.

I have followed the American Anthropologist style guide, where referenced citations are placed in parentheses within the body of my text and not in separate notes, e.g., last name of author, year of publication of work referred to, volume number, if any, and pages cited (Smith 1983:IV:221–222). An alphabetical listing of these references follows the text.

CHAPTER I

Life in a Lowland Village

INTRODUCTION

Robert Brownlee was a typical Scotsman: thrifty, pragmatic, direct, hardworking, and adaptive. We learn that he was well educated for a boy of his day and had a native curiosity that often motivated him to action.

His personality and character were formed in the tiny rural village of Bonkle, which is nestled in a picturesque setting of rolling green hills and patchwork farms close to the River Clyde in the Scottish Lowlands. In his memoirs, Brownlee mentions that his native village was part of an estate and built in accordance with the owner's strict plan. This aroused my curiosity and prompted a study of Scotland's feudal estates and villages. It turned out that Bonkle was one of a number of planned communities designed by estate owners between 1730 and 1830, and was specifically created to improve the estate of Sir Henry Seton Steuart. Scottish scholars have identified 126 such villages and continue to study them in the context of social and economic changes occurring in the 1800s. They are also interested in how these villages were modified through time and in understanding the factors that may have contributed to their decline.

More importantly, perhaps, Brownlee gives a rare description of daily life in one of these towns. After comparing his statements about education, income, religion, and work, with statistical reports of the time, we learn that he came from a typical Scottish family of the artisan class. The Protestant Church was a major force in everyday life and expected obedience to its doctrines, though its discipline had relaxed somewhat during Brownlee's time. Brownlee had a strong belief in the work ethic, and like other young men of his day, was apprenticed to a trade. His sisters and other rural women worked in various cottage industries. Walking was the main form of transportation. One can hardly doubt that trudging tangled moor and village paths in the brisk (and sometimes harsh) Scottish climate helped prepare Brownlee for his American adventures.

By 1836, when Robert was 23, Scotland had passed through a century of widespread change as the predominantly agricultural and rural society transformed itself to a nation of industry. Miles of new roads brought hamlets out of isolation and into contact with nearby cities, resulting in greater mobility and opportunity for the workforce. Improved communication opened vistas upon the world, and news of opportunity in the United States, Canada, and Australia catered to young and restless spirits in an authoritarian society. Robert Brownlee was one who decided the time was right to expand his horizons.

THE JOURNAL

At the request of my daughters I undertake something which depends wholly upon early recollection and deep impressions, made upon me while a boy of but few years. And all seems as fresh in my memory as though it had happened but yesterday. For instance: I remember when I ran in petticoats. I could not have been more than three years old at the time. I was playing with the children on the road when the cry got up, "There's old Lillie Mackey the beggar woman." The children ran leaving me behind. I had a small pen knife in my hand when I fell and the point went into my forehead and when I went into the house my sister pulled it out but it proved nothing serious.

I can also remember when I first went to School I had on that memorable dress made in one piece of home made flannel, but at this time they had added legs, with a back door, and two large buttons (handy for any emergency). This was the general dress for boys at School. Well do I remember where certain birds had their nests, as we had to visit them twice a day, both going and coming from School, which was two miles distant. All such things had to be attended to, even though our lessons had to be neglected, which would compel the teacher to use the taas [tawse], a strap of leather having three legs, in all about twenty inches long. This punishment was given on the hand, and hurt at the time, but was soon forgotten.[1] I must admit I was always among the leaders in mischief and had to be watched, for I was always fond of playing marbles and tossing buttons, neglecting my lessons. Our teacher was an old man, having an attendance the year round of one hundred scholars. In those days nothing but goose quills were used for writing, and he had to mend nearly all of these, besides listen to questions, look over our different sums on the slate, and keep order. I have often wondered how he ever managed to get along with such a babble of sounds; yet he lived to be an old man, and some of the finest scholars perhaps received their education at the Parish School, and any one who attended to his lessons advanced rapidly as he was a man of learning—a natural teacher.[2]

Time has passed. I am now some eleven years old when I am hired out to my uncle for five dollars a year to herd cattle. He had about twenty head of young cattle, twelve sheep, with some horses. I must admit that was the hardest earned money and the hardest time I have ever experienced. In the months of June and July the cattle would start with their tails over their backs, each taking its own course, and to keep them within their limits was very hard to manage, and should they get on your neighbors' land (which was hard to prevent) you would be sure to hear from them when you reached home, with sore feet, bruised heels, and grass cuts, which is cracks under the toes and very sore.

Laird Steel's land was one of my march lines; a creek also marked that of another. The cattle would generally run for the water, where I considered them safe, but as soon as the sun would go down they would pass out on his side. They couldn't have done much mischief had they stayed an hour, but that was not his way of thinking. Not saying anything to me he would march over to my uncle and tell. As a boy I had an opinion of him and thought if ever I grew large enough I would thrash him. And let me state right here, I came very near doing it, when I went to Scotland from California in 1852. I was attending a dinner party where the same Laird Steel was one of the number; it was all I could do to refrain from openly insulting him. He seemed very friendly, but I proved as cold as I could and would have nothing to say to him, not even answering a direct question. After he left I told the party my reason and they thought I would have forgotten it.[3]

From herding I went and broke stone with my father, as he was a contractor for making Parish roads.[4] I think I worked some two summers with him when I was apprenticed to my brother William for three years to learn to be a stone cutter. Nothing of note happened as I liked the trade. I believe in Scotland today the highest wages are paid for this outdoor labor. I still continued to work for my brothers, William and Alexander (as they had formed a partnership),[5] until I emigrated to America in 1836. But I may as well state where and when I was born before I leave Scotland.

I was born in Bonkle, Cambusnethan Parish, Lanarkshire, Scotland, April 24th 1813. Perhaps I may be partial to my native village, but I always, and will still continue to think it one of the neatest, handsomest [villages], having the best buildings, kept in the best order, of any place I have ever seen. The reason is obvious as the gentleman who owns the estate would not allow any buildings put up unless according to his plan. The village is built in the fork of two roads, and in this fork he made an oval plot and set it out with forest trees, with a thorn hedge all round, kept cut short. The houses in my day numbered eleven, placed around this plot of timber, being made of cut stone, and one story high, with a pediment in front of each. Each place has about one acre of a garden, which goes a long way in raising a family, with all the vegetables, goose-berries, strawberries and onions that a family needed.[6]

Let me here present a family which is no exception to the many. They lived in one end of my father's house.[7] He was a laborer, had eight fine healthy boys, all too small to be of any help. His wages would be fifteen or sixteen pence a day, or thirty-six cents in summer and thirty cents in winter. You can imagine how hard it must be to make ends meet. He had to pay house rent and buy coal, yet the most astonishing thing is at Sunday at church they appear all well dressed. You may say they go in debt. They never think of that as the law allows the creditor to sell them out.[8] His wife tamboured, which is embroidering a piece of muslin stamped with the design you wish to make in a frame six foot long and eighteen inches wide or by putting a whole web on the roller and unwinding it as required. She was a very fast worker and with long hours earned as much as her husband.[9] (My sisters and cousins worked at flouring, which was done on two small hoops about six inches in diameter for average wages of ten to fifteen cents a day of fifteen hours each.)[10] Their food was of the very plainest kind: for breakfast, oatmeal porridge with butter milk; for dinner, boiled potatoes, salt and butter milk, with oatmeal cake and butter milk. For supper, boiled potatoes, salt and butter milk was the common food. On Sunday morning, perhaps tea and loaf bread with butter and a boiled egg.

In my father's family we lived much better, as we were all mechanics receiving three shillings, or seventy-five cents a day. My mother kept a cow, and we always killed a fat pig. Besides, my father bought and killed a fat steer for winter supply. So you can judge that we lived well—always had meat once a day, with butter and cheese thrown in.[11] Those were happy days. In my father's family there were ten children: six sons (three were stone cutters and three were blacksmiths) and four daughters.[12] I am the youngest but one. They are all dead but sister Grace, who is six years older than I and lives in Canada with her daughter. I am going in my eightieth year, and if she is as well preserved as I, it would be very remarkable.[13] I am writing this without the use of glasses of any kind, writing entirely from memory, possess fine health, can sleep seven hours as well as ever, and am always ready for my meals. There is one thing in which I am deficient. I cannot get about in walking, it being very hard on me as I am troubled with rheumatism.

In the section of country in which I lived they were all members of some church. There were four different denominations: The Established Church of Scotland, was where my father's family attended, then there was the old Cameronian, the very strict Christians attended this, you must not laugh or dance. Then the Relief Church which was also well attended, last the New Lights, which was the one I attended before I left Scotland. Pretty much every person is a member of some one of these churches, [and] observed the Sabbath day very closely.[14] Every member of the family goes, and in private, families worship twice a day, if the Master of the house is at home, otherwise at nights. I may as well acknowledge here, that I've fallen far short of my early training. Having mixed with the world so long, has made my heart callous to the teachings of my youth. Yet I believe as strongly in the

Hereafter and the teachings of the Presbyterian church as ever I did, but am ashamed to say that I do not practice, nor profess openly the teachings of Christ to my family, and my fellow men. I pray that I may be forgiven for my indifference.

My mother was rather an exceptionable woman, was kind and charitable, ever ready to assist the needy or those in distress; I think a true Christian. My father was very kind and charitable also but of quicker temperament than Mother. Still a very exemplary man in honesty, integrity and industry—a good provider.

NOTES TO CHAPTER I

1. In many conversations I was told that Scottish teachers still believe that use of the tawse is effective in administering discipline. The form of punishment, however, was banned from all schools in Britain in 1982.
2. Since 1690, almost every parish in the Scottish Lowlands had a schoolhouse, and by mid-18th century, the majority of citizens could read and write. According to a study by T. C. Smout (1969:453–461), this was an incredible achievement. Except for Prussia, Switzerland, and limited areas in the United States, no other country in the world could make such a claim. Children from Bonkle and nearby towns walked a winding road through the woods—heavily grown with holly bushes, Scottish spruce, beech and oak—to the Murdestoun Estate School. The shell of the schoolhouse building stands today, a large, two-story, sturdy stone structure. Attached are the remains of the schoolmaster's commodious apartment. Classrooms were on the second floor of the larger structure, where there are a number of good sized windows. Some openings have been bricked in on the ground floor; this may have been patchwork, however, for they do not appear to follow any pattern that would suggest doors or windows. The ground floor area may have served as a barn then as it does today. The fact that the schoolmaster coped with over 100 children was not unusual; enrollment was also high in other parishes, in spite of the fact that children paid tuition. In Cambusnethan Parish, this was 1/6d. (one shilling, sixpence) a quarter for English, 1/9d. for reading and writing, and 2/6d. each for Latin and arithmetic (Sinclair 1792:XII:568–574). The 1826 *Returns to Parliament on the State of Education* (Smout ibid) indicated that, in addition to the three R's, a professor with a good background would also see that a child studied some algebra, geography, bookkeeping, and perhaps French. Moral and religious training were an

important, integral part of a youngster's education, and the Bible was among the first reading assignments. Murdestoun School used an 1824 King James version, and a local resident had carefully preserved the two small volumes—leather bound in red—which bore the school name imprinted on the inside flap. A child started school when he was five-and-a-half years old and continued for the next ten years, depending on his family's need for extra wages. In Smout's study it was further stated that even the poorest of parents sent their children to school, at least part of the time, and got along without luxuries in order to do so. Robert Brownlee does not tell us how much schooling he received, nor if his first job at the age of eleven combined part-time work and classes. Certainly as artisans on the higher end of the wage scale, his family could well afford to keep him in school longer. An eleven-year-old working child was not an unusual occurrence, however. For example, in 132 parishes in 1843, the mean first age of employment was 11.2 years, especially in the weaving trades and among the poorer classes (Levitt 1979:106). Nevertheless, the consensus among many writers is that in spite of the short time Lowland students spent in school the system not only managed to open their intellectual horizons but graduated a peasantry that loved to read and write and continued to seek knowledge. Robert Brownlee exemplified this tradition.

3. Fewer than 100 families of noble birth held title to feudal estates in Scotland; the great majority of landowners were known as lairds and bonnet lairds, subvassals of the nobility. After 1745, the most common form of land tenure became known as "feuferme": a laird would pay a noble a cash sum (grassum) as down payment for property and then pay pre-determined rent or feu-duty, fixed in perpetuity (Smout 1969:135–144). It is likely that the Steel family took title to parish land in this manner. The family is still remembered in Bonkle. They not only figured prominently in the history of the local church but had long lived on a farm still known as Summerside several miles south of Bonkle. John Steel lived there during the period in question (Cambusnethan Parish *Census* 1841) and he may have had good reason for chastising young Robert. The dispute took place during a period of agrarian change when farmers enclosed their fields to keep livestock away from crops. Robert probably was hired to implement this process.

4. Up until 1750, there were few all-weather roads in western Scotland. As a matter of fact, Glasgow was almost isolated except for contact by sea. Overland travel was slow and arduous: twelve hours to Edinburgh by carriage; two days by cart. Roads that did exist were roughly graded clay and gravel tracks, which made travel difficult between country hamlets

(Slaven 1975:36–41). Robert Brownlee's father, Alexander, was born in 1762, a time when population growth, industrial expansion, agricultural improvements, and a thriving domestic and foreign trade created a need for better roads. He must have found steady employment, for during the succeeding 60 years, workers laid some 1100 miles of all-weather turnpike to serve the major towns. He probably worked on the parish road being laid on the south side of the River Clyde in 1792 (Sinclair 1792: XII:568–574), the same year he moved to Bonkle (Steuart 1792). If so, he surely used a new and radical construction technique which Scottish engineer John Loudon McAdam first proposed in 1787. In contrast to the belief that only a subbase of massive stones could stand up to heavy traffic, McAdam insisted that it was the native soil that supported traffic, and that roads should be built to keep the subsoil free of moisture. He proved this by smoothing thin layers of broken stone or cinders on dry subsoil, covering them with crushed stone. The resulting angular material overlapped in such a way as to give a good, solid, and hard surface (Slaven ibid). McAdam's roads could also be quickly constructed with a minimum of labor and later demonstrated that they could, indeed, successfully carry heavy loads without deteriorating. The new technology was soon adopted in Great Britain and in the United States. In 1825, U.S. roadbuilders first used McAdam's simple principles to complete a wilderness road between Cumberland, Maryland, and Wheeling, West Virginia (Owen 1967:103). The McAdam concept has been improved in the 20th century only by the addition of concrete or asphalt.

5. In 1843, stonemasons in the Lanarkshire area earned among the highest wages in Scotland—some twenty-one shillings a week (Levitt, Smout 1979:115). Although Robert Brownlee did not record it, Brownlee masons built many of Bonkle's houses. These are represented by three types of Georgian-style buildings, characteristic of early 19th-century Scottish architecture—the double cottage, the multi-unit row house, and the two room bungalow. Mrs. Margaret Russell has lived in one-half of a double cottage on Allanton Road, known as Alcath Cottage, which was built in 1817. (Many Bonkle houses were given names as were later Victorian dwellings.) In addition to its original three good-sized rooms and two garret bedrooms, the cottage now features a modern kitchen and bathroom in the rear, along with electricity and heating. Mrs. Russell has lovingly preserved the historical attributes of the house: wood floors with their inlaid design; inside shutters, mouldings, flowered ceiling cornices; and a small, iron wall safe, still in perfect working condition. Outbuildings are also intact, although yesterday's byre or cow house is today's garage. The Brownlees also built two one-story multi-unit row houses

across the village green on Church Road. Robert's grandfather, William, owned one and incised "1785-WB" on one of the lintels. His father, Alexander, built the other in 1792, and it was probably the building where Robert Brownlee was born. Following local tradition, owners have made major changes and additions only at the rear of these buildings. Each of the two row houses had four separate one-room apartments measuring 14 x 17 feet, with 9-foot ceilings. At one time, there were 26-inch wide alcoves for beds or bedclosets, typical of the time. All cooking was done over the fireplaces, accessible in each room. The two-room bungalow was not as common in earlier days, mostly for economic reasons, but there is one in the village that dates to 1816.

By the 1860s, many Brownlees had left Bonkle and much of the property was leased to others. Some time after 1870, however, Robert's bachelor brother Alexander (Sandy) began to build Whitebank, a ten room, two-story house on Allanton Road, where he lived with his niece, Agnes Thomson Brownlee, until his death in 1883 (Cambusnethan Parish *Census* 1871–1891). Agnes Brownlee had taken entry to the ground in 1870, according to her feu contract with Sir Henry James Seton Steuart, which was dated April 15, 1878 (Cringean 1982). Whitebank, like other homes in Bonkle, has a slate roof and two-foot-thick walls of locally quarried sandstone blocks. This house has a number of features that set it apart from its neighbors: stepped gables; double, pitch pine doors; and many decorative effects around the door and entryway. Original features are preserved inside as well, including a gently curving staircase and balustrade still in place and kept in polished condition by its owner. Robert Brownlee's spinster grandniece (daughter of Agnes Thomson Brownlee) lived out her life in this house and is still remembered by older residents as "the Miss Brownlee." As a matter of fact, it appears that Miss Brownlee purchased much of the Bonkle property when the estate was sold, for residents recall paying feu duty to her until her death. Whitebank is on the preservation roll as one of the best examples of early domestic Scottish architecture. With this house, the history of the Brownlees in Bonkle ends. Whitebank and other houses in Bonkle are links to the history of the early village and its inhabitants, remaining as tributes to the masonry skills of the men who built them.

6. Bonkle village has an interesting history. It is a lovely little town about 18 miles southeast of Glasgow and was formerly located on Allanton, a 2673-acre feudal estate that had passed to succeeding generations of the Darnley Steuarts since 1421 (Brown 1859). Brownlee's comments regarding the landlord's authority in the village generated a number of questions about Bonkle's origins, and subsequent research identified the town

as being planned and conceived by Sir Henry Seton Steuart (1739–1858) in the late 1700s. Bonkle may now be added to Dr. Christopher Smout's (1970:102–106, 1981) roster of 126 "planned villages." These were brand new towns, built between c. 1730 and c. 1830, designed to support a specific economy: agriculture and estate interests; rural industry; fishing or manufacturing. Such towns are found throughout Scotland, and according to Smout (1970:75), "these planned settlements assisted a revolution in the economy of the estate and the nation [and were] expected to provide a completely new framework for life in the countryside."

The Brownlee family played a significant part in this activity, and the results are very much in evidence in Cambusnethan Parish. Up to the time suggested by Smout, the feudal estate and its tower house had been an integral part of the Scottish countryside and provided a livelihood for peasants who cultivated the farmlands as joint tenants. Housing in the early days was primitive (Dunbar 1966:233), and farmers and laborers lived in rudimentary, thatched structures of wattle, clay, turf or stones with mud mortar. Sweeping agricultural innovations during the 18th century began to alter all of this, as landholdings were reorganized into enclosed farms and progressive farmers adopted new farming techniques. Moreover, economic changes catalyzed the need to stimulate trade and industry in rural areas and to provide employment for labor displaced by enclosure.

It was during this time (and Sir Henry was no exception) that lords and lairds began to replace outmoded towers with country mansions, surround them with large and beautiful "policies" (gardens), to plant woods over formerly barren, treeless areas, and encourage tenants to enclose farms. If a village was to be part of the plan, it would have sturdy stone-and-lime houses with roofs of slate, and would fit in as part of the original scheme. Landowners contemplating estate changes and enclosure would normally hire a surveyor to draw up plans. Very likely, Sir Henry Steuart used this service, but it is certain that he did much of the planning himself for he was an eminent agriculturist, publishing in 1828, *The Planter's Guide* in which he outlined new methods for planting and transplanting trees. He also filled a book with notations and beautiful sketches that no doubt reflected his ideas for planning an estate. Unfortunately, these records were lost in a Wishaw library fire several years ago. As a result, we can only postulate the date of Bonkle's founding. It is true, however, that estate improvement and village founding went hand in hand, and it is known that Sir Henry replaced the old, crumbling tower house with a new country mansion about 1787 (Brown 1859).

A few years earlier, he had negotiated one of the earliest tacks, or leases, with Robert Brownlee's grandfather, William, a mason from nearby Hartwood. This was in 1785, the date I would assign to the town's establishment. In 1792, Sir Henry signed another tack with Alexander Brownlee, a roadbuilder (William's son and Robert Brownlee's father) for an adjoining piece of property in "Bonkill." From this information, local oral histories, and census records, it can be determined that Bonkle's function as a planned community was to house expert artisans: masons, joiners, blacksmiths, and laborers necessary to help Sir Henry build his new mansion, improve the estate, and erect houses in the village and on nearby farms. It has been shown that village development usually followed a pattern (Lockhart 1980, Smout 1970, Dunbar 1966, Houston 1948), and Bonkle appears to be no exception, in spite of the fact that it is a tiny village. A landowner chose a site near existing roads, if possible. Bonkle is on the Edinburgh-Ayr Road. A name was chosen, in this case, that of Margaret de Bonkyll, a long-removed ancestor in the Steuart line.

Owing to its specialized nature, there would not have been a ready supply of residents (farmers displaced by enclosure), and Sir Henry may have simply passed the word to attract residents, or he might have advertised in local newspapers as a few landowners did. Most residents, however, had long been in the parish or county. The Brownlee (Brownlea, Brownlie, Brounlee, or Brunlees) family name, for example, turns up in Cambusnethan Parish records as early as 1640. Sir Henry probably exchanged ideas with others contemplating reorganization, for his established regulations for the village compare favorably with those of other lairds. A long lease for the property was the rule. William and his son signed 999-year leases which passed in perpetuity to heirs (Steuart 1785, 1792). Feu-duty (See Note 3) and time of payment was specified. Leases also stipulated that houses were to be built in a right line with those on adjoining property, and were to be the same height. Doors, windows, chimneyheads, gavel-skews (gables), and corners were to be of hewn stone, "properly executed." Tenants were at liberty to use the estate quarries and to cut timber.

There is no doubt that building plots on Allanton and Church Roads were surveyed to face a central oval or village green, and the village can be recognized from Brownlee's brief description. The forest trees, old and gnarled, are there today, though the thorn hedge was removed some years ago. Both Church and Allanton Roads terminate at the woodlands of Allanton Estate. This, too, was often part of the design—to make the village part of the estate (Slater 1980:240), while, at the same time, providing an attractive entrance to the manor house. Bonkle village plans did not include a school or inn. There was a smiddy or blacksmith shop (long since torn down), but a church was not built at the end of Church Road until 1818. There have been a number of changes since.

The estate was sold in 1931 for the payment of taxes, and later the manor house was torn down. Sir Walter Scott once had a favorite path through the estate (Archibald 1981)—which is now only a memory, but many of the old houses stand, loved and preserved by their residents. A number of new dwellings encircle the original village, a haven for families who commute to downtown Glasgow, 28 minutes away by railroad.

7. Brownlee is referring to the fact that the laborer and his family occupied a one-room apartment in the row house. Each unit was self-contained and had separate entrances, fireplaces and bed-closets. In many cases, however, farmers and servants lived as one family and a laborer often worked for the same people as long as he lived (Jones 1970:4).

8. About the only way a laborer could go into debt was to pawn what little clothing or furniture he owned. My interpretation of Brownlee's statement, therefore, is that the pawnbroker (creditor) could sell these items if the laborer could not redeem his goods after a specified period of time, very often at exorbitant interest rates. This may have discouraged many would-be borrowers who had precious little with which to replace their belongings. Too, it is possible that a man could lose his job for debt. Scottish Poor Law, in force for three centuries, provided nothing for a destitute or unemployed worker, and very little for the sick or elderly (Levitt 1979:128). Both church and state held that an unemployed worker should be punished for his "sin" of idleness and that the sick and elderly should be cared for by families or sent to almshouses. State authorities also believed each parish should accept responsibility for its poor and unemployed. But, for the most part (Smout 1969:325), citizens were too proud to turn to the parish for help. A workingman, therefore, had to try and subsist within his means and save if he could. It was not until 1845 that the Poor Law Reform Act gave some relief to unemployed workers.

9. A high percentage of parish women were able to work at tambouring, a type of needlework that could be done at home. The wages these women earned were necessary towards making ends meet and elevated a family's standard of living. They used a tambour needle (similar to a crochet hook) to decorate yard goods such as muslin or fine cambric and worked the printed design with closely-spaced lines of chain stitch (Caulfield 1972). The size of the frame suggests that the material would later be used to trim or decorate dresses, curtains, or caps.

10. The girls were embroidering fine muslins. Both tambour and embroidery work were forms of home labor that employed literally thousands of women in the rural countryside, and representatives from Glasgow and

Paisley manufacturing houses periodically delivered the needed materials to women in the Lanarkshire area (Slaven 1975:86, Smout 1969:405).

11. Brownlee's few comments have confirmed many points brought out by Levitt and Smout (1979:23–41). For example, most Scots ate little meat in 1843. Residents of North Lanarkshire generally enjoyed a better and more varied diet because they earned higher wages and meat consumption was commonplace. They also ate more cheese and butter in North Lanarkshire and neighboring North Ayrshire (home of the famous dairy cow and Dunlop cheese) than anywhere else in Scotland. The average feu in Bonkle was 60 x 104 feet, providing ample space for growing vegetables and keeping a pig, cow and chickens. There are stone and brick outbuildings still standing which formerly served as chicken coops or small byres, with ample pasturage beyond the gardens.

12. Robert's parents, Margaret Russell and Alexander Brownlee, followed custom and did not have an engagement. Instead, they announced their intention to marry on Friday, April 17, 1795, just twelve days before the actual ceremony (Cambusnethan Parish *Records* 1634–1819). He was 33, she 19. Such age differences seem to have been characteristic of the Brownlees and other Scotsmen as well. When the men married, they were usually in their mid-30s to early 40s. Wives often were as much as 20 years younger. On the other hand, a number of women remained spinsters, or married late if they married at all. Very often, two brothers from one family married two sisters from another. Often they were first cousins, a not uncommon arrangement, possibly because there was not a broad base for marriage partners. Marriage was patrilocal, and a woman usually went to live in her husband's village. If widowed, however, she very often returned to her native village to live with parents or a brother's family. Sons often left home to seek work in other parishes. At death, all parish citizens were buried in the same ground at Cambusnethan Parish Cemetery. Most members of the Brownlee family lie under one large tombstone, interred in tiers of eight around the four sides.

Large families of eight to ten children were the rule. Younger ones were spread around to live with grandparents. An older daughter might act as housekeeper for an aged uncle; perhaps a younger one might be a servant to an aunt. In a town as small as Bonkle, however, it would be easy to keep close ties with all family members. They would often be in the house next door or, at most, across the street. This also relieved the pressure of large families in a small space. The eldest male was usually named after his grandfather; one daughter always received her grandmother's maiden name; and other children were named after favorite aunts and uncles. Women retained and used their maiden names in conjunction with their married names (as far as Brownlees are concerned, at least, this tradition has continued to the present day). Women could also own and inherit property.

The Brownlees were long-lived: 74 was the average age of seven of Alexander and Margaret Brownlee's children. Robert, Thomas, James, and brother John's sons all emigrated to America. Brother Alexander never married. Another brother, William, had only daughters. One brother, however, married a Brownlee cousin, and thus the name and Brownlee property passed on to those children—in this case, only daughters. The last member of this family, Miss Elizabeth Russell Brownlee, remained a spinster and the Brownlee name did not survive in the village beyond her death in 1939.

13. Sister Grace was then living with her daughter Christina, and son-in-law, James Russell, in Carluke, Ontario, Canada, a town that was named for the Scottish village just a few miles beyond Bonkle. Exemplifying the Brownlee longevity, Grace was 88 when she died in 1894, and Christina 82 at her death in 1929.

14. The moss-covered shell of Bonkle's first church, the Muirkirk of Cambusnethan, stands hidden by a grove of trees on a lonely moor some two miles from Bonkle. Over the years, stonework and debris have tumbled inward, gradually filling in the cavity. The date 1740 is still clearly discernible on a remaining stone lintel, a reminder that the story of Muirkirk is closely aligned with the long and complicated history of the Church of Scotland.

In 1690 Parliament restored the Presbyterian system, and a number of groups split off in reaction to proposed changes. The Cameronians, who dissented at that time, comprised a small group adhering to a strict Calvinistic doctrine. The next group to leave the parent body became known as the First or Original Secession Church. These people were followers of Rev. Ebenezer Erskine, an opponent of patronage (state support). Seceders from Cambusnethan Parish were among the first to form a new congregation, and in 1737 the Muirkirk of Cambusnethan was established. Members traveled to the moor from twenty-two scattered parishes and conducted services in a tent until 1740, when their permanent structure of stone and thatch was finished. The church, during this time, wielded a strong arm.

Kirk Sessions' minutes for Cambusnethan Parish are filled with major and minor "sins" committed by parishioners, who were sentenced to atone for their misdeeds. One Grizzel Brownlie, for example, was forced to sit in the "place of public Repentance" for the sin of adultery in 1755.

The congregation continued to meet on the moor until 1818, when it moved into a new church in Bonkle. In the meantime, however, the congregation went through a number of changes. In 1747, members of the Muirkirk of Cambusnethan Secession Church split over an issue concerning the Burgess Oath, questioning if it was lawful to take the oath required by burgesses of cities where they acknowledged the true religion publicly preached and authorized by the laws. The majority of the congregation upheld the Burgher side; the dissenters assembled as Anti-Burghers. There was further controversy in 1800 when the two groups split into the New Light Burghers, New Light Anti-Burghers, Old Light Burghers, and Old Light Anti-Burghers. Muirkirk sided with the New Light adherents, who supported toleration in religion. This, of course, occurred in the period when Brownlee said he attended the New Lights Church. (Burleigh, 1960:323, remarked that New Light seceders usually were people with "sturdy independent minds" who came mainly from rural areas and Lowland towns.)

A few years after Brownlee left Scotland, the United Secession Church and the Relief Church formed the United Presbyterian Church, and in 1847, members of Bonkle Church became known as United Presbyterians, thus becoming reaffiliated with the Church of Scotland in 1929. Today, Bonklians attend services in a picturesque stone church built in 1878 on the site of the earlier meetinghouse.

(This historical information was derived from a series of sermons commemorating the 200th anniversary of Bonkle Church, by the Rev. James Winchester, 1937.)

CHAPTER II

A Greenhorn in America

INTRODUCTION

Confident that his masonry skills would be in demand after the great fire of December 1835, Robert Brownlee made up his mind to sail for New York, where he arrived the following spring just as the city was rebuilding. He readily found work. Although New Yorkers took their daily life in stride, the young man from the Scottish Lowlands was fascinated by everything new. Most of all, he was impressed by the amount of money he could earn.

Perhaps Brownlee was more comfortable in a rural environment, however, for he did not sojourn long in New York. Instead, he took advantage of opportunities to cut stone for state houses in Raleigh, North Carolina, and in Little Rock, Arkansas. Brownlee's later reminiscences offer a brief glimpse of life in 19th century America as he moved from place to place. His observation of the Charleston Salt Works, for example, notes the time when West Virginia's economy depended on salt production long before the coal industry became important.

Brownlee also left a little travelogue, in which he mentioned that in 1837, Americans did not just "pick up and go" in a direct line when they traveled from one place to another. The story of his wanderings is of particular interest because it takes place during the nation's transition to railroads. At that time, the United States' newborn railroad system totalled only 1000 miles of track, distributed in segments across eleven states. Many miles of turnpike did connect with major towns, but as population dwindled toward the west, so did these roads. Shipping was the major and most efficient mode of transportation, but utilized only the waterways.

Brownlee and his fellow migrants on the frontier availed themselves of all transportation methods as they journeyed from place to place, and his story mirrors that of all traveling Americans in 1836. They braced and slept upright as stages swayed and bumped over back-breaking corduroy roads. They sat patiently as the new trains chugged at a crawl and endured time-consuming stops to take on wood and water. Like Brownlee, they sometimes went fishing while they waited for a grounded schooner to be released by the tide. Brownlee's impressions describe a time when journeying Americans needed an adventurous spirit combined with endurance and patience, to suffer the vicissitudes of travel before improved roads and railways appeared on the scene.

THE JOURNAL

As I am about to leave Scotland for America I may as well state why. The New York papers referred to the great fire in that city in the years of 1835 and '36 and that there was a great demand for mechanics, particularly stone cutters. I was working some three miles from home, and at ten o'clock in the morning everything was running as usual, when the idea struck me that I would go to America. I stood musing for a few moments when I was asked, "What was the matter?" When I told them I had done my last work in Scotland they did not believe me, but when I put on my coat they thought differently, for I started home three miles and met my mother and told her I was going to America, and that I wanted money to pay my passage, she being my purser. This astonished her. She tried to persuade me out of the notion, but that was no go. So I started 16 miles to Glasgow and 22 miles to Greenock by water, when I met a friend and stayed with him all night. Next morning, we went to a shipping office and engaged our passage on a barque.[1] Our passage cost three pounds or $15 and to find our own board and bed, and that it would sail in two days.

From Greenock I took the steamer to Glasgow. By rail it was seven miles home, where I reported progress,[2] and they were very much astonished, so they could do nothing but cry. Mother began to realize how things stood, only two days in which to make shirts out of home made lint called harn shirts,[3] strong enough to last till you got tired of them, which was not very long after I landed. The tailors were required to make me clothing, as of course they could not be gotten in such a new country.

While these preparations were going on I was visiting my friends and relations, and besides I want you to know, I had sweethearts to be attended to. [And,] I suppose making promises to write like all young folks on their first legs. This I do know, that for three nights I had no sleep before I started. It is 16 miles to Glasgow, brother James was walking along with me, and he said I slept nearly all the time, when I would make a lurch and that would waken me for a few minutes. In due time all was ready and leave taking and a few "Fare you w'e'lls" with a few tears, I parted with parents and many others, never more to meet on this earth, hoping we may all meet in a better place never more to part.

They made a box half filled with oatmeal cake, and oatmeal mixed among the cakes with butter, cheese and boiled eggs. There was no use in boiling [the eggs] as we had a fine galley on which to cook, with some sea crackers. I don't remember whether we had meat or not, but don't believe we had.

The name of the bark was 'Tasso', carrying twenty-one passengers and some of those were children. We were six weeks and three days in making the trip, and with the exception of sea-sickness, had no trouble. I can assure you that for three days in the Irish Channel, I would just as soon the vessel would sink as to float; I never have been sick, knew nothing about how it felt, and to be introduced to sea-sickness all at once, was rather severe. I have never experienced anything like it. I have suffered with sickness often, caused from fever and ague, taking many vomets in my time, and this situation will compare well with the feelings of sea-sickness; but when once relieved, you can rest quietly. It is quite different at sea, for the pitching of the vessel continues, and every time she rises your stomach seems to turn inside out, the downward motion is just as bad, besides the rolling motion, you haven't any time for rest, and as the stomach is entirely empty, the straining continues. On the third day the mate gave me my choice—

whether to swallow a piece of raw pork, or to drink a quart of seawater. I chose the latter, and in a very short time, as the weather moderated I got all right, and the box with my provisions was then in great demand.

I think we sailed the latter part of March 1836, had a pleasant time, and landed in New York May 10th. On nearing the city the fruit trees were all in blossom, and such quantities of them made things look grand, and I had never seen so many before. As there was not any sickness aboard, we landed immediately, but left my things behind. My chest of clothing "By the by" was no toy, its dimensions being some four feet long, by two feet square every way; my meal box was not much smaller. So you see I had to find some place in which to store them. I had a letter of introduction to David Sterling, a stone-cutter by trade. I found him and got a job in the same shop, and a boarding place, where I had my freight stored, and commenced work next day on the Hudson River, 20th street and 8th Avenue. This then was in the outskirts of town, while now in 1892 it is in the center of New York city.

I had no difficulty in holding my own so far as work was concerned; but I had trouble with my hands blistering, for a few days. The boss was a complete Yankee, but a good man. He put me on piece work, and this was the kind of work which did not pay very well, therefore I had to work the harder to make the average wages, which was $2.00 a day. I fell short the first two weeks as he paid us at that time. The second pay day I averaged $2.25 and from then on $2.50, which was equal to ten shillings. Perhaps I was not proud to think I was so fortunate, and was making a fortune right off.[4] This is not all. We had coffee and beef-steak for breakfast, roast beef and pie, for dinner, with fish Friday. What a difference from boiled potatoes and salt. I enjoyed the change immensely, and my first letter home was full of the great change in food, and of the wonderful sights to be seen.

For instance—the first day I went up town, I saw 30 yoke of oxen hitched to one pair of very high, and wide wheels, which were fastened to a stone said to weigh 30 tons, to be used on the new Custom House on Wall street. When I first saw them they were unhitching some fifteen yoke from the front, and fastening them to the hind part. I was at a loss to know the cause but was not left long in the dark, for it was a downgrade to the building, so when they started the leaders, the driver behind began to probe the steers in the heads, when they held the load from going too fast, and in that way the stone was taken with all ease where wanted. What astonished me was, there was no crowd following them. I supposed to them it was nothing new, while to me it was the greatest wonder I had ever seen, for I had never seen oxen hitched in any manner.[5] I was a "Green-horn" you must allow, and was always seeing new wonders, and the way it was being done.

In the shop where I worked they were ever seeing something in me to laugh at. I could hear them commenting on what I said, or did, and I must admit was much annoyed with myself, for my Scotch tongue was all I knew how to express myself by, and of course it caused them much merriment, to my great mortification. I had not worked four weeks before they found out on pay day, that if I couldn't speak as good English as they, that I could earn more wages; and that in itself was the means of diverting themselves at my expense. I want it distinctly understood, if I say it myself, I was the model young man in the shop, and you may wonder why. It was in this way; at that time in the shop all were in the habit of going four or six times a day to the first "Whiskey-Mill" and of getting a drink, each one of which cost three cents, and the different bosses throughout the town never objected. I was never accustomed to see anything of the kind done before, [and] did not approve of the custom.

I worked in New York some four months, and in the mean time sent my mother $100.00 as a token of love and affection. When I went home in '52 they told me she was proud of her prodigal son. That is a long time ago, yet when I think of such things they are pleasant memories on which to ponder, as I believe my youthful days were more to be commended than when I was more advanced in years. Not that I have been accused of "Sheep-stealing" or with running away with somebody's wife; it was simply this: I had not mixed so much with the world and its different temptations.

In September 1836 the architect of the State House of North Carolina came to New York in quest of stone cutters; to work on the Capitol at two and a half a day. David Sterling and myself started at once on a sail vessel for Petersburg, Virginia, and from there on a railroad as far as the Roanoake [River], and from there went to Raleigh, North Carolina. I think it was eighty miles by stage. The stage was engaged for three trips ahead, and they only made three trips a week. So David and myself concluded to walk, and to have them bring my chest of clothing when it suited them. So we walked the distance in two days, through rather poor country, except on the banks of the creek bottoms. The farmers were poorly housed. I suppose [they] could not afford to live better as they were too far from market, and railroads in North Carolina were not as yet built, and the one from Petersburg to Roanoake I think was nothing but wagon tire spiked on sleepers [stone blocks], and the train had to take on wood and water every ten miles.[6] The distance may have been sixty miles over the poorest country I have seen anywhere. Craw-fish land in every sense of the word. Over their holes they would build a small tower ten or fifteen inches high, in case of high water, so we were told. The timber is nothing but scrubby pine about the size of your leg and perhaps fifteen or twenty feet high. I was badly impressed with the land, for there was not one settlement on the sixty miles.

I had a little adventure on the schooner coming up the James River. The vessel got aground on an oyster bank where the hands went out and took aboard all the oysters they wanted; also all the crabs they cared for, then came aboard and tied up the boat. I could see from the deck the crabs close by so I took the boat and net and caught as many as I wanted. But I foolishly started bare-headed, and bare-footed, so I could wade among the riffles. The tide commenced to go out, and as I undertook to return to the schooner, and commenced pulling, the crabs would catch my bare feet, and the boat drifting down the river looked rather bad for me, for I knew nothing about [it]. I suppose never tried to pull an oar before. David told me to skull the boat. By so doing I could stand up and be out of reach of the crabs. The long and short of it was when I got aboard I was overheated. The Captain thought I was going "To kick the bucket." They poured the coldest water all over me and gave me brandy which made me sweat all over, then I could breath more easily and next day was all right, although it came very near being a sunstroke. For ever after that I could never endure the hot sun as well as other men. The lesson of catching crabs came very near being my last, and I should not have gone alone as that was the only boat the schooner had. I could not eat oysters then but was fond of crabs.

Mr. Sterling and myself landed in Raleigh in the evening and commenced work next morning on the State House of North Carolina, which is built of granite, the four fronts being polished and with heavy cornices all around [and] having large granite columns with massive Ionic Caps. It is the finest building on which I ever worked. It was all done well as you could have [in] your own time. All that was required was to make a clean good job. Mostly all of the stone cutters were Scotch and Irish. There were sixty stone cutters of us besides carpenters and blacksmiths. The architect and foreman were Scotch, both very fine men.[7]

The commissioner—Mr. Daniels was a very fine man, was President of the State Bank and he of his own accord gave me a letter of introduction with a very high recommendation to the commissioner of Public Buildings in Arkansas. The Bank paper of North Carolina was below par, so he gave us a draft on the Bank of Tennessee which was almost as good as gold in Arkansas. The State House was nearing completion and as I was among the last taken on, I would of course be among the first discharged. So seeing an advertisement for stone cutters to do the Stone work of the Capitol of Arkansas, [three other] Scotchmen who had landed in New York as I had and were about the same age, [and I,] concluded to try our fortunes in Arkansas. I will give their names as we were together until the work was finished. James McVicar, Samuel McMorrin, and John Cooper, all good workmen and of steady habits.[8] After working sixteen months in North Carolina we had saved nearly all we had made, and think I had something like $600.00, the rest about the same. We expected if we got the contract for the stone work we would need all we had to pay expenses. So you see Mr. Daniels did us a good turn in giving us a draft for our money before leaving Raleigh.

I must admit North Carolina is a very poor country as a whole, as there are good lands on the river bottoms but the up-lands are of a gravelly nature, not good for corn or cotton. You could judge from the farmers when they came to market, for they would have nothing but a few eggs, a little honey, and some coon skins—perhaps a few deer skins. As a whole they are a poor looking ignorant set, as few of them could read or write. The most wonderful thing I ever saw them do was, when they would come around to look at the building, they would all squat down on their "Hunkers," and would sit in that position for an hour. Seemingly they have no ambition for anything. For what I saw, I am bound to say the morals of Raleigh are very easy, that is, the feminine part.

I think I have finished with North Carolina when I tell of my first hunt on Christmas day. It was a black, frosty morning. Our game consisted of cotton-tail rabbits, with quail thrown in; there was no lack of dogs, and boys to beat the scrub pines [and] we had decent sport. I heard a dog barking out in the open field, and went to see and I saw a sight that made my hair stand on end; only one dog and he had no teeth, so the coon had it all his own way. They were fighting in water about four inches deep. I did not want to shoot, so I concluded to catch the coon alive and show the boys my trophy. I waded in and waited my chance and caught him by the tail, and carried him out to dry land. He weighed twenty-eight pounds so I had to swing him around from one hand to the other as he was making every effort to get hold of me, and I was hollering for help. On hearing me, some thirty boys and men, and twice as many dogs came, but that coon held his own for a long time. Of course you think I was proud, and you think exactly right for once.

A party of three besides myself are about to leave North Carolina by stage, to a point on the Ohio River called "Guyandotte" [today's Huntington, West Virginia]. It took the stage seven days and nights to make the trip, and we were never in bed but once during that time, and then for only about four hours, as we were about to descend the Blue Ridge Grade, into the Kanawa River Bottom.

When we started from Raleigh it was December 20th, I think, 1837—in mid-winter and the roads in many places were laid with small trees, called "corduroy roads." If a person wants a good shaking up, let him take a ride over such a road; and once will satisfy him. There was a General from South Carolina on his way to Congress, who was well dressed and of middle age, and wore a stove-pipe hat. You should have seen that hat at the end of the second day. It was on one of these roads where he got his first bounce, which sent him and his hat up against the roof of the stage. Of course, profanity was above par. We younger people could sympathize with him outwardly, but enjoyed the same inwardly. We did not admire him in conversation, always, "Big I and little You."

I think we landed the second night by daylight at Richmond, Virginia, and then started up the James River. This was a beautiful country in a high state of cultivation, having fine roads, and thickly settled with fine farm houses, and good fences, which was quite a change in the appearance of things. The winter-sewn wheat looked green, and reminded me of the land on the River Clyde in Scotland; where I used to see green wheat during the winter months. The names of the different towns, and distances, I have quite forgotten, as they never made a deep impression at the time, as did the killing of the coon.

I recollect of coming through Stanton [Staunton, Virginia]. The reason I suppose was the sight of the Insane Asylum struck me forcibly at the time, as I had never seen anything of that kind before.[9] Also [I remember] ascending the Blue Ridge Mountain, as we all had to get out and walk, the ground was frozen hard, and the air very cold, and we could walk much faster than the six-horse stage could travel. On top of the mountain there was a toll-house occupied by a green-Irishman. I was astonished to see him there in his primitive glory, and must admit was green to think an Irishman could not get there as well as myself. On ascending the mountain, we passed the Virginia Sulphur Springs which is a great resort in the summer, for its mineral qualities.[10]

After leaving the Springs we had to ascend somewhat, and it was somewhere near here that we got the four hours sleep, from 10 P.M. till two A.M. When the moon rose we started down grade with the six horses on a run most of the time, down the hill-side above the river. It was a grand sight. About sun-rise the stage stopped and let us look at the Hawks Nest, which was a grand scene, as one could look down to the river, which was one thousand feet below; and to drop a stone would strike the river.[11] The next place that we passed was Charleston Salt Works,[12] and about sun down we reached the Ohio River at the mouth of the Kanawa. Here we took a steam boat for the mouth of the Arkansas River.

We left Raleigh on the stage Monday morning and arrived on the Ohio on Sunday evening so you see we were just seven days in making the trip. You may wonder how we slept. It was not so bad as it might seem, all being young and full of excitement, and when the stage was full it was very easy to sleep. For instance—for four nights there was a Negro girl who sat on my right, Sam McMorrin was on my left, and we had our overcoats on all the time, with a large comfort around our necks, and by sitting stiff and straight, you could catch small naps. I was never cold on my right side, as the reason is plain.

We went aboard the steamer "Cinderella," to the mouth of the Arkansas River, and landed at a small town called "Napoleon," on Christmas Eve. When we came down stairs in the morning, we were invited to take egg-nog, which, by the way, was not hard to take. The view of the Mississippi from here is a grand sight, being about one and a half miles wide, we were told, and moving along at the rate of four miles an hour. Napoleon is at the mouth of the Arkansas River, which looks small in comparison to the Mississippi. Napoleon is a small town, yet it was astonishing how many people were to be seen say by twelve o'clock in the day, canoes with two to four passengers were arriving all the time, and woodchoppers from the different wood yards, until by twelve o'clock they became very noisy—fighting and swearing and using the bowie knife freely. There was one man killed, but no notice taken of the fact.[13] We, the green ones, took our guns and went into the woods to hunt squirrels, and at the same time keeping a watchful eye on the river for a steam boat to go up the Arkansas river to Little Rock, the Capitol of the state, and three hundred miles by water. We got aboard a steamer that evening, and arrived in Little Rock in due time.

NOTES TO CHAPTER II

1. Fire swept New York in December 1835 and destroyed the heart of the city—some 674 buildings in all. This was followed by a flurry of building activity in 1836, when workers constructed 1,635 buildings (Stokes 1915:V:1737). As a result, experienced mechanics looking for adventure and willing to risk the tedious voyage could find immediate employment, and many took the gamble. For example, among the 22 passengers on board the *Tasso*, five were stonecutters, two were joiners, and one was a laborer. Three clerks, a shoemaker, and a hatter (some with families) rounded out the group seeking its fortune in America (U.S. State Department 1820–1897). The *Tasso* was a 314-ton vessel out of Boston (Appleton & Co.), and subsequently engaged in the lucrative hide and tallow trade along the California coast in the 1840s (Bancroft 1886:IV:562,569).
2. Brownlee is unclear here, but he probably walked from Glasgow to the nearest station on the Wishaw-Coltness Railway. Small segments of the

line started opening up after 1832 (Slaven 1975:42). Then as now, most Scots preferred to walk.
3. A coarse cloth was made from flax or hemp refuse.
4. By comparison, top pay for a mason in the Scottish Lowlands was about 21 shillings (Levitt, Smout 1979:115) or about $4.75 per week.
5. Clydesdales did the heavy work in Scotland. These famous draft horses were first bred in the Clyde Valley, where Brownlee was born, and a Scots farmer used at least three to draw his plow (Sinclair 1792:XII:568–574). A team of eight could haul about eight tons.
6. The Petersburg and Roanoke Railroad covered 59 miles (Dunbar 1937:1084).
7. In addition to being "very fine men," Town and Davis of New York were distinguished architects, acclaimed for their designs of American buildings in the Greek Revival style. The beautiful building in Raleigh was only one among many state capitols designed by the firm. The "foreman" Brownlee refers to was David Paton from Edinburgh, who supervised construction between 1833 and 1840 (Waugh 1967, Hamlin 1964).
8. The three men, however, were not Brownlee's shipmates on the barque *Tasso*.
9. The first asylums were starting to dot the American countryside at this time because of an increasing belief that insanity was curable (Rothman 1971:111–131). Brownlee commented on this new social phenomenon because there were no such institutions at that time in Scotland. Families or churches cared for the insane where he had lived, or, more frequently, they were incarcerated in jails, almshouses, or workhouses. The Western Lunatic Asylum (later, the Western State Hospital) admitted its first patients in 1828 and was one of the first U.S. institutions established specifically for treatment of the mentally ill. The Staunton asylum looked like a southern mansion and was built on 80 acres of tree-studded, rolling hills in view of the Blue Ridge and Allegheny Mountains. Here, doctors abandoned the restraints and chains of the past and gave their patients good food and introduced them to crafts, light labor, and exercise (Hurd 1916 III:719–732).
10. Now known as White Sulphur Springs, this popular spa must have fascinated the newly-arrived Scotsman. The Springs was a fashionable vacation resort in 1837, catering to the planters of the Old South. It provided many cabins, a large dining hall, a kitchen and bakery, a ballroom, and stables for 80 horses (West Virginia 1941:426–429).
11. Today, visitors can stand on the edge of the New River Gorge in West Virginia, and view Hawks Nest Tunnel, which diverts New River through the south flank of Gauley Mountain to a hydroelectric station three miles

away. In 1836, however, the fish hawks that gave the area its name still nested on the towering rock formation which rose 585 feet above New River.

12. Brownlee and company were traveling in Kanawha River Valley. Salt production had been a booming business here since 1805, and furnaces and tub mills along the road between Malden and Charleston provided employment for thousands of workers. Production peaked at three million bushels in 1850, then declined, as salt producers turned to coal mining (West Virginia 1941:444). The travelers continued in a westward direction toward Huntington (formerly Guyandotte, West Virginia), located near the junction of the Ohio and Guyandotte Rivers.

13. Napoleon is part of the riverbed today. In 1837, however, it was a wide open, roaring river town and one of Arkansas' chief outlets to the Mississippi. The Mississippi and Arkansas rivers encroached, finally submerging Napoleon, and by 1874 it was "a town no more—swallowed up, vanished, gone to feed the fishes; nothing left but a fragment of a shanty and a crumbling brick chimney!" (Clemens 1957:187).

CHAPTER III

An Arkansas Traveler

INTRODUCTION

In 1837, Arkansas was the American frontier, where the "wild west" began. Robert Brownlee writes colorfully of a time when the bowie knife and dueling pistol settled disputes, when backwoods justice was certain, swift, and very often cruel. It was a time when it was prudent to practice the principle of *laissez-faire*. During that period, the rivers of Arkansas provided her highways, and the frontiersman was never far from his main source of transportation and recreation—his horse. Here, the ague, or malaria, was a constant threat and returned each year to plague Arkansans. As could be expected, Brownlee adapted to the spirit of the times as he set about making a living.

He continued cutting stone as long as there was a demand for his masonry skills. He and his friends worked on a number of Little Rock buildings, including the Old State House. The designers of these buildings are often applauded for their contributions. We can, perhaps give further historical credit to men like James McVicar, Samuel McMorrin, John Cooper, Robert Brownlee, and other, nameless, itinerant laborers who brought architectural plans to fruition.

In the years following the panic and depression of 1837, when many Arkansans faced financial reverses and hard times, Brownlee looked for new ways to support himself. He learned to lay brick, to build chimneys and houses, to carve gravestones, and to farm and clear land. His attempt at farming did not reap great profits because these were also bad times for the farmer. In spite of this, Brownlee observed that the pioneer spirit of generosity and cooperativeness prevailed, extending beyond the farm. With an associate, Brownlee built a brick kitchen for a friend. The same associate helped Brownlee build his own brick house in 1847. Brownlee's memoirs also identify a small Georgian dwelling in downtown Little Rock as one he built so long ago.

About this time, there was a renewal of family ties when Robert's two brothers moved to Little Rock. Robert was still far from settling down, though. By his own admission, he was much more at home in the company of men because he did not know how to "sweet talk" the ladies. But when the opportunity arose, Robert Brownlee was ready for further adventure.

THE JOURNAL

I may as well state here that Arkansas had just been admitted into the Union of states that summer [June 15, 1836]. The Legislature was in session when we arrived, and the day before there arose a dispute in regard to the premium allowed on wolf scalps. The lie was given between Mr. [John] Wilson, speaker of the Senate and Mr. [J. J.] Anthony. They met, one with a chair, and Mr. Wilson with a bowie knife, who gave the fatal blow under the chair of Mr. Anthony, who died right there. Wilson was cleared, as it was proven in self-defence.[1] You must remember that Arkansas was composed of the very worst class of men, murderers, counterfeiters, horse-thieves, and all those who were compelled to leave their native state for their country's good. In 1837, Arkansas was the resort of all cut-throats and escape the gallows crowd—murder on the street was a very common event, and all they had to do to make their escape was to flee to the woods and canebrake and join some other gang.[2]

For instance—there was the Regulator Party, and the Moderator Party, both at swords points, and whenever they met, they knew each other, and some one had to die, as they waylaid one another and would fire from ambush. It was a very common event, and nothing would be said or done, for it was not safe to express one's opinion, or you would be spotted for it, it being hard to tell to whom you were talking. I think it was in the year 1838 that there would average one murder every two days.

I never saw anyone hurt but an Indian in Little Rock, and I think he was hung in a very strange way for horse stealing. He was sitting on his coffin in a wagon, when they drove the horses under the noose, which was suspended from a tree, and placing it around his neck, drove the wagon out from under him, leaving him hanging in the air. The laws of the land were only in name, as you could not enforce them, as the jury would never agree, or if they found them guilty as charged, they might expect at some time or place, to pay for their decision, with their lives. The best policy was to attend to your own business and not pass an opinion upon the affair, as ignorance was the best policy, as you could not tell friend from foe, and "Mum was the word."[3]

I have tried to present things as they were at that time, and by the fall of 1838 Little Rock had improved very much. Mechanics of all grades were moving into town, brick layers, plasterers, painters, carpenters and printers—so that the rowdies had to behave themselves, or leave town. The mechanics were very clanish one to the other, and generally speaking, a better class of citizens were there. The Courts were more respected [and] justice was to a certain extent administered.

I will try and give a statement of how we progressed in getting the contract for the stone work. The Commissioner of public works had contracted with a Scotchman to do the stone cutting, so we waited for some two weeks, and were about to leave the state, when the Commissioner heard we were about to leave, and [as] the Scotchman was making no showing, he proposed to him, to take us as partners, which he did. After a few weeks we got rid of him as he was of no force.[4]

First we had to hunt for stone quarries, which we found thirty miles up the river, and finished the stone work of the State House, which cost something like eleven thousand dollars.[5] When the state concluded to build a penitentiary, we did the stone work, also that of the State Bank, and a stone wall, which was built partly around the State House.[6] We did very well, but suffered a great deal from sickness.

In 1840 we were rushed by the brick layers, in getting the stone jambs for windows and doors, for the penitentiary. I think there were eight stone cutters. But the trouble was in getting the stone down the river, which had to be brought some eighty miles on a flat boat, which carried about eighty tons. John Cooper and myself were up getting stone out of the quarry when we were both taken sick, but managed to get down to Little Rock, where Cooper died.[7] I came very near going too, but had taken both calomel and ipecac. I was much the weakest when we started down, but the Doctor said the medicine had saved my life.

The year 1840 was the most sickly season I ever saw, and besides we had to work in the sun all the time, and often in the year at the quarry the water we used was green, as we had to use that from the cypress ponds. We boiled it sometimes, but not often, and it is no wonder we had chills and fever—nothing but quinine enabled us to be able to do anything, and calomel, with Sappington's Pills. Each man carried either one or the other in his pocket, and whenever he felt a chilly sensation would take quinine or a vomet and by taking so much medicine made him very weak, which sickness was generally in the months of July and August. The every day ague was bad enough, but the third day ague would last some four hours, and the fever afterwards for eight or ten, with a severe head-ache and burning fever.[8]

I think we finished stone cutting between 1840 and 1842, therefore, we had nothing to do. You may remember John Cooper, one of our partners had died, so it left J. McVicar, Sam McMorrin and myself. We concluded to buy Indian ponies, had rifles made to order, and were preparing for a hunting trip. I still had the shot gun I had brought from Scotland, and in the mean time we got acquainted with a farmer, who, by the way, was a Scotchman. We met him at a shooting match, where somebody would put up a beef and charge so much for the quarter, the hide making the fifth quarter, which was worth as much money as the beef, so you had to pay 25¢ for each shot, and in that way had good sport.

I really forget how John McHenry took such a fancy to us three anyhow, but he took us home to his farm, and I think I must have stayed off and on for six or eight years.[9] In that time we hunted mostly all the time with hounds, and think we had ten to fifteen dogs, and had fine sport, a Negro to saddle our horses and put them away on our return. I think Mr. McHenry worked about fifteen slaves and they were able hands.

As a slave holder, he was a good master in one sense of the word. Although not hard on them himself, he had an overseer who was forever passing the whip, and seemed to think it grand to hear them begging for mercy. He was a young German, of about twenty years, and naturally cruel. He and I had many words about his management, and he always went armed. There was a run-away Negro, who came from a distance and was hanging around the Negro quarters. When he heard it, he got his shotgun ready and loaded it with 24 buck shot. As the Negro wouldn't stop when he told him, he fired and killed him—as far as I know there wasn't anything done to him, as a run-away Negro coming around your place enticing your hands away was held by the slave holders as a legitimate mark for your gun. One of his own men ran away and the overseer fired his gun (which was loaded with quail shot) at his feet, which stopped him with the shot in his feet—take him away from the Negro and he was very agreeable.

While we were staying with Mr. McHenry, Sam McMorrin and myself built a good brick kitchen and cellar, and cut two mill stones for him as an acknowledgement of his great hospitality and kindness.[10] He had a very fine family—a girl of ten years and a boy of some five.[11]

Sam McMorrin and myself were professed whigs of the Henry Clay stamp, had voted on several occasions, and declared our intentions in North Carolina in '37 and got our naturalization papers in Arkansas in '39. Therefore, we both voted for General [William Henry] Harrison and [John] Tyler in 1840; and if I am spared, in a few days will vote square for the former's grandson to fill the same exalted station in the gift of the people. We have just received notice of the death of Mrs. Harrison, October 25, 1892, and the people of the great Union sincerely sympathize with the President in his great bereavement. Doubly so it having occurred on the eve of another election. I notice by the papers that both parties by their central committee require that there be no public parades or open demonstration till after the funeral, which shows great respect for the honored dead.

To resume—James McVicar was appointed Warden at the penitentiary of Little Rock. A very fine position, although he gave it up for the Gold Fields of California, but he left [there] and returned to Arkansas and died.[12] Sam McMorrin and myself did what stone cutting was done, such as monuments for the dead. We cut one for the grand master mason, with all the Masonic Emblems, for which we got

$800 I think. It was cut from free stone.[13] We also built a stone fence which occupied us all summer, and was valued at $1500, instead of which, we took 360 acres of improved land, which was nearly all fenced, and covered with the finest shell bark hickory, and black-walnut with the best of white oak timber. I made many improvements on the buildings, and tried farming, such as raising corn. I tried wheat also but [it] mildewed and was [of] no account. I then tried to raise cotton but forget how it turned out, anyhow, we had to haul it thirty miles.[14] I hired two white men for $10 each a month, a Negro woman for the same sum to cook for us and to help in the field. I was told afterwards that she did more hoeing, and picked more cotton than the two white men together,[15] for they were out hunting and idling away their time. You may wonder why I tolerated such work—it was simply because the stone cutting which we had in town paid us better than working a farm which was thirty miles away from us.

I could raise plenty [of] corn—60 bushels to the acre, if the ground was half worked. The trouble was there wasn't any market. To show you—when I was getting ready to start to California, I sold two cribs of corn for twelve cents a bushel and then only guessed at the amount on hand. Fresh pork cost two and a half cents a pound on foot, stock of any kind was very low. I think I stayed on the place off and on some five years, and enjoyed living very much. I always loved the country and so continue to do, for you are away from temptation that prevails more or less in any town. Besides you can hunt, and I always kept two or three hounds and game was plentiful of all kinds. I liked to hunt on horseback with dogs and a shotgun, although I must admit I was never much of a horse man. In those days I generally got off my horse to shoot, but after a while, I became as I thought, quite clever with the gun as I killed frequently. I think to me nothing is so musical as the sound of a hound on a fresh trail and you trying to reach some place of vantage, even though the saddle should work forward on the horse's neck. A "green horn" forgets all this in the moment of excitement.

I think it was in 1842 that my brother James and wife, and brother Thomas with three other Scotchmen right from Scotland, by way of New Orleans came to Arkansas. My brothers started a blacksmith shop in Little Rock, in which town I made my home when not working on my farm. I don't think they made much in the shop, which was partly their own fault. They had no enterprise and were unused to the country's ways in that new place.[16] I have learned to do most anything that comes along. It may not be as well done as a professional mechanic, but never mind, you will improve after a while and the public will not find fault.

For instance—Sam McMorrin and myself built brother and wife a good, substantial brick house and kitchen. Perhaps it did not look as clean as it might have done, as we had to be shown how to strike a joint, and to properly bed our brick.[17] Ever after that we built chimneys all over the country, and I can assure you brick laying is no part of a stone cutter's trade, nor yet is handling the plow, gathering cotton, or shucking corn, and above all, clearing land; for when we took possession of our farm, there was any amount of fallen timber, which had to be gotten out of the way, and neither of us had ever chopped with an ax, and the logs would often be from one foot to three in diameter—and what was to be done as they were so thick you could almost step from one log to another. One of our neighbors told us to "Nigger the log." The inquiry was, "How was that done?" He told us, and by following his advice we succeeded first rate for by burning them into lengths so they could be handled and rolled into large piles, where we burnt them up; that's the secret of "Niggering logs." It was done by taking the small chunks and limbs and placing them across the logs in different places, say about fourteen feet apart, and setting fire to them. By attending to your fires morning and evening, in three or four days you would have done more than four choppers could do.

Log rolling is like corn husking, when every neighbor turns out to help, and with a yoke of oxen, twelve or fourteen men with hand spikes, would astonish a stranger by the amount of work done. Such is the custom of the West to help and oblige in any way. I found them so, when the corn fodder was ready to be gathered. I knew nothing about it, but they came and helped me when it was ready, in curing the same. Nothing would afford them more pleasure than for you to go and stay with them over night or even a month, if you only saw fit. To sit and talk hunting, and of the ways of the outside world, made them undoubtedly the most hospitable people in the world I ever saw.

Instead of hauling a few eggs and coon skins to market as people of North Carolina did, you could see three or four yoke of oxen hitched to a wagon hauling cotton, loads of corn or dressed pork. They are much better housed also, seemingly in the midst of plenty, and their land is much superior in Arkansas. The river land cannot be beaten anywhere. There are so many creek bottoms which are all of the best quality. The only drawback being that of sickness, which prevails wherever the land overflows, as it does every year on the river. This is the best soil and produces equal to Louisiana.

I must tell you about the bear I killed close to the house. Brother Thomas was out visiting me and while eating our dinner, the Negro woman who was looking down in the field, called out to me, "Massa Robert, there's a bar shuah and sartin." And on looking we saw it was a black bear coming over the fence, so I gave brother Thomas the hunting pony and told him to go a certain place on the road, and stand. The bear came his way and pretty near ran over him. I took three hounds and a bull dog and went where I last saw the bear, the dogs struck the trail right off up the side of the mountain, and he soon got away from me. I took another course close by the house, when I could hear by the dogs that they were coming straight for me down hill; the bull dog was biting the bear at every jump making it a running fight, the hounds were doing their best. The bear went up a large pine tree within fifty yards of the house and myself. I had buck shot in my gun and as the bear went out on a limb, I fired right under him and he fell dead within six feet of me, and then I let him have the other barrel of squirrel shot in the head—that ended the fight. Brother Thomas came up as I shot, and was much pleased as the bear came near running over him, the bull dog was biting him so he never noticed Thomas.

I got tired of the farm and rented it. Then Mr. McMorrin and I bought 360 acres of Government land at a dollar and a quarter an acre on which to prospect for lead, as there had been considerable excitement about finding big bunches of lead ore, and that it carried great quantities of silver. We went and saw the ore they had in sight, perhaps fifteen tons, almost on the surface of the ground. Miners came from Dubuque mines and pronounced these good, and they bought up all the land adjacent to the claim and we bought the next best, built a house and furnished food to any one who wanted to prospect on our land. If they found anything we were to get one half. The first summer there were a good many sinking shafts, but always failed to find ore in paying quantities, so they all left, and even my partner, Mr. McMorrin, got disgusted and left.

There was one, an Irishman, who joined me in hunting a fortune.[18] We sunk a shaft about sixteen feet through very hard rock, in the joints of which could be seen good ore. The water was very bad and everything had to be blasted, the seams of the rock being about eight inches thick. It was in setting off a blast that I nearly lost my life. My partner had been down and helped drill the hole and had started up to be ready to pull me up when the charge was in, we had to work quickly as the water came in so fast it covered the hole, so we threw a shovel of live coals to hasten the explosion. I had put in the charge and given one tap first, but hit a little harder the second time, when it exploded right in my face (We used an iron needle in those days instead of the fuse). It broke the tub used for hoisting in fragments, and my foot was in the tub ready to be hoisted out quickly. How I ever got out alive is a mystery to everybody. The last thing I remember was a blue streak of fire coming out of the hole—I never fell when I came to myself, but was reeling against the wall of the shaft, [and] could not get my breath for some time. I suppose the powder smoke had something to do with it. I examined myself very quickly and found my leg was badly injured and my left arm was powerless, but my right arm and right leg were pretty good, and my senses had returned, and I knew I couldn't live long in that smoke.

During all this time my partner was at the windlass and was calling to me—was I killed, and to save me I couldn't answer him, and he going on like a crazy man. I managed at last to say, "Hoist." I had my right leg on the hoop of the tub and hold of the rope with my right hand, when I arrived at the top and breathed fresh air. I was nearly fainting, and he did not catch me when I landed, and I saw I was going to fall right down where I had been, when I cried, "Catch me." He was none too soon, as I could not help myself. After he got me out and I was standing alone, he let me go the second time. Then I told him to keep hold of me and to call the Negro boy, and to take me to the shanty.

That poor Irishman seemed perfectly crazy as he so proved, for he kept calling me, and in a few days made an attempt to cut his throat. The Negro boy was aged about thirteen. He met us about half way, when I told him to run and tear one of my shirts into strips and that if I lost my senses to tie up and bandage tightly every part that was bleeding, and then get on horse back and ride to the next camp (two miles away), and tell them to come as fast as possible, as I was bleeding to death and could not see for blood. Sure enough, they were not long in coming and did what they could for me. They then started for Little Rock to where my brothers lived. They got a Doctor and he prepared a bed on a stage coach, and started right off. I remember them putting me in the stage, and of them carrying me into the house. For several days when those miners came to me I lost my mind or presence of mind entirely. I heard them talking and saying they would have to cut my left arm off, any how, my left hand, when I begged them not to allow anything of the kind. If I went, I wanted to go altogether.

It is 43 years since my blowing up in the mine, and while I am describing the blue smoke coming up out of the hole, I am to a certain extent undergoing the same feeling now, not in reality but by a nervous sensation. My heart beats so strongly and fast that it hurts me. I suppose my mind is realizing and is really seeing and going through the same sights that so forcibly impressed me at the time. I have often told how it felt and looked, but never felt this way before. I suppose it is because I am writing all by myself and my mind [is] fully absorbed in my subject.

I may as well relate about a trip I made with an Englishman, R. Jennings, up Fourche Le Fee [Fourche la Fave River],[19] some thirty miles, to establish getting out staves for the English market, and he wanted me to go with him, and I must allow with the hardest set of citizens I had ever seen. Thirty miles back from the river, (he had oxen to haul his goods back), there was a fall in the stream of six or eight feet, and he proposed to have a mill [there] some day. There was nothing but cane brake for miles and the settlements were scattered through these cane brakes and the people were nothing but horse thieves, counterfeiters and anything that's bad in the catalogue.[20] The Englishman's goods consisted of molasses, tobacco and whiskey, of course. It would not be worthy the name of "store" if there was none of the "crathur."[21]

He gave a ball in honor of, and wishing success to the enterprise, and of course we went, carrying a coffee pot of molasses, another with whiskey to make black strap, which is a mixture of whiskey and molasses. The first time I ever saw it the women were as fond of it as the men. Well to make a long story short, we got back safely. We took about eight gallons each and when we started home it was all gone, and they were in fine trim to settle all past difficulties. The women had as much to say as the men.[22] That country on the Fourche Le Fee is the finest of land with a dense cane brake from ten to twelve feet high, and the path is generally a cow path, where the canes meet over your head. There is the very best of timber which indicates the quality of the soil which was then all Government land.[23] Even the prairies are good farming land.

Arkansas contains much good soil and is a good poor man's country, by farming, enough to make bread and butter. The woods furnish all the meat you want, the wild turkey, deer, bear, opossum, coon, and squirrel. Besides, hogs get fat on acorns and pigs [on] hickory nuts. And hundreds of backwoodsmen live as I have now stated and raised large families, I may safely say in ignorance, but kind and hospitable to a fault. Such I always found them, and that of the best quality, the finest of any kind.

I have been in the state some twelve or thirteen years. Society has improved very much, people on the street are not afraid of being assaulted, the laws are strictly observed and horse stealing is a thing of the past, thieves being mostly confined in the State Prison.

They have about five different denominations of Churches in Little Rock: Presbyterian, Methodist, Baptist, Christian, and Roman Catholic. The Methodists are the most numerous, and have their annual Camp Meetings, which last several days, and seemingly do much good, as they are very sincere in their profession. These meetings are well attended, all camp on the ground, the Camp being laid out in streets, and as orderly as can be. Policemen are appointed for night and day and I have attended several and never saw anything out of the way.[24] When in Little Rock, I attended the Presbyterian Church, and although not so many in number, still have a fair congregation.

I always made friends, and in Little Rock it was no exception, as some of them were very dear to me, that is among the men part. I was never any account in charming the girls my way, and their way did not seem to have any internal attraction for me. I did not use, besides did not know how, to apply blarney, or speak in idle talk in any way. When I had anything to say it was said, then I was done; so therefore was never much of a "lady's man."

I think it was in '47 or '48, that I became acquainted with Mr.

[Alexander] Lamont's family. [They were] Scotch people having two daughters, and two sons. I was more in their company than with anyone else,[25] and when convalescing from the effects of the explosion in the mine, the girls used to come and see me, which cheered me up wonderfully. I was staying with brother James' family, and used to tease the girls about getting married. Mary was both old enough, and fat enough, being the very picture of health. The younger one, Annie, was a tall slender girl of some thirteen or fourteen years of age. I used to tease her the most, and tell her I was going to wait for her, more in jest than anything else; but I have often heard things said in jest, which turned out true, and in four or five years I came back from California and married Annie, and here we are today in 1892, in the midst of plenty with a family of six—three boys and three girls, all grown up, the girls all married, and enjoying good health.[26]

NOTES TO CHAPTER III

1. This scene is a well-documented segment of Arkansas history. The Legislature was debating the Wolf Bill in December 1837. Should wolves be exterminated in Arkansas by offering a $3 bounty for each scalp? John Wilson, Speaker of the House, was opposed and argued that hunters would bring in skins from out of state. J. J. Anthony proposed an amendment that offended John Wilson and during the argument that followed, Wilson drew his bowie knife. Anthony countered with his. A colleague tried to separate the combatants with a chair. Wilson advanced, shoved the chair aside, plunged his knife into Anthony's chest, withdrew it, wiped the blade clean with thumb and forefinger, then calmly walked back to the Speaker's desk. Anthony died on the floor minutes later. Wilson was tried in another county. He hired a mob to demonstrate in his behalf, it is said, and was acquitted as expected. That night, he and his supporters celebrated and paraded through the streets playing on drums, trumpets and tin pans (Fletcher 1947:62–63).
2. This was no exaggeration. Fletcher (1947:65–66) called the years between 1820 and 1840, the "duelling, knifing, brawling, period." Most did not wait for a challenge. They settled disputes then and there, usually with the bowie knife, more commonly dubbed the "Arkansas Toothpick."
3. A number of writers have penned horrifying and dramatic accounts of backwoods justice during the 1840s including: Friedrich Gerstäcker, *The*

Regulators in Arkansas, 1845; Charles Summerfield, *The Desperadoes of the Southwest*, 1847; and John W. Middleton, *History of the Regulators and Moderators*, 1883. During this time, hundreds of poor farmers eked out a living in the Arkansas wilderness. Criminals also fled from justice to the woods, and very soon became a problem for the area farmers. Without a court, sheriff or jail, farmers and hunters eventually united as the Regulators to rid their country of these miscreants, whom they called the Moderators. The two groups often fought pitched battles until the loser retreated to the canebrake. Once apprehended though, captives were usually tortured for admissions of complicity, and at the same time, witnesses frequently dropped out of sight due to fear. Each faction served as its own judge, jury, and on-the-spot executor of punishment—mainly by hanging.

4. Richard C. Hawkins was Commissioner of Public Buildings in 1842 (Arkansas *House Journal*, 1843). Thomas Thorn and a partner named Cook (Kennan 1950:IX:37) had been responsible for the stone and brickwork of the State House since 1835 (Robinson 1980). Brownlee and friends, Cooper, McMorrin, and McVicar, apparently became partners in McVicar and Company and assumed responsibility to do State House stonework in about 1838; Thorn retained the contract for the brickwork. Records also show (Arkansas *House Journal*, ibid) that James McVicar and Company was paid $6,100.50 for "Building stone wall and stonework of State House, &c."

5. Gideon Shryock, the famed architect from Kentucky, designed Little Rock's first Capitol, a handsome Greek Revival style building that still stands on a rise overlooking the Arkansas River. The Capitol's main building was completed by the time Brownlee commenced work in 1838. Therefore, he must have worked on its two wings, whose brick walls were painted and plastered to represent masonry block. McVicar and Company, therefore, surely laid the foundations of native stone. The building must have been impressive for its day because a number of Forty Niners on their way to the California goldfields took time to note its appearance in their diaries. In 1849, Charles Pattison of New Jersey wrote that the Capitol "was a splendid building" and was "the ornament of the place," while Lorenzo Aldrich of New York remarked that the capitol is "rather a fine building, being composed of brick and coated with a plaster having the appearance of marble." By September 30, 1842 (Arkansas *House Journal*, 1843:6), $33,733.62 had been paid out of a $37,000 appropriation to complete construction. The Old State House was the seat of Arkansas' government for 75 years. When the Legislature moved to a new Capitol, the building was used as a medical research laboratory, and

later as the War Memorial Museum. Extensive restoration begun in 1947 has helped the Old State House regain its glory. The 1836 House of Representatives and the 1885 Supreme Court chambers are now beautifully and expertly restored, while former offices contain displays which interpret Arkansas' historic past.

6. It is unfortunate that Brownlee did not expand his discussion on the stone wall. Other than the above citation and his reference that McVicar & Company was paid for building a stone wall, Brownlee's mention of it is the only other known reference. He does, however, give one additional piece of information: it "was built partly around the State House." According to Lucy Robinson, Director of the Old State House, the location of that wall is a mystery. It has been established that a five-rail fence surrounding the State House for many years was replaced in 1870 by an ornamental iron fence set in a stone-coping wall (Kennan 1950:IX:39). With reference to the State Bank, it seems possible that Brownlee worked on the Real Estate Bank, since the Little Rock branch of the State Bank had been open for some time prior to Brownlee's arrival. Neither bank stayed in business very long. Banks began to close down in stages after the general panic and depression of 1837, leaving thousands to face financial ruin (Ferguson 1966:70–72). Brownlee apparently carried his bank in his pockets for he seems not to have been affected. His Scots' thrift may have stood him in good stead as it appears he had plenty of money to lend in 1841.

7. I stumbled on Cooper's gravestone in a remote corner of Little Rock's Mount Holly Cemetery. It says that his friends, James McVicar, Sam McMorrin, and Robert Brownlee carved and erected the marker in his memory. Cooper was 28 years old when he died on August 24, 1840.

8. Brownlee's symptoms suggest malaria, a disease that caused enormous distress to thousands of frontiersmen. The anopheles mosquito was the culprit, although in 1840 men did not know that. The problem was magnified in Arkansas because its profusion of rivers provided miles of breeding ground for the pest. Some have said (Arkansas 1941:278) that the Arkansas variety of ague (also known as bilious fever, marsh fever, or chills and fever) caused the greatest suffering. The medicine show and its itinerant peddler who hawked patent medicines was a familiar sight in those days and there is no doubt that a good supply of Dr. John Sappington's pills was on hand. Sappington commenced marketing his quinine pills on a wide scale in 1832 and became well-known for his expertise in the treatment of malaria (Hall 1971:1–7).

9. John McHenry was one of the younger sons of Archibald McHenry, a pioneer Arkansan of the 1820s, and inherited his father's 1432-acre farm,

home, and slaves around 1835. This property, about 10 miles south of Little Rock, was situated upon the first traveled road in Arkansas, known as the Southwest Trail. For many years, Ten Mile House, McHenry's large, two-story, brick home, was a stage stop on the trail. This is the first information Brownlee gives that he and his friends spent a good deal of their time there, probably until 1848. Margaret Ross (1955:3–9), who has researched the McHenry family in depth, says that John McHenry married Catherine Thorn of Bordentown, New Jersey, and we can thus postulate that this was a sister of the selfsame Thomas Thorn, brick contractor for the State House, and whose tombstone in Mariposa County, California, notes that he was also born in Bordentown, New Jersey. There are no birth or death records for John McHenry, but according to Ross, he must have died between 1846 and 1848, because his wife, Catherine, married Sam McMorrin in 1848. McMorrin then, must have lived on in the McHenry home until his death in 1854 at the age of 72. McVicar also was close to the family. One of John McHenry's younger brothers, Jesup, accompanied McVicar to the California goldfields in '49. And in 1855, McVicar returned from California to marry John's sister, Amanda McHenry Miller (Ross ibid). Ross says that many details are vague on birth and death dates for Archibald McHenry's known children. A reference in the 1870 California census for Mariposa County suggests there may have been another McHenry brother, Morrison McHenry, who was born in 1833 in Arkansas. He was a roadmaster in Mariposa County and was married to Susan E., age 39, also of Arkansas.

10. The McHenry home, now over 150 years old, still stands on its extensive plot but is showing signs of age. Some of the outbuildings and the brickworks are gone, but the old brick walkways are discernible through a tangle of grass. Though she favors the earlier date, Margaret Ross (1955:3–9) claims the house was built some time between 1825 and 1836, and is one of the oldest in Arkansas. It was designed by Gideon Shryock of Kentucky, who also drew the plans for the Old State House, which was constructed between 1833 and 1842. Brownlee's memoirs relate that he and McMorrin met McHenry some time between 1840 and 1842, so the kitchen would date after 1840 but before McHenry's death in '46 or '47. This information may help researchers fix a more definite date for the house and outbuilding construction. The kitchen and cellar that Brownlee and McMorrin built are in use. The one-room kitchen is a small replica of Brownlee's Georgian-style house in Little Rock, with high chimneys at each end, staggered brick edging under the eaves called modillions, and a central doorway. The kitchen, separated from the main building, is partially obliterated today by the addition of a curved wooden

hall, designed to connect it to the house, and by a later outbuilding, possibly a smokehouse, to its left. The cellar appears to be intact, but the kitchen roof badly needs repair. Interior and exterior brick walls have been whitewashed. The interior of the kitchen has enjoyed some modernization, with the addition of cupboards and modern appliances now covering one fireplace. Robert Brownlee might be proud to know that his brickwork appears to be in fairly good condition except for erosion around the remaining fireplace at the opposite end of the kitchen. This fireplace is still intact with its pioneer fittings. The house has deteriorated since its restoration in 1935, but the present owners recognize the building as part of the Arkansas heritage and are planning to refurbish it once again.

11. According to Ross (1955:3–9), John McHenry's only known child was Bonaparte John McHenry, born in 1846. It has been difficult to trace many of the McHenry members since it is believed that a number of them are buried in unmarked graves somewhere on the plantation (Ross ibid). Brownlee's reference to a daughter may very well be true. Not only did he spend a good deal of time with McHenry, but his recollection of people, dates, events, and places checks out well with known facts.

12. McVicar was born in Fifeshire, Scotland, on April 1, 1814, and emigrated to America when he was 21. He was elected and served as warden of the State Penitentiary in Little Rock from 1842–1846 (Bennett 1982). In 1845, he became Grandmaster Mason of the Grand Lodge of Arkansas (Ross 1955:3–9). He enlisted in the army on July 1, 1846, and served as quartermaster sergeant of Colonel Yell's cavalry regiment at Buena Vista (Arkansas History Commission, 1913). McVicar joined Brownlee in 1849 on the trek to California, where he opened a trading post at Indian Bar on the Tuolumne River (Woodruff 1850:August 6). In 1852, he took over the Dill and Tateman general store in the town of Mariposa, California (Mariposa County *Records Book* II:91). He also purchased a number of town lots, ranchland, and mining properties in and around Mariposa between 1852 and 1860 (ibid). During this time, McVicar also served as Justice of the Peace for Mariposa County (Mariposa County *Supervisors' Minutes Book A*:436, 524, 541). He had returned to Little Rock in October 1855 and in January 1856 married Amanda McHenry Miller, sister of his old friend, John McHenry (Ross ibid). Some time after 1860, McVicar started to sell out his Mariposa property. His last transaction was recorded on August 24, 1869, when he and his wife sold a lot on Bullion and 8th streets (Mariposa County *Deeds Book Y*:181). They may have returned to Arkansas at this time. McVicar died in 1872 and is buried in the Masonic plot in Little Rock's Mount Holly Cemetery. Amanda

died in 1871 and is buried in Calvary Cemetery, Little Rock. They had one son, James William McVicar.

13. It is not difficult to locate this prominent monument in Little Rock's Mount Holly Cemetery. It was dedicated to William Gilchrist, First Grandmaster of the Grand Lodge of the State of Arkansas. He died on September 15, 1843. Brownlee and McMorrin cut an obelisk that rises about 16 feet from a nine-foot wide base. (McVicar is also buried in this plot dedicated to former Grandmaster Masons, but his simple marker is unadorned.)

   For 140 years Arkansas' historic families have been laid to rest at Mount Holly and are commemorated by one of America's finest collections of grave markers. Because of these criteria, Mount Holly is one of the few cemeteries in the country included in the National Register of Historic Places. Robert Brownlee and Samuel McMorrin would no doubt be proud to know that this stone, along with others they might have carved, helped to achieve this status and will be preserved on this historic site as part of the Arkansas heritage.

14. The farm was southwest of Little Rock and twelve miles west of Benton on the Perryville Road. Except for modern highways and more recent settlements, the area appears little changed today. Seventy acres were under cultivation in 1850. Brownlee described the farm as having "a good, substantial double-hewed log dwelling-house, containing 2 rooms and a spacious passage, a good kitchen, smoke house, corn crib, and stable, a well of excellent water, and two remarkably fine springs within a yard of the door" (From an ad Brownlee placed in the *Arkansas Gazette* on April 12, 1850). The three Brownlee brothers and Sam McMorrin jointly owned the 260 acres after March 2, 1842 (Pulaski County *Deed Book B*:303). Brownlee sold his share of the property to McMorrin for $200 on July 26, 1852 (Pulaski County *Deed Book D*:50).

15. There were a number of ways Robert Brownlee could hire a Negro during the days of slavery in Arkansas. First, there were many free Negroes in the state who were available for hire. In some cases, owners would deliver a slave in lieu of a debt. More commonly, however, owners would lease their Negroes for specific jobs or specified periods of time. They were sought for construction work, railroad and road building, farming, cooking, or as domestic servants. By law, the slave could not "hire his own time" (Taylor 1958:59–91); his wages went into his master's pocket. Arkansans paid top hiring prices for Negroes, and the ten dollars Brownlee paid was within acceptable limits of the day.

   Though Brownlee said he did have some words with McHenry's overseer about his management of the Negro, the reader might ask why

Brownlee said so little on the issue of slavery. Possibly this had a great deal to do with his pragmatic nature and decision to remain uninvolved in areas that he believed did not concern him. Scottish Historian Gordon Donaldson (1976:206) provided an additional observation for consideration: "The egalitarianism of the Scottish society helped Scots to accept peoples of various social backgrounds, and it has been suggested that the existence in Scotland itself of two races and two languages made the Scots less sensitive than many Europeans to differences of race and colour and therefore readier to establish and maintain good relations with natives."

16. For a number of years, James lived in Robert's Little Rock house rent free but paid the state and county taxes on it. He also owned two slaves, two pleasure carriages and four horses (Pulaski County *Tax Records*, 1848–1852). In 1849, he founded J. Brownlee & Co., a livery stable at Main and Elm streets (*Arkansas State Democrat*, May 18, 1849). James eventually returned to Scotland, where he died in the small town of Carluke in 1880 at the age of 70. Thomas, on the other hand, emigrated to Northern California in 1852 and set up the first blacksmith shop in the town of Vallejo. He also spent some time in the mines at Virginia City, Nevada, but later returned to California where he worked in the Navy Yard machine shop on Mare Island near Vallejo. He was 68 when he died in 1884 (DAR 1936:IV:75).

17. Brownlee and McVicar would have expected their houses to be standing today. Scotsmen built houses that way—to last! They would have been amazed, however, to learn that their houses had become museums in the Arkansas Territorial Restoration complex, which depicts life in early 19th-century Little Rock. The Brownlee and McVicar houses and two other 19th century structures sit in a park-like enclosure bounded by Scott and Cumberland between Second and Third streets (Block 32) in downtown Little Rock, a short walk to the Arkansas River or Old State House. Care of these buildings has been undertaken by the Territorial Restoration project, and they have been restored to prime condition. Their interiors have also been brought to life by period furnishings.

William E. Woodruff, founder of the *Arkansas Gazette*, once occupied the house on lot #12 adjacent to the Brownlee home. Jesse Hinderliter operated a grog shop in a commodious, two-story building (Little Rock's oldest standing structure) on lot #7 and on the other side of the Brownlee house. Brick contractor, Thomas Thorn, later bought the building and ran it as a boarding house (1840 census records list 89 people on the premises, 49 as slaves). It is possible that Brownlee and McVicar found rooms here when they first came to Little Rock. Thorn also owned adjacent lots #8 and #9. James McVicar purchased these and the Hinderliter house on February 16, 1842 (Pulaski County *Deed Book N*:458), then sold lot #9 to Robert Brownlee on July 12, 1842 (Pulaski County *Deed Book O*:21). Extensive research by the Arkansas Territorial Restoration has shown that McVicar erected a frame house on lot #8 in 1849. It was moved across the small park during restoration and is the only one of the four buildings not on its original site.

The Brownlee house has been known as the Noland House since Col. C. F. M. Noland was thought to have lived there in the 1850s. However, with the information Brownlee has supplied in his memoirs, supported by deeds, tax records, and an ad that appeared in the *Arkansas Gazette* on April 12, 1850, it is clear that Robert Brownlee owned the property, and with the help of Sam McMorrin, completed construction of his Georgian-style brick house in 1847. The same ad contained a description and sales information for his Benton farm and silver mine. It appeared six months after Brownlee's arrival in California and suggests that it did not take long for him to decide to stay. The ad stated that "the proprietor has determined not to return to Arkansas, he will sell any or all the above valuable property considerably below its value; either for cash in hand, or for one-half cash, and the residue in 6 and 12 months, with interest at 10 percent." James Brownlee continued to live in the house and pay its taxes (Pulaski County *Tax Records*, 1848–1852). Brownlee sold the little brick house to Roderick L. Dodge during an 1852 visit to Little Rock (Pulaski County *Deed Book W*:245). The property subsequently changed hands a number of times until the State of Arkansas took possession on July 12, 1939 (Pulaski County *Deed Book 263*:315). By then it was dilapidated, weather-worn and much changed. Little did it resemble Brownlee's description in the *Arkansas Gazette* (April 12, 1850), when he advertised for sale: "A NEW 1-STORY BRICK DWELLING HOUSE; On the west side of Cumberland, between Cherry [now Second] and Mulberry [now Third] Streets, and Lot No. 9, in Block No. 32 . . . in the city of Little Rock. The house contains two neatly finished rooms separated by a spacious and airy hall. On the premises are an excellent kitchen, smokehouse with cellar underneath, and other out-buildings, together with a well of the best water in the city."

Photographs taken before restoration in 1941 show a tattered old building with a raised-seam roof, one chimney missing, another falling in, and a sagging front porch where none had been before. A four-room extension had replaced outbuildings at the rear, and the well was in a tiny weed patch hidden by debris. Restorers removed the additions, raised the house and set it on a new foundation, rebuilt the chimneys, and rehoused the well. Since the original kitchen would have been a separate structure (*Arkansas Gazette*, March 3, 1940), one was built in brick and suitably outfitted at the rear of the house near the well. To achieve symmetry, a twin building was erected on the other side of the well and was furnished as an office, although Brownlee mentions no such room. Archaeologists are presently working to reveal locations of the smokehouse and other outbuildings. Despite the minor liberties taken during the initial restoration, the Brownlee house was skillfully reborn. Two authentic mantlepieces, the front door with its handsome sidelights and transom, and the three doors that open to the back porch (which was reconstructed in its original location), have all been reworked with care and fidelity. Historians found period pieces to furnish one room as a living and dining area and the other as a bedroom, just as it might have been in Brownlee's day. Here, Robert Brownlee might be pictured lying in his bed as he recovered from the wounds that he received in the 1848 mining accident, while his brother James and sister-in-law, Isabelle, tended to his needs. It is appropriate that the house has been renamed to honor its builder.

18. Brownlee probably purchased the property in the spring of 1848 after reading several articles in the *Arkansas State Democrat* (April 21 and May 19, 1848) that reported a recent discovery of quantities of lead ore with a high silver content. One company that owned mines in the area—Moreland, Moulton and Hunt—reported that every 1000 parts of ore contained three parts silver and was selling for $113.12 a ton. Brownlee, of course, made no "fortune." He described his mining property in the same ad in which he advertised his house and Benton farm: "VALUABLE LEAD AND SILVER MINES recently discovered and now being worked, in Pulaski county, on the north side of the Arkansas River, and about 10 miles from Little Rock. These lands were selected with a special view to their containing mineral, and, from the indications on the surface, it is believed that as valuable discoveries of SILVER, LEAD, ZINC, and other ORES, may yet be found on them as at the other rich diggings contiguous to them" (*Arkansas Gazette*, April 12, 1850).

19. The Fourche la Fave River flows through the Ouachita National Forest in west central Arkansas and into the Arkansas River near Perryville. It is possible that Brownlee and Jennings met during State House construction. In the Arkansas *House Journal* (1843:6), under expenditures for the State House, R. T. Jennings received $4,207.50 for painting.

20. In his *Wild Sports* (1854), the German writer, Friedrich Gerstäcker, draws an excellent picture of life in Arkansas in the late 1830s and early '40s, confining his stories to firsthand experiences. He spurned city life, pre-

ferring instead to live and hunt in the forest area near Fourche la Fave River. The woods supported dense stands of canebrake and because of sparse population, provided good cover for lawbreakers. It is not possible to pinpoint the exact region that attracted Brownlee and Jennings, but they may have gone somewhere near present day Mena.

21. An old Scottish word meaning "all that stuff."
22. Gerstäcker called these "frolics," which were held to celebrate the completion of various community endeavors such as a "log-rolling frolic," or a "quilting frolic." Brownlee and Jennings may have staged a frolic to celebrate their business deal. The party might have been very much as Gerstäcker (1854:220–223) described it:

> I lounged toward the place of destination, leaving my rifle at home . . . Here all was in movement; the whole neighborhood had assembled, and the rough backwoodsmen formed many strange groups; some in hunting-shirts, like myself; some in woollen homespun coats—but the greater number without their upper garments. Several fires were lighted, and cooking was going on in various modes, while, in a shady place near the house a group of women were occupied in boiling a 'powerful long coffee.'

When he arrived at ten o'clock in the morning, Gerstäcker said they had already begun dancing, which would go on until sun-up. Music was supplied by a series of fiddlers, not necessarily in top condition due to the liberal quantity of spirits available to all. Gerstäcker went on to say that the ballroom comprised:

> The interior of a log-house, about sixteen feet by twenty. . . . The air within was hot, almost to suffocation, but the sight was at times too pretty, at times too comic to be quickly deserted. Indeed, most of the girls, beating time with their little feet in jigs, reels, and hornpipes, were pretty enough to chain to the spot any worshipper of natural beauty. . . . Some changed their dresses five times between noon and the following morning. It would be as incorrect to dance for a whole night in the same dress as in Europe to appear without gloves.

23. Gerstäcker (1854:20) confirms this, adding that the first settler on the land retained prior rights to its purchase.
24. These meetings were the outgrowth of a religious revival that began in the early 1800s in a few Presbyterian colleges in the east and south and gradually moved west and toward the frontier. It was not long before the Methodists also started to hold open-air meetings that welcomed both sinners and salvation seekers. Brownlee may have heard that some worshippers became hysterical when they received the "divine spirit" at such meetings—a religious experience that would have been quite unlike those he had known as a boy.
25. Alexander Lamont was born in Aberdeenshire, Scotland, in 1796 and emigrated to Cuyahoga County, Ohio, with his wife, Elspeth (Cameron),

in the 1830s. Arriving in Little Rock during 1847, they stayed there for three years before moving to Boone County, Ohio. They had four children. Daughters Mary and Annie were born in Strathardle, Scotland, in 1828 and 1834 and married the brothers Thomas and Robert Brownlee, settling with their husbands in California in 1852. The Lamont sons, James and George, were born in Bedford, Ohio, in 1842 and 1844 (DAR 1936:IV:274), and were brought by their parents to the West in 1854. Both the Lamont and Brownlee families became long-time respected residents of Napa and Solano counties in northern California.

26. Brownlee has jumped ahead of his story and it is necessary to go back to the winter of 1848, when he was recuperating from his mining injuries in his Little Rock house. During this period of inactivity he might have reflected on the experience, and perhaps thought about new ways he might make a living. Because he had been so active all of his life, he must have been getting more and more restless as he began to feel better. It will never be known what plans he might have had in the back of his mind, for once again, a far-off event changed his life—the discovery of gold in California. Just as in 1836 he suddenly decided to sail to New York, he now quickly made up his mind to go to California.

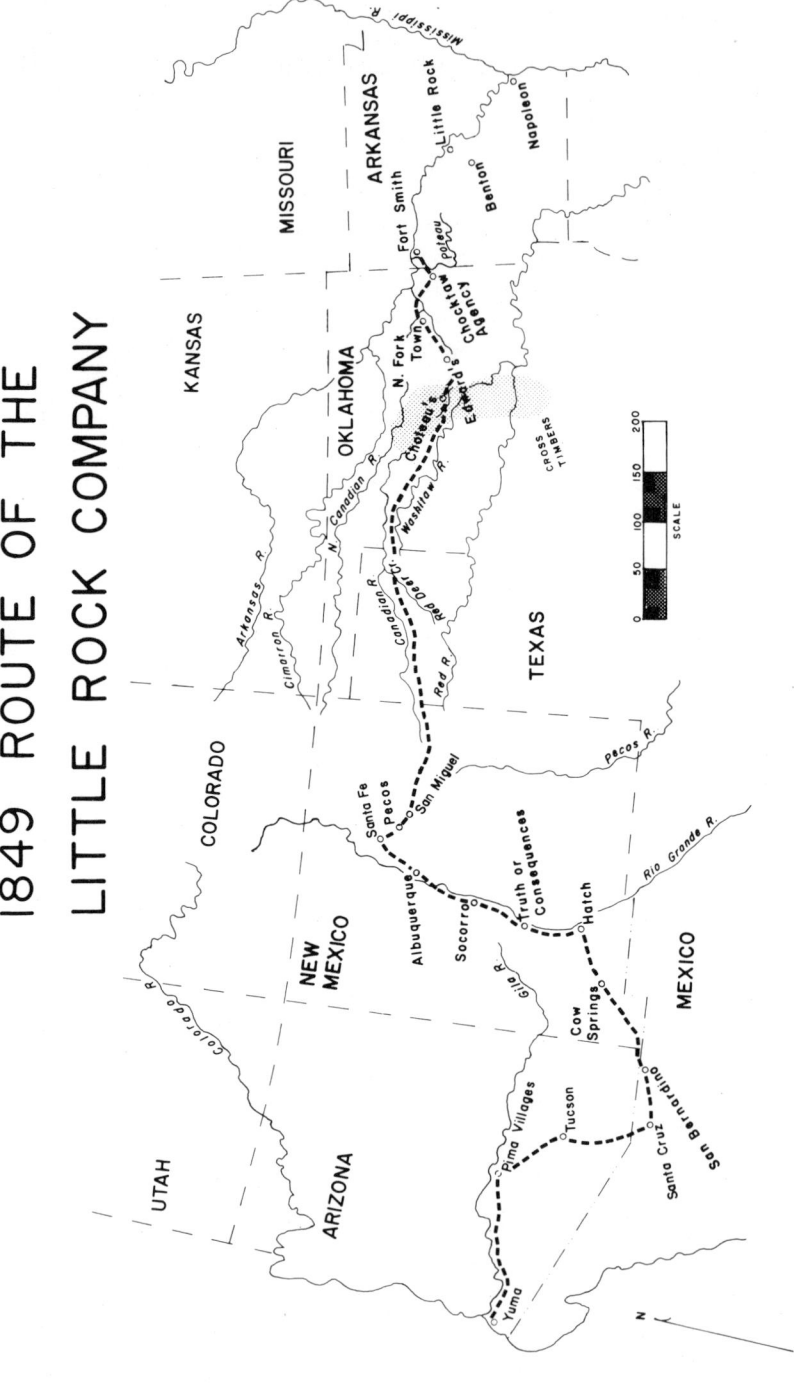

CHAPTER IV

To See the Elephant[1]

INTRODUCTION

President Polk's State of the Union message was the headline story on Friday, December 22, 1848. When Robert Brownlee opened his *Arkansas Gazette* he must have read the President's confirmation of rumors that had circulated and escalated for months—that there was indeed gold in California and plenty of it. Brownlee and a number of his Little Rock friends wasted no time in making preparations for the long trek West and were on the road by mid-March. Their activities were repeated around the world as gold fever spread to every state in the Union, to Australia, Mexico, South America, Asia, and to Europe. Ultimately, some 90,000 adventurers set sail or came by land, and during the final months of 1849, began the historic stampede into California.

Brownlee was optimistic that his expectations would be fulfilled and like other Forty Niners, set out despite fear of cholera, which was then crippling U.S. cities. He went in spite of unknown hazards of travel on unfamiliar tracks over rugged mountains and parched, saline deserts. He and his friends hoped to find plenty of water and forage for their animals and gambled that both their provisions and health would hold out. They also prepared for the possibility of attack by hostile Indians. In retrospect, these men helped speed up the westward movement; never before had so many traveled so far and settled a new state so quickly. The migration also was unique because it involved primarily a force of men who, for the most part, planned to return home as soon as they had gathered their fortune in gold.

Brownlee's narrative is the first that has come to light describing the journey made by members of the Little Rock and California Mining Association. He says that the men decided to follow a new road on the first leg of their journey, one that went across the plains between Fort Smith, Arkansas, and Santa Fe, New Mexico. At Santa Fe, the men decided to turn southwest on a trail meandering through New Mexico and Arizona. Brownlee and his fellow Arkansans were among some 18,000 goldseekers who crossed the Colorado River near modern Yuma in 1849, then negotiated the rugged trail through the Southern California desert toward Los Angeles or San Diego.

Because few men left written accounts of their adventures along the Southern Trail, Brownlee's observations add a new dimension to the overland story. He recalls that though they moved through hundreds of miles of unexplored country, the men were able to replenish supplies in remote New Mexican towns. Usually, local townsfolk staged a fandango for the tired and dusty travelers. Despite rigors of an overland journey, Brownlee retained the curiosity and energy of a modern-day sightseer. While at Santa Fe, for example, he observed St. John's Day festivities, which were celebrated with the colorful and exciting sport of *Correr el Gallo*. He remembers his visit with peaceful Pima Indians who tended their farms on the Gila River, and relates encounters with the wily Apache and Yuma Indians, whom he met as free and proud warriors.

The Little Rock Company faced its toughest challenge on the Arizona and California deserts, where temperatures were well over 100°. The effort to locate water became a daily problem as men and animals neared the end of a long journey. Eagerness and excitement for the venture had diminished somewhat, especially since the death of two comrades, who rested in graves back on the trail. Nevertheless, Brownlee and his fellow travelers remained remarkably adaptive despite coping with numerous obstacles and many long days in the saddle. They arrived safely at the Colorado River crossing near Yuma in average time for overlanders: five-and-a-half months. Their journey, however, was not quite over.

THE JOURNAL

I was confined to the house some two or three months [after the explosion], when the news reached me of gold being found in California. I think it was on Christmas day, when they fixed me up for the first time to go out, it may have been the same day on which we heard of the gold. When my friends came to me I told them I was going to start for California as soon as I got well enough, which I think I did in the middle of March.[2]

As I have not left Arkansas yet, I had better wind up before speaking of home matters. In arranging to start for California I had much to do, and was at first not able to attend to it properly. I had half of the farm for which I gave fifteen hundred dollars, the house and lot worth two thousand, and three hundred and sixty acres of land, which was bought for mining purposes. Besides, I had loaned Colonel [Thomas] Thorn sixteen hundred dollars in 1841 at 8%. He cleared out and went to Texas with forty or fifty Negros and left me in the lurch. I commenced suit and got something like nine hundred dollars, about the sum to which the interest would amount.[3] You must bear in mind, I spent lots of money in mining for lead in September 1848, I think it was. Besides [I had] Doctors' bills, which made me very short for ready cash. I had to get a good outfit with plenty of provisions, so joined a mess of four with a teamster, which made five of us in number—just three too many. We had to have a wagon made and to buy four mules with harness, and a saddle horse for each man. We took everything from Little Rock, as we could not buy anything on the road. After a while, we were ready to start.

We were to rendezvous at Fort Smith, about three hundred miles up the river, at the mouth of the north fork of the Canadian, which took us almost to Santa Fe.[4] We stayed in Camp at Fort Smith some time, waiting on different portions of the train, more for self protection than anything else. There were some teams, which had to come four hundred miles to connect with us, and as the roads at that season were very soft and miry, it took them a long time. After a while, about the latter part of March, some sixty wagons, with from four to six mules to a team, and each man with his saddle horse and rifle, joined us. Some had shot-guns and others pistols. I took an old shot-gun and cut the barrels off to a length of ten or twelve inches, also a good supply of bullets, besides buck-shot.

As we are about ready to start, I will go back to Little Rock and bid them all good-bye. You must remember I am yet very weak, my arm in a sling, had to be helped on my horse, which my brother got for me and was a fine, stout, young and gentle one, for which I paid eighty dollars; and eighty dollars for the mule and harness; forty dollars, one fourth of the hundred and sixty for a new wagon; and about a hundred dollars more for provisions and general outfit. The captain [James McVicar] and his Lieutenants examined every wagon to see if they were all properly provided for, if not, they could not join the company. Besides every one had to be in good health, so that the company would not be detained on account of sickness.

I mounted and called on my friends to bid them good-bye. While on my way to Fort Smith, I called on Mr. [Alexander] Lamont's family and saw the old folks and the girls, shook hands, and started up town, and parted with brother, and many others; when I joined some of our company who were about to start to overtake the wagons, which had been gone several days. We didn't come up with them until we reached Fort Smith.

After awhile we made a start, but as the roads were very soft, loads heavy, and mules green as well as the men, we made short drives,[5] and as feed was very poor we made slow time, until we passed the Cross Timbers, which is a belt of small trees about as thick as your arm, growing on red clay. There's where we had to work in good earnest. Every morning about fifty men with axes were detailed to go ahead and make corduroy roads, all the way through that belt of timber. After lifting the mired teams out of the road, it had to be re-fixed for the next, as the road got worse every time a wagon passed, so it would often be in the night when we would reach camp. I think the Cross Timbers as they are called, run East and West, some half mile wide.[6]

After passing the timber we came upon very fine farming land, no wood in sight, except on streams. I think we were now in Oklahoma Territory, for we traveled parallel with the Cimeron [Cimarron River], and could see the timber.[7] We had a stampede here, among the saddle horses. As the mules were driven up, each man was supposed to catch his own. They were all caught while the horses were feeding all around, when all of a sudden some five or six of them that were loose started, just as hard as they could put. Whatever startled them no one ever could tell, for we were in an open country. We followed them on horse back but they were never caught, as they took up the waters of the Cimeron River. Orders were then given that when the mules were driven up, each man except the cook must help catch and fasten every animal.

We had now passed through the Cherokee Nation, which was the prettiest country, and finest land I had as yet seen, being partly timbered with walnut, pecan, shell-bark hickory, ash, oak and wild-cherry and having a black rich loam. The people's houses were mostly of brick. They had good fences having lots of Negroes and all as well mannered as the White community. The next was the Choctaw Nation,[8] who also had a good country, although not as good as that of the Cherokees.

We lost our horses in the Seminole Nation, where there was but little timber, but good grazing ground, as the grass was wonderfully fine in this country. We had just camped, when we were surprised by the "Wildcat," the Seminole Chief. There were about a dozen Indians coming home, half drunk from a party, when the Chief came boldly into camp, and inquired for the captain, and on seeing him said that he was a poor looking captain, and he thought he could whip him, then called for tobacco which was given him. He then left saying we would hear from him again. That was our first night to stand guard, and my name being among the first, I shouldered my shot-gun, loaded with buck-shot, and stood sentry two hours. We fully expected to see him return with more Indians, and if he had there might have been blood shed, as we were not going to suffer any indignity to our captain, but he never came back.[9]

About here was where the first buffaloes were seen, and we were so fortunate as to get one. There were five old bulls feeding when first seen, and when they started off, each man took after one. I had a good horse which was not afraid of the gun but my arm was in a sling so [I] did not have a very good show.[10] Mr. Thebolt [F. J. Thibault], an old hunter,[11] on his mule happened to get ahead of one, and as he passed, fired; twas then we had our first buffalo meat, and our last, as we never killed another. I was close by when he shot, and when it fell dead, the others crossed over its body, over the False Washitaw River, and got away; as the river was some hundred yards wide, we had to give up the chase. We returned to help dress the bull, and to prepare for packing, as we were now some four miles from the train. That old bull was a hard looking case, not a hair on his body, and his skin looked like that of an elephant.

While we were skinning him, all our horses were loose save mine, which fortunately I was holding, every one of them stampeded down the river, and my horse was like to get away from me, and had he succeeded, I suppose we could never have caught the rest, as there would have been nothing fast enough to have headed them. I mounted and followed. They were a long way ahead, but the river being very crooked enabled me to cut across from point to point, and check them a little, when I was able to grab the stake rope of the leader, and by this time some of the boys had come up and by talking to the horses, got them quieted down, so we could catch them. It was coyotes that frightened them, as they were seen when the horses started, and bear in mind, stampeded horses are crazy. When we got back, the buffalo was in pieces, so that it could be packed. What feasting we had that night. We had a kettle which held five gallons, so when camped, put it on the fire with marrow bones, and other fancy pieces, "tid-bits." My mouth waters yet to think how we enjoyed the feast. We had enough cooked to last us two or three days.

I now really forget how many men were in our company. There were sixty wagons and say three men to a wagon, which would make one hundred and eighty persons.* It takes a great quantity of bull beef to fill all these mouths. Some of them were too lazy to try to provide in any way, others homesick of the worst kind, the most dejected looking men you can well imagine, and could scarcely eat when it was prepared for them. Men of families might be partly excused, but for single men there was no excuse. To laugh and make fun of them had no effect, as they would tear off by themselves, where they could whimper and whine about the great privations they were suffering. And all for what? They did not believe they would ever see any gold, and thought the whole thing was gotten up to deceive, and to be the

*See Appendix 1

means of depriving them of comfort to which they had always been used—to even think they would have to cook their own food, make their fire, carry water wherever they could find it, besides to have to cook with buffalo chips. Besides, the bread they made was mixed with saleratus and the more they put in, the more the stomach refused it. Served them right. You could hear the growlers, and the weak-kneed murmuring to one another; such men as those are a great hindrance and annoyance at all times. The company were traveling too fast or not fast enough, always finding fault, as though that would do any good.

Of such men were three of my mess, among whom were two brothers, who had been used to being waited upon by slaves, the third was a printer; the teamster was all right, and did his work cheerfully, without a murmur. I proposed to do the cooking, the others to get wood, water, fuel, and to pitch the tents; the teamster hitched and unhitched his team, helped to herd the mules through the night and hunt for good pasture and water. Some days the stock would be driven quite a distance from camp, therefore the teamsters were expected to be with them all the time, to stand guard and keep them together, to drive them up in the morning by sunrise, so we could have an early start. In traveling we found, that by starting early, we could make good time, travel twenty or thirty miles, and get into camp before dark, and could see what we were doing while cooking, and in pitching our tents. Our mess did first-rate at the start, but as we were getting farther West, would do nothing that they could avoid doing, and commenced whining, and of course you know I wouldn't stand any such nonsense, and told them that they had to do, as they all agreed to at the start. This helped for a few days, when it got back, and was perhaps worse than ever. The teamster and myself pulled together, and to make a long story short, remained so until we reached Santa Fe. Here we dissolved the mess of which I will speak when we get to Santa Fe.[12]

I suppose we were now two thirds of the way there. Perhaps I had better go back and bring the train along, which keeps moving and gets along nicely, through a fine country, void of timber, but covered with grass and plenty of buffalo signs. One of which drew our especial attention—it was a small circular ring about twelve feet across, perfectly round and seemingly much used, as the ground was greatly worn and they were very plentiful [buffalo wallows], the bulls get in them, bellow and paw the earth. Let it be understood, we have no wood, nothing but buffalo chips to cook with, but they make the finest and quickest fire for baking bread. Our cooking utensils consisted of a frying pan and a dutch oven. On the lid of the latter was an edge piece all around and by breaking the chips fine and placing on these covers and setting fire to them could bake on top first-rate.

I hunted on the road and most every evening would have something fresh: a rabbit or bird of some kind; sometimes a deer or antelope, perhaps a prairie dog. These latter are about, well maybe larger than a squirrel, head and tail as much like a young puppy as anything you ever saw, their feet resembled a squirrel's. As you approach them, they will sit up and bark so much like a dog, you would be easily mistaken, although the noise is not quite so loud. They are fat, and on what they thrive we never could find out, as there is no grass in their towns, save fine goose grass, and that is not disturbed in the least. There is a much traveled road between their holes, which are I believe, all connected, so how they subsist has been a mystery to everyone. You can never find water where they are, but plenty of rattlesnakes and owls, all three coming up out of the same hole. Where you see one you would be sure to see the other. We often had occasion to camp in a dog-town, but were very careful about snakes, as there would always be one or two killed every day. This is not all, the stench the dogs produced was very unpleasant. Nevertheless they were good eating. Their holes went almost straight down, and if you shot them they were likely to roll down out of your reach.[13]

We are about to cross the Arkansas River, that is the North Fork, where the water sinks almost out of sight. Where we were going to cross the river was about two hundred yards wide, and we forded the most treacherous quick-sand I ever heard of. Half of the train had crossed safely. Our team happened to go a few feet from where the others went, when the two off mules got in the quick-sand, and the two nigh ones were on firm sand. I was close by, and took the harness of the two mules, when I was nearly sticking myself. In a few moments the mules were cleared, wagon unloaded, and our ferry rope attached to the tongue of the wagon. As the wheels on the upper side were out of sight, after lifting and with about fifty men on the rope pulling, the wagon was gotten out safely. The mystery with me is why the solid sand, and the quick-sand should be so distinctly separated, just as completely as though done by hand.[14]

The next place of any interest was the old Pico [Pecos] Mission, which is at the junction of the road from St. Louis to Sante Fe. The place was in complete ruins, no roof, the walls in many places being down. It was built of stone and mortar of some kind, had once been a large building, and showed considerable mechanism. The walls contained nothing but cells, say four feet square at the mouth, and extended back six or eight feet, five or six tiers high, and of square timbers of considerable lengths, with some decent carving on wood. Whoever built and occupied the place, there are no signs of now, as there is no one living around. What those cells were used for is the wonder, if not for sleeping apartments. They were situated somewhat like a honey comb, one over the other with much regularity.[15]

The next place of interest was a natural pass through the spur of the Rocky Mountains, [which] looked just as though it had been pulled apart, and left a rift in some places not over one hundred feet wide, and in others much wider, where the earthy matter had washed away. As I am only writing from memory I may not be correct in my distances, but think the pass was one and a half miles long, and perhaps in some places one fourth of a mile wide, and may be two thousand feet high; in one place in particular the wall on the left, entirely overhanging the road for some distance. A small stream of pure water flowed along and was in great demand, as this was about the middle of June and very warm. Under that hanging rock it was cool and pleasant. The pass I think is a wonderful freak of nature, and there must have been some powerful convulsion to have parted, or split apart such a high mountain. Perpetual snow had been in sight for several days, perhaps not at the pass but close by. You must bear in mind that traveling on this immense plain is exceedingly monotonous, with scarcely any timber in sight, and not any mountains. So when we approached the Rocky Mountains, and could see their tops covered with snow it was a welcome change. It seemed to me we were passing the end of the Rocky Mountains, for to our left we could not see any high mountains covered with snow, but they were plainly visible on our right.

It was in this place that General Kearney [Stephen Watts Kearny] was attacked by the Mexicans in 1846. They built and barricaded the pass to prevent his advance, close by that overhanging rock; how the battle ended is a matter of history.[16] Anyhow Kearney passed out victorious, and a short ways from there was caught in a snow storm, of which we saw plenty of evidence. It may be twenty or thirty miles from the pass to Sante Fe, and the road was lined with dead carcasses of horses and mules, lying just as they fell, the skins perfect, the eyes gone, but you could raise the skeleton on its feet and it could stand; and at a little distance looked life like. The altitude is so great, that putrefaction did not take place. We passed a small town of Mexicans close by the pass. I think [there were] some three or four thousand people. Anything in the shape of vegetables, cheese, butter or eggs, we were always looking out for.[17]

Now we are in Sante Fe. I think it was a walled city of considerable size. The United States had troops there to preserve order. The town was some ten miles from the mountain and there was a small creek of the finest kind of water which came from the snow. The land was very poor around the town but they raise some corn near the creek, but the quantity was so small, and the ground so poorly worked, it was of very little value to supply a town. We stayed there several days, and bought grass, which had to be packed on jack asses for several miles to feed our mules.[18]

I spoke some time ago of not getting along with our mess, so I withdrew and joined John W. Clark, as he did not get along nicely with his mess either. We managed to rig up a four mule team, bought a light wagon, and Mr. Clark, although never used to horses, proposed to drive, while I was to cook. The change proved very fine, as Mr. Clark was industrious taking good care of the team, and was always hunting for good feed for them, and by so doing, our team was the fattest in the train. As he was much younger than I, [he] always looked to me for advice. He was perhaps six feet two inches tall, and rather slim, of a light complexion. When we started they talked of not taking him along, as he looked consumptive, but before we reached Santa Fe, they found out he could stand more fatigue than any one in the company, and [he] never whined; and if he had no water, was always ready to go hunt for some, or to go ahead and look for good camping grounds. As the train came into camp the wagons were drawn up in such a way as to form a corral to drive the stock into, to be caught, also into which to drive them when attacked by Indians.[19]

I know we were in Sante Fe June 24th as the Mexicans hold that day as a Holy Day. American Officers as well as Mexicans were all well mounted, and immediately after church was dismissed the Priest came to the plaza, and threw a chicken on the ground; when every man on horse back took after the chicken, and whoever caught it put around the plaza just as fast as he could, trying all the time to prevent the others from getting it. I had never seen such fine horse-man-ship—they would stoop down at a full run, and pick up the chicken, when some one else would get it away from them. I did not see much sport in the thing, but certainly admired the horse-man-ship.[20]

As the main train never entered Sante Fe, but moved along, they were four days ahead of us, and as there were only three wagons of us, we made fast time, and overtook them at Albuquerque where they were preparing to cross the Rio Grande river, which is a bold quick stream. The Tennessee company had overtaken ours, and jointly as they passed a grove of pines, felled and split timber to make a flat boat, and hauled the stuff some twenty miles, each wagon taking a portion. It is astonishing how quickly a lot of men can take timber from the stump, and make it into planks, and make wooden pins to fasten all together. The boat was ready to be launched, and our long ferry rope fastened from each side, with plenty of men to pull, so it was just pulled from one side to the other, and did not take long to ferry our company across. The land on the Rio Grande is of the best quality, the river bottom being some three or four miles wide.[21]

I think the next town was Seccora [Socorro], which was [a] considerable Spanish town. It happened to be the Fourth of July and the two companies sent a committee to buy sheep or goats, to have a feast to finish the holiday with, in fine style. I was one of the number, and think we bought twenty-four goats and some onions for our company. And you may just believe we enjoyed the same hugely. There was speaking and singing, and we spent the whole day in feasting and high living. Such is not often seen, nor a more patriotic set of men.[22]

We followed the Rio Grande for some distance, passing some small settlements. I think we left the river at a small town called [Doña] Ana.[23] We had an adventure with Apache Indians—one of our men was out hunting, when an Indian surprised him by walking towards him saying, he was a good Indian, [and] he jumped up behind him on his mule and told him to go to his camp, which he did. We saw them coming as fast as they could, when the Indian jumped off and asked to see our captain. He wanted to trade horses and mules, so I traded my horse right off, for a fat mule, as my horse was leg weary. The Indians all spoke Spanish, and it was well for this man that he understood the language.[24]

As we moved along we came to another rift in the mountains not as wonderful a pass as the one we have described, yet it is most wonderful how the passage is made, not over the mountain, but through the mountain, and on a level. On leaving that pass we had a down grade, just enough to cause the single-trees to strike the heels of the mules, still not enough to put the lock on the wagon.[25]

It was some thirty-five miles to the waters of the Mimbres, now called Demming [Deming] by the railroad guide. The Tennessee company came up and reported that some of their company had found gold towards our left. Twelve men among whom was myself, went some distance and looked, but found none, but later gold had been found in great quantities in that vicinity.[26]

The main train never stopped, but went on and was two days ahead of us. The second day we couldn't find any water, but a way to our right a little could see plenty, also wagons, mules and men, which seemed so real that some of our men wanted to go to them, but after traveling some time we recognized them as our own company, could see them washing, and drawing water, and see the mules feeding. At this time we must have been ten or twelve miles away, and it was nothing but mirage, and of the most deceiving kind. Men who want water very badly, and who even know all about mirage, will allow themselves to follow the delusion to their own sorrow, and many to their death.

I never suffered for water but once, which was on the other side of Sante Fe, but it was partly my own fault. A young man and myself left to go around what seemed to be a round table mountain, instead it was a long one, and we traveled all day and hadn't any water; towards sun down we crossed over and struck the wagon road. It was now dark, and we did not get into camp till ten o'clock at night. This was the Tennessee Company and they had camped without water, but gave us all the assistance they could, each of us getting about a pint of coffee, as they didn't have any more to give. Our Company had gone on about three miles ahead; in the morning we were hunting for our horses and couldn't find them, so concluded they had gone on ahead to catch our train, so we started on foot to overtake them before they left camp. The roads were dusty, besides it was very warm, and to our dismay the train commenced to move off when we were yet a mile away, so when we overtook the last wagon, we were completely given out, for the lack of water; we emptied all the coffee pots and sucked the grounds; held them in our mouths to cool our swollen tongues. We came upon a dry river bed where some one had dug a well some eight feet deep, the quick sand would not allow them to go any deeper. A man handed a tin cup full of sand and a little water, and every man had to take his turn. I got one or two tin cup fulls of sand and water, put the cold sand in my handkerchief and held it on my tongue, which was now getting too large for my mouth. I was thus much relieved.

Providence had been ever kind to us all the way, and even now when everything looked blue He came to our rescue, something like when Moses cleft the rock, when water rushed out to quench the thirst of the Jews in the Wilderness. It seemed marvelous that such an amount of water of such fine quality could be stored away within two miles of us, but one of our men returned and reported that he had found a perfect lake of water up the river, so the train was not long in getting there, as the mules seemed to smell the water. It was stored between two knolls of ground. In the bed of the river there was a ledge of lime stone rock, which crossed it and held the water; in quantity there seemed enough to float a Steam Boat, but by the next evening there was just enough for camp purposes.

There were a great many animals in our train, say 400 head, and the Tennessee Company had as many more. The Clarksville, which was an ox train, had say 600 oxen, 200 saddle horses to get all the water they could drink, and after having had to fast for two days without a drop and making big drives were very thirsty. The two mule teams got to water about noon, and about sun down the ox train sent men ahead to tell us, that the women and children were about given out. Some twenty men volunteered to return, and went back with ten gallons of water for each horse, among which was my horse, so I at last got him safely. I sent a water train back, which I have no doubt saved some lives. The ox train got in next morning, and when they got in sight of the water, you could not stop them long enough to unyoke them, and the families had to be gotten out before they reached the water so there was not any damage done. It was fortunate that the teams did not all arrive at once, or there would have been some accident. When we left camp that evening, water was getting very low. But I have given a lengthy description, and was to blame for starting around the seemingly round mountain, which instead was the end of a long one.[27] As we struck the plain, I killed an antelope just at sun down, so we had plenty to eat, and gave some to the Tennessee Company.

We are now in the territory of Arizona.[28] The country as we proceed does not compare with the land that we had passed, being more sandy, nothing but bunch grass, and that looked as though nothing would or could eat it; but to our surprise the stock ate it fine, and there was plenty to spare. Water was sometimes scarce, but as yet we had had enough. One morning we came up to a small lake [Playas Lake, New Mexico], some one hundred feet across. The water looked fine, but on tasting it proved as salt as the ocean with plenty of fish to be seen. We caught some of them, and each one had four legs as distinct as a lizard has and were about the size of herring. We, or at least I did not eat any of them. The wonder was, where did the salt water come from, as I suppose the pond must be five or six thousand feet above the level of the sea.[29]

The next place is Guadalupe Grade. On approaching the mountain the country is quite level, and all of a sudden you come to the jumping off place which was a fall of two thousand feet. The road was slanting and went down almost perpendicularly, and it took every man to help the wagons down—one set with a lever on the upper side to keep them from upsetting—another set with a rope to keep them from going too fast; and in one place in particular they had to be lowered by the ferry rope. After working hard all day we reached the bottom safely, and found plenty of good water, saw plenty of wild turkeys but did not have the time to go after them.[30]

About one mile below was a walled town, level country and everything in good order. We camped close to town, and from that hill came a fine clear creek, and with others like it soon formed a good large stream. We arrived in town about sun down, and they were having a very solemn procession, the Priests chanting something, and when they stopped the women would let out the most solemn sounds, more like a wail—then the procession would start [and] go a little farther and go through the same performance again. We were told that a few days before, the Apache Indians had stolen one or two children, and some jack-asses.

The women came out and washed our clothes, and we gave them a cup full of salt, for which they washed all day. Young women and men went under our wagons, and licked the salt which had dripped from the bacon, off of the boards, they being crazy for salt. Santa Cruz is the name of the town and is in Mexican Territory.[31]

We passed several old missions, some entirely deserted,[32] which at one time had been thickly settled; but the Apache Indians have been too many for the Mexicans. And let me say right here, almost too much for "Uncle Sam," as he has not as yet gotten the better of them. He has them on reservations, feeds them well while they stay, yet they are not satisfied, but every once in a while steal away, and commence killing. About the very place I have been describing, they are very treacherous, and you cannot place any confidence in them. I suppose we came down the Santa Cruz river about a hundred and fifty miles, where the river sinks in the sand. We had to dig for water, where we found plenty and of the very best quality.

We have now passed a fine little town, containing a beautiful church, built of sun dried bricks, and well finished on the inside; a credit to whoever did the work.[33] We have now arrived at Tuscon [Tucson], the largest town we have seen but Sante Fe. Here we got plenty of ripe grapes, onions, eggs and cheese, all in exchange for a little salt. The town is built on the Santa Cruz river, although you cannot see the river, plenty of water can be had by sinking a few feet. We left here with everything full of grapes.

I can remember very well. It was a hot day, when a young man and myself were riding along, when we saw water in a ditch, and concluded to have some and to fill our canteens, so reached down as far as we could to get the coldest. By so doing we got that which was most strongly charged with alkali. We drank freely and I noticed a burning sensation so ate a piece of pork, which eased me right off. He did nothing for himself and died next morning when we buried him. I think it was some thirty miles from Tuscon. His name was William Fagan. I had known him from a boy. That was a sad day; one of our party offered up a fervent prayer, and I don't think there was a dry eye in the crowd.[34]

Having camped without water, we were compelled to move the main train after burying our young friend and this was not the end of our trouble as there was another victim, a Negro, who was a slave to the man who offered the prayer. His sickness also was caused by drinking alkali water. When the train left he was not dead, but to all appearances could not live long, so six volunteered to stay and help the suffering man who was lying on an India Rubber bed which was blown full of wind, and belonged to his master. In the afternoon there appeared a small black cloud a little above not over a mile from where we were camped and how it thundered and rained there. We could see and hear the rain falling, while with us there was not a drop. But to our astonishment, the water came down in one bold unbroken front some two feet high, not running fast as the land was level, and what we could do for the sick man had to be done quickly; as it would have drowned him if left alone.

We tried to build a dam around him, but the water came faster than we could build, and was by this time knee deep. On looking around we saw a small dry knoll, where we carried the sick, and it was well we did so, for we were holding him suspended in the air, as the water had bursted in our dam. The water ceased running as fast as it was rising, and in one hour you could not see anything of the cloud burst. You would think we had plenty of water to drink, but not so, as the ground was so charged with alkali that it was impossible to drink it. Perhaps the mules used it, as they were tied where the water was running by them. All this time the Negro was getting weaker and for us to stay there could not be thought of, and before he died we had his grave dug six feet deep and timber cut the right lengths over the vault dug in coffin shape. As soon as he stopped breathing we rolled him in his blanket and laid him away; to await the great Judgment Day. This was a sad crowd, leaving two of its members in camp, and may well be imagined, was not very encouraging to us, as we hadn't had any water fit to drink for two days.[35]

We left camp about sun down and traveled till day light, when the mules must have sleep, as well as ourselves, or all would soon give out. We laid down beside two large cacti, and slept about one and a half hours, then started and traveled till about noon, when we caught up with the train. Here we got water, such as it was, it had to be boiled before using. We rested one hour and started for better camping grounds. We struck the Gila river where [there] was plenty of the best of snow water from the mountains. Shortly we came upon the Piemo [Pima] Village, finely situated on the banks of the Gila, where they had irrigating ditches, with plenty of corn, large fields, pumpkins, beans and watermelons; not large, but comfortable adoby houses for [the] Indians. I think we camped with them two days, and traded for corn and corn stalks. As they plant corn any time in the year, they always have it green. Besides we bought shelled corn to carry us through the American Desert. I think Clark had six bushels, procured in trade, he had some vermillion that took their eyes, [as] they were very fond of bright colors. For instance: McVicar had on a new red flannel shirt, which the squaws would give anything to get. They treated us well and we did them. They lived in the Gila bend, and it is forty miles to the next water.[36]

We started in the afternoon and traveled until daylight, gave the mules about two gallons of water each, and two hours sleep, then we again started through the dustiest alkali roads, which made the eyes and nose sore. The sun was hot and the dust like a cloud, as there was not the least sign of any wind, but some of the prettiest whirl winds would start in the dust and go away up to a great height, when they would hang, some in the shape of umbrellas, and would stay so often an hour at a time. We could not leave the road as the ground was covered with every form of cacti, some six inches, others forty feet and the small ones were the ones to be dreaded, being as sharp as needles, the horses could not stand them.[37]

One of our party, Major Haroldson [H. Haralson], an old man of about sixty years, wanted water very badly. As we could see the timber on the Gila river, he started away ahead of the train, pushing his horse beyond its strength, [but] it gave out, and as I was well in advance of the train, [I] came up with him sitting under a mesquite bush or tree about fifteen feet high which gave him some protection from the sun, and his horse was nearly dead. The Major's tongue was sticking out of his mouth, and was perfectly flat. We had some water in our canteen which we gave him, and helped him very much, and when giving him the water, were compelled to hold his horse to keep him away. The balance of the party came through safely; the Major was one who would never help himself, or provide for such emergencies.[38]

We reached the Gila river, when I plunged in clothes and all, and drank till I was fully satisfied. The water was as warm as new milk. When we last saw the river it was a large body of water, and very cold; now it was a small stream, [having come] 160 miles around the Gila bend. We now had plenty of water, but no feed for our teams, so had to cut down small cotton wood trees and let our stock eat the bark.

Clark and myself started ahead, to try and find feed. We traveled until mid-night, not thinking any other teams would follow, but McVicar's two teams, and a white man with a black family, came up and camped with us; so this ended our traveling any longer with the main train. We out traveled them, as we started in the afternoon and traveled all night, as the dust was not so bad then, and there was no feed for the teams, and we avoided the hot sun. The heat was intense all the way down some two or three hundred miles, and we suffered more the last four or five days than enough, but the new full moon enabled us to travel by night. We reached the mouth of the Gila river at mid-night, when we took the mules and washed them all over, getting the alkali out of their eyes and skin.

There were two wagons of Cherokees camped, who told us that about two miles out there was fine pasture for our animals, and that they would go and show us the way. Our stock needed feed very badly so we started, and as the sun arose we were surrounded by the Yumas in a very hostile manner, [they] came right among the wagons, and you may be assured we were somewhat alarmed; as our company was rather small, and three or four gone with the stock, and we being separated from them, placed us under many disadvantages. We could ill afford to send after our mules, but had to, and Governor [Thomas S.] Drew's son [Ransom], of Arkansas, volunteered and brought them all in. The Indians were still speaking, and I must acknowledge there was one old chief, about six feet tall and as straight and well proportioned as could be, [who] made a speech after which they disappeared as fast as they came, slipped into the water and were gone, and we could see nothing of them but their noses. Anyhow we harnessed up and started, accompanied by the Cherokees who proved to be of great service in standing guard.[39]

After traveling about ten miles we struck the Colorado river, at a large sand bar, and here there was nothing for our animals but cotton wood bark; we had to feed some corn as we were about to start across a great desert of eighty miles and we had to get across the river in quick time which we did. We got four cotton wood logs, dried and cut them about eight feet long, put a wagon bed on them, calked as well as we could, lashed all together tightly, making a very serviceable ferry boat. We were very fortunate in securing the services of four Indians who pushed the ferry boat over, one swimming at each corner. I went with the first load, with provisions and guns, and the men went with the mules. And before night we were all across safely, but with no feed, and what was worse, no cotton wood to give them, so the corn came in good play.

By this time, many wagons had arrived on the other side; and many pack trains, which went straight into the water, and swam their trains right over. There was one man, who gave way about sixteen feet from the land, one of our men went to his relief with a rope, and he was none too soon, as the man was sinking for the third time, when he was pulled ashore. The Cherokee doctor got him across one of the water kegs, rolled him back and forward on it and pumped the water out of him; and in three hours he started with his crowd, and didn't even say—thank you.[40]

NOTES TO CHAPTER IV

1. "I haven't seen the elephant yet," and, "I finally saw the elephant," or, "I have seen enough of the elephant," are varying forms of an expression commonly used in gold rush journals and letters. In the days of '49, these words meant that the writer had (or had not) achieved the ultimate in adventure, had survived considerable deprivation and hardship, and had achieved his goal in spite of all (Botkin 1944:304). The origin of the expression, however, was traced to Philadelphia some time around 1820. The *Arkansas State Gazette & Democrat* reported on May 17, 1850, that

high society had gathered to watch a pageant; it was to be a gala affair. It seems that the script called for an elephant to spend several hours on stage. During the performance, two men who provided foundation for the bulky elephant figure whiled away boredom in their stuffy confines with some bottles of strong spirits. Thus the elephant became tipsy, reeled, missed his footing and fell into the orchestra pit. Confusion gave way to laughter and "everybody held their sides [as] music, actors, pit, gallery, and boxes, rushed from the theatre shrieking between every breath, 'HAVE YOU SEEN THE ELEPHANT?'" The expression was particularly common in the gold rush lingo by 1849.

2. This is true. In the meantime, while Little Rock newspapers played stories about facile profits and fabulous wealth beckoning the adventurer to California, Robert Brownlee, James McVicar, Thomas Parcell, and Henry Keatts organized the Little Rock and California Association. The results of the proceedings were reported on January 16, 1849, in the *Arkansas Banner*, announcing that the men had outlined a preliminary route, suggested an inventory of provisions, and struck upon a March 25 departure date from Little Rock. The men reconvened in the Little Rock City Hall on January 31 (*Arkansas State Democrat*, February 9, 1849) and selected officers to lead the group. James McVicar was elected captain, Henry Keatts and James Murphy were named 1st and 2nd lieutenants, respectively. Alden M. Woodruff (son of the editor of the *Arkansas Gazette*) was to be orderly sergeant, while George B. King would serve as commissary. Thomas Parcell, who helped organize the emigrating company, decided to ship to the goldfields and arrived long before the others (*Arkansas Banner*, October 2, 1849). Most emigrating companies formed along military lines and adopted by-laws for their mutual protection. The Little Rock Company was no exception and published its Articles of Association in the *Arkansas State Democrat* on February 9, 1848. The by-laws masked the real purpose of the trip—to gather California's gold—by stressing that the expedition was to be mainly exploratory and would "trace out the nearest practicable route . . . to the mouth of the Sacramento river . . . explore and make settlements in the valley, and on California bay." The suggested itinerary would take the men along the Fort Smith-Santa Fe Trail to Santa Fe, then south along the Rio Grande River to a point near the modern town of Truth or Consequences, New Mexico, where they would turn west and follow the Gila River on a pack trail that General Stephen Watts Kearny opened in 1846 (hereafter referred to as the Gila Trail. See Appendix II for description). The company later learned that the Gila Trail was unsuitable for wagons, so it bypassed the

trail junction and traveled over the wagon road that Col. Philip St. George Cooke and his Mormon Battalion opened in 1846 (hereafter referred to as the Southern Trail. Notes describe this route in detail as the emigrants moved along). Association by-laws also limited membership to 100 men, who were permitted to take their slaves. Many did, and released the men from bondage after arrival in California which was to be a free state. Rules limited mess size and specified the maximum wagonload and the number of mules to haul it. Many good intentions went by the wayside as the travelers progressed: they heaved contents of overburdened wagons, they split and reformed messes, and they sometimes left the main train and formed smaller groups in order to travel faster and take better advantage of forage and water (See maps on pages 50 and 206).

3. Brownlee obviously knew Thorn very well, and it is curious that he referred to him only twice and very briefly at that. From the way he talks about Thorn in his memoirs, it appears that he also had told many stories about the man. Fortunately, Thomas Thorn appears in historical records time and time again, so parts of his role may be pieced together. Thorn and Brownlee must have met during construction of the Old State House in 1837, when Thorn held the contract for the brickwork. Thorn also owned a good deal of prime Little Rock property, which he sold to McVicar in 1842 (Pulaski County *Deed Book N*:458). Since Thorn disappears from Arkansas records at this time, Brownlee's story helps us complete the picture. Thorn left for Texas shortly after completing the sale of his Little Rock property and remained there until 1849, when he headed for California with his wife and Negroes (Collins 1949:28). He was in Los Angeles by November 27, 1849, according to a letter from W. W. Stevenson, a former resident of Little Rock (*Arkansas State Gazette and Democrat*, March 15, 1850). He settled in the southern mining region of California, at a small hamlet by the name of Quartzburg, not far from Agua Fria where Robert Brownlee would prospect. The Bear Valley road skirted the house Thorn built, a road Brownlee would also take many times on his future pack trips to Stockton. It is impossible to say when Brownlee saw Thorn again, but one can imagine their surprise if it happened to be a chance encounter. Moreover, it appears that the two men renewed their dealings, for Brownlee tells of receiving $300 in gold dust from Thorn in 1852 (See Chapter VII). Thorn served as Quartzburg's Postmaster (Davis:1853, January 5). He was also known as Quartzburg's leading citizen. He called and presided over the Mariposa Quartz Convention, whose minutes were published in 1851, and became a partner in

some sixteen quartz-bearing veins (Collins ibid). Collins also wrote that Thorn erected a log cabin which Sam Ward termed, "Thorn villa," where a wayfarer would receive generous hospitality, "a clean bunk, a tidy supper with the luxury of milk (then a great rarity in all of California), and generous provender for his beasts." A friend, Charles Davis (ibid), savored Christmas dinner at Thorn's "victualing house" and in addition to enjoying Thorn's "agreeable company," he praised Mrs. Thorn's dinner of rare roast beef, cabbage broth with pork and potatoes, and dessert of apple pie. A year later, Davis (1854: January 6) reported that Thorn was dying of consumption and that his wife was also very ill. Their two daughters and a Negro woman continued to run the boarding house, while others tended the small store. There are no signs of Quartzburg today. Its oak-covered hills are now part of a privately owned ranch. The family graveyard remains, though well-hidden in a stand of trees. Thomas Thorn's tombstone records that he was born in Bordentown, New Jersey in 1806, and died in 1854.

4. Fort Smith, Arkansas, is situated at the junction of the Poteau and Arkansas Rivers. The north fork of the Canadian River flowed into its main stream at North Fork Town, 40 miles west of Fort Smith. Beyond this point, Arkansas travelers faced a westward trek of some 800 miles before reaching Santa Fe. For the most part, the Little Rock Company followed a road opened by Capt. R. B. Marcy on the south side of the Canadian River. Marcy left Fort Smith on April 5, 1849, under orders to survey a national road from Fort Smith to Santa Fe (the trail was subsequently known by that name), and to provide a military escort for emigrants. Grant Foreman details the Captain's report in *Marcy and the Goldseekers* (1968), which describes the route to Santa Fe and is an excellent source for further study. Thousands of emigrants took this trail (many in advance of the escort) between March and August of '49. From accounts in available literature, it may be estimated that 40% of all the emigrants who took one of the southern trails to California started out on the Fort Smith-Santa Fe Trail.

5. The Little Rock Company left Fort Smith on April 16, 1849 (*Arkansas State Democrat*, April 27 and June 1, 1849), and drove its teams fourteen miles to the Choctaw Agency near modern Spiro, Oklahoma. Here the route forked. Captain Marcy's new road went in a westerly direction along the southern bank of the Canadian River, another trail went almost due west to North Fork Town near the junction of the North Canadian and Canadian rivers, while a third route turned northwest to cross the Canadian a mile above its junction with the Arkansas River (Foreman

1968:161). The Little Rock Company took the northwestern road and continued to North Fork Town on Little River, Edward's Trading Post, then crossed to the south side of the Canadian River at Choteau's Fort, where they joined Captain Marcy's road. A company member wrote a long letter home recounting his adventures during the first 200 miles of travel:

> We are now 26 miles from Little River and 25 miles from the Cross Timbers . . . we . . . crossed the Canadian on the 24th, the North Fork on the 25th, and Little River on the 1st of May. We passed through some of the finest country, richest land, and most beautiful prairie I have ever seen. We have met with some delays on account of the road being so wet; and had considerable work to do in the way of ferrying rivers, pushing our wagons up the hills . . . Capt. McVicar came near being obliged to abandon one of his wagons. One of his wheels gave out, but he was fortunate enough to obtain another that fitted exactly (*Arkansas State Democrat*, June 1, 1849).

Alden M. Woodruff's May 3 letter (ibid) described some of the other vicissitudes encountered by the men from Little Rock:

> Yesterday we moved camp two miles to find a dry place; and it is the only comfortable place I have seen for four days. The ground we occupied from the 2d to the 5th was a perfect mud-hole. During the last three or four days it has rained incessantly, and such thunder and lightning! It was terrible. The sun came out today, and every foot of ground, and every bush and shrub in this vicinity is covered with wet blankets, boots, saddles, &c., &c.

6. The Cross Timbers was a hardwood forest with very dense undergrowth which effectively separated the prairies from the great plains. It varied from about five to thirty miles in width and extended north and west from the Red River in Texas to terminate near Choteau's Fort in Oklahoma (Hollon 1955:63).

7. The men traveled parallel to the Canadian River; the Cimarron was many miles to the north. In 1849 this was Indian territory (Oklahoma did not become a territory until 1890) and a number of Indian tribes had been farming, trading, and hunting there since the 1830s, having being removed from their native lands in the southeastern United States. Members of five major tribes included were the Choctaws, Chickasaws, Cherokees, Creeks, and Seminoles.

8. The emigrants made their first stop at the Choctaw Agency, a busy little Indian Village about fifteen miles southwest of Fort Smith. The opening of the Fort Smith-Santa Fe Trail was a boost to Indian economy. Both Chickasaws and Choctaws settled near the road and sold surplus stock and produce to the western traveler (Foreman 1934:112–113). Other Indians took advantage of the opportunity to increase their assets, and

Foreman (1968:165) tells of an enterprising Shawnee chief who, in company with members of his tribe, obtained mules and buffalo from western tribes and then, by following their trail, sold the items to needy emigrants.

9. Wild Cat, or Coahoochee, was a formidable Indian. McReynolds (1957: 199) called him "the boldest and most resourceful war chief of the Seminoles." For six years, he had outwitted the U.S. Army in Florida, thus postponing his tribe's forced relocation to Oklahoma in 1841. The Indian impressed George Sniffen of the Havilah Mining Company, who commented (May 31, 1849): "at Edward's trading house on this side of the river, I saw and shook hands with 'Wild Cat' the celebrated Seminole Chief. He is a stalwart noble looking man about 6-1/2 feet in height and dressed in a beautiful Indian costume, brilliant with silver ornaments, beads and cloth. I told him how glad I was to shake the hand of such a great Indian brave and warrior, with which compliment I suppose he was well pleased for a smile broke out upon his gloomy face like the sun suddenly shining out after a shower." The following December Wild Cat left the Seminole country in Oklahoma and, together with a group of his own people, Creeks, and Negro families, went to Eagle Pass, Texas, where they built an Indian colony. He died there of smallpox in 1857 (McReynolds 1957:257).

10. The travelers were now on the south side of the Canadian River near present Purcell, Oklahoma.

11. Thibault kept a journal of the Little Rock Company travels from which the *Arkansas State Gazette & Democrat* published a few excerpts in 1851, some of the best that have come to light. Unfortunately, the journal has not survived. Thibault was one of the proprietors of a jewelry store in Little Rock (Pope 1895:252) and returned to Arkansas in 1851 to resume his business. He left a number of descendants, many of whom live in Little Rock.

12. Brownlee was 36 years old at the time and had had much experience in the world, while a good many of the Little Rock Company members were in their early twenties (California *Census* 1850). The cross-country trek probably hastened their maturity!

13. The black-tailed prairie dog (*Cnomys ludovicianus*) populates most of the Great Plains, though today in diminished numbers. These vociferous rodents subsist on grass and weeds that grow around their villages. Owls and snakes are two of many natural predators.

14. This river was probably Red Deer Creek, flowing out of the Canadian River between today's towns of Canadian and Miami in the Texas Pan-

handle. Captain Marcy (Foreman 1968:222) described this area and explained the phenomenon by saying that the quicksand absorbed much of the flowing water which further evaporated in the daytime. At night, when evaporation was less, the water flowed over the sand.

15. Captain Marcy's road from Fort Smith joined the Santa Fe Trail near the town of San Miguel, New Mexico. The Pecos Pueblo is several miles northwest of this junction. Hernando Alvarado found a thriving village that supported some 2500 Tanoan farmers when he first saw Pecos Pueblo in 1540. Over the years these native farmers constructed a pueblo of sun-dried brick four to five stories high with over 600 storage and living rooms. A protective mound of earth covers most of the aboriginal living quarters today. There were two parts to Pecos: the Indian village, and a church which Spanish padres built in the 1700s. Brownlee was one of the few diarists to observe its carving, although four years prior to his visit, Lt. W. H. Emory (1848:30) had noted that "the cornices and drops of the architrave . . . are elaborately carved with a knife." Archaeologists presently working in the pueblo might be interested in an exhaustive description written by one Phineas Blunt in his diary during May 1849. Its details would greatly help in any eventual restoration, since Blunt not only took measurements, but described many rooms and architectural features in detail, particularly within the church. He observed that black and white images painted on the ceiling and timbers were still visible but that "the whole is in a state of decay, the roof in one place has fallen in. Over the altar [are] these characters F C A R O E U S with letters recessed, being more easily read by standing at the back of the altar." The "cells" Brownlee referred to may have comprised the convento, the mission padres' living area, which was connected to the church. The adobe shell of the church still stands, but is greatly changed since Brownlee viewed it in 1849. Pecos' population declined steadily after 1700, resulting from an epidemic and continued warfare with the Comanche of the eastern plains (Kidder 1962:85–86). The last seventeen survivors had left ten years before Brownlee's visit.

16. The United States declared war on Mexico in 1846, and General Stephen Watts Kearny, Commander of the Army of the West, was ordered to take Santa Fe. The army marched along the Santa Fe Trail and easily claimed the small town of Las Vegas in San Miguel County, New Mexico. Kearny promised the residents that the United States would guarantee freedom of religion and protection from marauding Apache and Navajo bands. After passing Pecos, Kearny proceeded on to Santa Fe by way of Glorieta Pass, which was "a gateway which in the hands of a skill-

ful engineer and 100 resolute men, would have been perfectly impregnable." According to the report of Lt. W. H. Emory (1848:31), here Kearny expected resistance from the Mexicans but General Manuel Armijo, however, decided not to contest and retreated with his army. Kearny subsequently raised the American flag over Santa Fe on August 18, 1846, without a shot having been fired.

17. This would have been San Miguel del Bado, a small settlement fourteen miles southeast of Pecos. In 1849, San Miguel was "composed of about seventy-five adobe hovels, one story high. . . . There are several stores of groceries within the place, their principal business being the sale of inferior liquor at a 'bit' a glass" (Chamberlin 1945:XX:51). Many emigrants enjoyed their first taste of Mexican hospitality here and C. E. G. (Edwin Galloway) of the Little Rock Company noted on June 20, 1849, that the citizens of the pueblo "got up a fandango for the emigrants, and most of our company attended. The Mexicans waltz beautifully, and go through the Spanish dance to perfection." Dr. Fagan, also with the Little Rock Company, declared that "we can go to a fandango every night or two. . . . We frequently take occasion to make ourselves agreeable to the señoritas and although there are none of us much distinguished for our gallantry among the fair sex, I assure you our efforts in this line have been eminently successful among the brunettes" (1849: Santa Fe). An anonymous correspondent summed it up saying that "the way the native population waltzes is a caution to cripples" (*Arkansas State Democrat*, August 17, 1849). Attending a fandango was, perhaps, an amusement that attracted the younger men, for Brownlee did not mention these affairs. Whether or not this assumption is true, whenever emigrants arrived in a New Mexican town, there is little doubt that some local resident invited all to one of these festive dances.

18. Most members of the Little Rock Company bypassed Santa Fe and went directly to Albuquerque. Brownlee, Clark, and Galloway decided to spend a few days in the city (DOJ 1849:2), and the latter sent this report to the *Arkansas State Democrat* on August 31, 1849:

> I can hardly imagine how this town is supported. The country around it is barren. At the North stands a snow-capped mountain [part of the Sangre de Cristo range], while the valley in which the town is situated is dry and sandy. The streets are narrow. In the morning this place is crowded with articles for sale. A Mexican will walk about the town all day to sell a bundle of grass worth about a dime. They are the poorest looking people I ever saw. They subsist principally on mutton, onions and red pepper. The proportion of poor to the rich is about 1000 to 1. Groceries are very high here, but dry goods are about as cheap as at Little Rock.

William H. Chamberlin, a member of another emigrating company, echoed reports about Santa Fe and commented (1945:xx:55) on the facets of New Mexican life style, especially disapproving of the fact that the women drank, gambled, and smoked. As a result, he said that "Santa Fe is a very immoral place. The population is composed of Mexicans, Indians, and foreigners from all parts of the world. The public square and gambling houses are crowded with idle loungers, male and female; the character of but few of the latter will bear a virtuous test."

19. Brownlee and John W. Clark continued the rest of their journey in company with James McVicar, Jesup McHenry, Ransom Drew, Seneca Brownfield, William Garrity and two Negroes (Brownlee 1849: September 16).

20. Brownlee was among the few diarists who recorded impressions of the St. John's Day festivities in Santa Fe called *correr el gallo*. Josiah Gregg (1844:1:241–242) called this "one of the most attractive sports of the rancheros and the peasantry, and that which more than any other calls for the exercise of skill and dexterity." He went on to describe his version of the sport in detail:

> A common cock or hen is tied by the feet to some swinging limb of a tree, so as to be barely within the reach of a man on horseback: or the fowl is buried alive in a small pit in the ground leaving only the head above the surface. In either case, the racers, passing at full speed, grapple the head of the fowl, which being well greased, generally slips out of their fingers. As soon as some one, more dextrous than the rest, has succeeded in tearing it loose, he clasps spurs to his steed, and endeavors to escape with the prize. He is hotly pursued, however, by the whole sporting crew, and the first who overtakes him tries to get possession of the fowl, when a strife ensues, during which the poor chicken is torn into atoms. Should the holder of the trophy be able to outstrip his pursuers, he carries it to a crowd of fair spectators and presents it to his mistress, who takes it to the fandango which usually follows, as a testimony of the prowess of her lover.

21. A man purported to be Caspar S. Ricks, founder of the city of Eureka, California (Coy 1929:235), left a diary in which he recorded the daily experiences of the Little Rock Company as it traveled between Albuquerque and Santa Cruz, Mexico. There is no doubt that the account of this adventure is accurate. However, the author was not the real founder of Eureka. The first page of the diary is missing and there is no reference to the writer's name. We do know that the Caspar S. Ricks who founded Eureka, arrived in California by way of Panama on August 18, 1849 (Irvine 1915:233), and that the diary's author (DOJ 1849:2–5) was in Albuquerque on June 27, 1849, when he decided to split with his mess and

move "on in company with another wagon belonging to Brownlee and Clark." The anonymous traveller went on to record that the emigrants arrived at the Rio Grande crossing (about a mile and a half below Albuquerque) on June 30 and took their place in line along with other companies waiting to cross the river. They pitched tents in a heavy rain and lived in wet and muddy conditions for the next two days. He noted further that there was no wood and that travelers resorted to dried stalks of sugar cane to cook with and help dry things out. By now, after several months on the road, most of the men probably took such things in stride. Their plight, no doubt, was somewhat relieved when a nearby resident invited all to the inevitable fandango.

22. Hundreds of Independence Day activities took place at scattered spots along the wilderness trail between New Mexico and California as overlanders took time off to proclaim their patriotism with speeches and the traditional firing of guns. No doubt many felt pangs of homesickness as they celebrated far from the folks at home. Nevertheless, these men from diverse backgrounds and with different life experiences appeared to share joy for life and give thanks for the opportunity to freely search out their destiny in the vast, new country. The Clarksville, Little Rock, and Captain H. H. Davis' Washington company spent the Fourth of July at a spot midway between Albuquerque and Socorro (DOJ 1849:6, King May 4, 1941). Each company appointed a committee to select a marshal for the day and three assistants to help him (DOJ ibid). The emigrants obviously had a good time, and several wrote their impressions which later appeared in the *Arkansas State Democrat* (September 28, 1849). One reported that Mr. A. B. Bates of the Clarksville Company gave a prayer, Dr. James Fagan of the Little Rock Company recited the Declaration of Independence, and the Rev. Mr. Annis offered an oration. This was followed by a military parade. Another correspondent described the subsequent celebration: ". . . we drank to the health of our friends at home, and the prosperity of our country, in an assortment of brands. One mess brought out some of the best Holland, another Cognac, while your humble svt. and a few others were lucky enough to find at the bottom of a trunk some sparkling Champagne, reserved for the occasion. At sunset we fired a grand salute; and in the evening we had a fandango, at which, by special invitation, there were present quite a crowd of Seignoritas. They waltz 'devinely,' and their dancing is '*dem foine*'" [damn fine].

23. Travelers moving south out of Albuquerque kept to the western bank of the Rio Grande. Roads there were sandy. As the Forty Niners moved along, they were often forced to negotiate rocky, gravelly bluffs that close

in upon the river. The banks of the Rio Grande were lined then, as today, with stands of cottonwood, and the dusty company would often set up camp in their cooling shade. Here, a lucky fisherman might bag a twelve pound catfish, or a hunter might bring back a partridge or rabbit to flavor the evening stew (DOJ 1849:11–13). By comparing emigrant diaries with modern topographic maps together with J. R. Bartlett's *Narrative* and present reconnaissance of the area, it appears likely that emigrants left the river in the vicinity of modern Hatch (about fifteen miles north of Doña Ana), ascended to a broad tableland, then continued in a southwesterly direction toward a mountain known as Cooke's Peak. Those who came north out of El Paso kept to the east of the Rio Grande until they reached a prominent butte known as San Diego Mound. Here they forded the river, according to Bartlett (1854:1:215), and continued north along it until they came to the trail from Santa Fe.

24. The emigrants were about 32 miles southwest of Hatch and near Cooke's Peak when they met with the Apache. Alden M. Woodruff (1850: February 6) verified this experience: "It was at that place, and the only one, that we saw Indians. Mr. Thibault had strayed off from camp, hunting, and fell in with three Apaches. When he first saw them, they were riding at a fast gait, and seemed to be on the trail of something, and did not perceive him, until he hailed them and presented his gun. They halted, and asked him, in Spanish, if he was an American? He replied that he was. The Indians said they were friendly to Americans, and one of them took up behind and brought him into camp." The Clarksville Company also was encamped here, and on July 21, A.D. King (*Arkansas Gazette* May 18, 1941) wrote that the Apache later came by "with certificates of their friendly disposition, claiming good conduct of us, saying at the same time that 'Americans is much awaner,' or very good." He added that "they are a fine looking race of Indians, carrying with them at all times their spears, bows and arrows and implements of war. The squaws ride invariably man-like. The manner in which they claim an endurance of our friendly disposition is to give them presents, which we did." The Apache had not yet become a real problem to travelers who were just passing through, and contacts for the most part were concerned with trade. However, the Apache had long resented Mexican settlers intruding on what they considered to be their territory. Traditionally, these Indians followed a nomadic hunting-gathering tradition with limited farming, and permanent settlements threatened their way of life.

25. It was just south and east of Cooke's Peak where Brownlee said they "passed through the mountain." Bartlett (1854:1:220) referred to this as a

"mountain defile" and said that the trail went in a southwesterly direction for three miles before turning northwest toward the Mimbres River. A segment of the trail is clearly defined on topographic maps as the later route of the Butterfield Stage. Vestiges of the road can be viewed from highway 180 midway between Deming and Silver City, New Mexico.

26. This took place on July 25 and 26, 1849, while the men were encamped near *Ojo la Vaca* or Cow Springs (DOJ 1849: 20–22, King 1941, May 18). Cow Springs is 20 miles northeast of Deming and a major crossroads. This junction is located on private ranchland today. The men were considering searching in the area of the Santa Rita Mines, long since abandoned by the Mexicans as a result of Apache raids. The Clarksville, Tennessee and Little Rock companies each contributed a small contingent of men to prepare for an overnight expedition. In the meantime, according to the unknown author of *Diary of an Overland Journey* (DOJ ibid), Henry Keatts of the Little Rock Company was for some reason violently opposed to an expedition to the proposed location and gave some extravagant accounts of finding gold at another point some distance behind on the trail. Though the writer said some of the men believed this to be a hoax, nevertheless, they had seen a sample of the gold and excitedly abandoned the original plan and retraced their steps. Brownlee was, no doubt, a member of this group. Of course they found no gold and the diary's author recounted how the disappointed hikers returned to camp empty-handed feeling deceived and foolish. Chances are good that the Tennessee Company to which Brownlee refers came out of Fayetteville, Lincoln County, Tennessee, and was led by a Major Robert Farquharson. They had left Fort Smith on April 14, 1849, two days before the Little Rock Company (Shouse 1977: 512–513).

27. Diary accounts say the dryest stretch of the march was between Cow Springs and Playas Lake. On July 27, the author of *Diary of an Overland Journey* wrote that the Little Rock Company had started on the day's journey without water as they expected to find supplies midway on the trail. Instead, the author learned that they "had to go forty miles without water, and not having made any preparations for it, we reasoned the case for a while and . . . concluded to try it [though] we suffered greatly for water . . . and just about day we came to the place where Cook lays down as having sufficiency for 50 animals, there we got what water we ourselves could drink but very little for our mules since men with ox teams were ahead of us and had a cup and bucket dipping out the water as fast as it oozed in." A. D. King reported on July 29 that when he arrived at Cooke's "watering place . . . The men in front of the train had

watered it all to their horses." It was not until the following day that the men located a good supply of water at a spot west of Playas Lake. There, King said that "the turf or sod around these pools is some 10 inches, under which appears to be a hollow for the earth shakes around the pools. Many of our oxen fell in those pools. One broke his neck by the fall."

28. The area east of the Colorado River, north of the Gila River and extending to the Rio Grande, combined to form New Mexico Territory. This was ceded to the United States in 1848 by the Treaty of Guadalupe Hidalgo which ended the Mexican War. The strip of land south of the Gila to the present day international boundary, remained part of Mexico until the Gadsden purchase in 1853. The gold-seekers, therefore, actually traveled through Mexico until they crossed the Colorado River at Yuma.

29. The Cow Springs road went toward Playas Lake in southwestern New Mexico. In the Chihuahuan desert are found numerous *bolsons* "large purses," which are inland basins with no drainage to the sea. Runoff water from surrounding mountains created these shallow lakes and evaporation left layers of calcareous clays and alkaline crustations (Jaeger 1967:33). Playas Lake is an irregular and elongate lake bed, which angles southeast for about fifteen miles and stretches to about a mile at its widest point.

   Charles Edward Pancoast (1930:230) was also fascinated by the four-legged amphibian, and complained that they ran rapidly about the camp picking up pieces of bread and other cast-off food. The Arizona Desert Museum in Tucson, identifies this dark brown, orange-striped creature as the barred tiger salamander (*Ambystoma tigrinium*), commonly found in Arizona and New Mexico.

30. The Guadalupe Pass road is located in the Peloncillo Range of the Guadalupe Mountains, about four miles east of the Arizona-New Mexico border, and inside the international boundary. This was one of the best documented portions of the trip to California, and emigrants wrote lengthy and lively reports of the crossing of this segment of the Southern Trail. They had been conditioned to expect difficulties negotiating the way, for many had read Col. Philip St. George Cooke's narrative of his 1846 journey.

   Cooke had come south from Cow Springs on a trail used for centuries by Indians, Spanish, and Mexican traders. The path snaked west over the Guadalupe mountains near the present international boundary, where it was intersected by another well-used trail coming north out of Janos, Chihuahua. These trails were the only link to settlements in Arizona.

Since Cooke could not find the Guadalupe Pass trailhead, he and his men were forced to blaze a new path 1½ miles north of the main trail (Cooke 1848:554), a path which would have been totally impractical for loaded wagons, according to Forty Niner H. M. T. Powell (1931:123). Forty Niners found and traveled the existing trail.

Both Glenn Dumke, *Mexican Gold Trail* and Charles Peterson, editor, *Western Historical Quarterly*, told me they had flown over this area, but as far as I could determine, no one has attempted to locate and describe the pass. Because of this, the trail has been incorrectly traced on many published maps. Some show it angling southwest from New Mexico into Arizona far north of its actual location. Others show the pass to be in Arizona, vertically paralleling the New Mexican border for many miles. Some maps do not show it at all, and others locate the pass far to the south in Sonora, Mexico. Questions were inevitable; where were Guadalupe Canyon and Guadalupe Pass: Arizona, New Mexico or Sonora? Part of the answer appeared when the trail was found reproduced on a 1918 USGS Topographical map. Was the trail still there and identifiable?

I first visited the area in 1981, when I learned that a good portion of the Guadalupe Pass trail is on private ranch land and not negotiable by any vehicle. Fortunately, the owners Diana and Drummond Hadley were willing to help in the search. At Diana's invitation, I returned in August 1983, some 134 years to the day since Robert Brownlee and the Little Rock Company crossed Guadalupe Pass. With the aid of the 1918 map, we had several objectives. The first was to locate and follow the emigrant trail and photograph landmarks which had been previously sketched or described by emigrants: the summit; the 1000-foot descent; and the mass of towering rocks, which Bartlett of the U.S. Boundary Commission had sketched in 1852. Secondly, we wanted to find what I have called "Cooke's cutoff."

The "summit" was one of the emigrants' first stops as they entered the pass from the east. Here, A. B. Clarke (1852:74) saw "probably one of the finest views in nature" as he "looked down on an extensive valley luxuriant with grass, and studded with hillocks, with mountains of different heights at its circumference."

Bartlett (1854:II:331) described the 1000-foot descent as a "chalky hill . . . exceedingly smooth and steep," while F. J. Thibault (1851:July 11) of the Little Rock Company said that "one miss drive, and a wagon whirled to destruction" and where "no one felt inclined to trust himself on the back of his animal for fear of performing a somerset over its head. To take a seat on the verge of this descent, and view this mountainous and broken landscape, would fill the beholder with dread."

Thibault wrote about "Bartlett's Rocks," as Diana Hadley called them, saying that "the scenery was truly grand. . . . One might see towering rocks, like huge chimneys, with cavities where could be sheltered all the men in our train—other places where it appeared nature had been trying her freaks, by moulding these rocks into a thousand fantastic shapes."

Once on the trail, the term "pass" was found to be a misnomer. There is no natural pass across the mountains. Rather, the road or trail follows contours close to the summits with several steep ascents and descents (most over the 5000-foot level) and then makes a winding but gradual descent to the northwest to a point where it comes into Guadalupe Canyon.

The summit that A. B. Clarke described turned out to be a broad, windswept, and treeless tableland (5300 feet in altitude) that looked east toward the Animas Mountains, the verdant Animas Valley lying at their base. Except for an occasional ranch, the valley has escaped man's encroachment and remains much as it was in 1849.

The 800 to 1000-foot descent was viewed from a distance—a steep angled gash cutting through the undergrowth. Though we rode this portion uphill, we could understand why emigrants had to use ropes to control the wagons. The trail was hard packed, finely ground rhyolite tuff, a very slippery material when dry, and eroding easily when wet.

Below this descent, at about 4800 feet, there was a small valley where Bartlett's Rocks appeared in silhouette. This sandstone formation presented a dramatic scene as it rose in jumbled confusion above a small, running stream. There was a broad, flat clearing nearby, which would have made a good camping spot for the western bound emigrants. Though Thibault's description may seem exaggerated to those familiar with a western landscape, emigrants coming from the prairies would have found terrain quite different from that at home. The area remains in wilderness, with no introduced species of plants, and no destruction of environment. The only sign of man is an occasional fence to separate neighboring ranches. Now and then a red-tailed hawk circles to break the stillness.

On our return, we struck out cross-country to try and find Cooke's cutoff. It was easy to experience at first hand the pioneers' descriptions of the terrain. The trail was barely discernible around hillsides or through thick stands of juniper and pine, the horses picking their own trail. Cooke's dilemma was all the more appreciated as we rode from hilltop to hilltop in search of his old trail. Few traces were found (it may never have been used again). The place where Cooke's trail rejoined that of the emigrants was also hunted, although there are few possibilities in this rugged country. Cooke may have been a mile or so off when he first entered the area but he had to be very close to the main trail as he proceeded west. After leaving Bartlett's Rocks, the trail begins a gradual, northwesterly descent into Guadalupe Canyon. Once in the canyon, many emigrants probably took a sharp northeast turn to rest and take advantage of a nearby spring, "the Spring of Contention," after which companies traveled southwest down Guadalupe Canyon at an altitude of 4000 feet. Towering rock walls contain a winding stream shaded by centuries-old cottonwood and sycamore. Capped Rock, also sketched by Bartlett, is a prominent feature in the canyon. The trail follows and crosses the stream bed for about six miles. At a point just inside the international boundary, the stream turns sharply south. Probably at this point the emigrants left the canyon and proceeded to Rancho San Bernardino.

Members of the Little Rock Company negotiated this road on August 1 and Thibault penned his impressions thus:

> Well might the boys say, we have overtaken the "elephant" at last. In descending this creek, the enormous heights would confine us to the narrow limits of the stream and for every few hundred yards a new scene would burst upon our sight. I would at times experience a degree of wild excitement—while gazing about me at the giant mountains, and listening to the rush of waters, and the noise and bustle of the drivers and teams, through this difficult pass. And often have I stood on some commanding height, and wished that those friends we had left behind, might for a short space of time be transported to my side, that they too might enjoy those lovely scenes of primitive nature, that lay stretched at my feet for miles and miles in extent.

31. Before arriving in Santa Cruz, however, the future prospectors camped at the ruins of Rancho San Bernardino, Sonora, an 1821 Mexican land grant which its owner, Lt. Ignacio Perez, had to abandon in 1837 because he could not control Apache raids. John Slaughter, a cattleman and tough and formidable sheriff of Cochise County, bought the land in 1884. The old grant straddles the U.S. and Mexican border today, and the Johnson Historical Museum of the Southwest has restored the Slaughter compound, which is several miles east of Douglas, Arizona. It also serves as a wildlife refuge. The old San Bernardino adobe hacienda has settled into a mound and is located one mile south of the Slaughter buildings on the other side of the border. Here, the anonymous diarist (DOJ 1849:27) traveling with Brownlee and Clark noted that some of their men had good luck hunting wild cattle, descendants of the old San Bernardino herd.

When Col. Cooke came this way in 1846, he continued to Tucson by way of the San Pedro River. The emigrants bypassed his road, continued west, and followed the Santa Cruz River to Tucson. It was about 90 miles to the tiny Mexican town of Santa Cruz from San Bernardino (Marcy 1863), and the Little Rock Company arrived on August 9, 1849. Santa Cruz was one of nine frontier posts that the Mexicans established to guard northern Sonora, but the Apache had no fear of the town's garrison and continued their raids. As a result, many of the town's citizens moved away. By 1849, the town's population had dwindled from a maximum of 1500 to 300 (Dumke 1945:147). About 1000 people live in the quiet farming village today and often travel to Nogales, Arizona, for supplies along a forty-mile winding dirt road, probably the same route followed by the emigrants. It was at Santa Cruz that McVicar learned that the Sonoran Governor proposed to levy a $40 tax on each of the company's wagons. McVicar showed that he was a no-nonsense man, and he reportedly announced that they "were going ahead and if they demanded a duty of us we would pay it in powder and lead" (DOJ 1849:30).

32. The first of these was the abandoned frontier mission church of Tumacacori, preserved now as a National Monument. In December 1849, Judge Benjamin Hayes (1849:116) noted that "it had a melancholy appearance. The walls of the church still stand, no roof, and only the upright piece of the cross. It looked desolate indeed." Another was the deserted presidio of Tubac, where "there was not a human soul to enliven all this silence. It was a most eloquent stillness" (Harris 1960:76–77). Today, Tubac Presidio State Historic Park protects the remains of the old Spanish fort, and the surrounding village has become an artistic center, featuring many galleries and studios.

33. Mission San Xavier del Bac was built circa 1783 to replace an earlier mission that the Jesuit explorer-priest, Francisco Eusebio Kino, had founded in 1700. Since then, the church has worked continuously in behalf of the nearby Papago Indians. Known as the White Dove of the Desert, many consider it the most beautiful mission in the southwest. The annual San Xavier Pageant celebrates the mission's founding and pays tribute to a blend of cultures and past traditions of the Spanish, Papago, Yaqui, Mexican, and Anglo people of the area.

34. George W. B. Evans (Dumke 1945:152) of Texas, witnessed this scene and wrote of it in his diary. Brownlee's recollections, however, were not much at variance with his '49 version as detailed in a letter to his brother (1849:September 16):

> It pains me to announce the death of Dr. Fagan. Fifty miles this side of Tusson [Tucson] he had been complaining, for a few days rode in the wagon, and as we

had neither grass nor water, we were compelled to make a long drive to obtain both as man and beast stood in need of them. That night, August 22d, he was taken with a bleeding at the nose and mouth, which reduced him very fast, and a quarter to 9 o'clock next morning he died with his hand in mine without a struggle. He appeared sensible but said nothing nor made any request. Every attention possible was rendered him, as we had in our company Dr. [James L.] Fort from Washington, Arkansas, who did everything in his power for his relief. We in our destitute condition interred him under a large Muskite [mesquite] tree, and secured the remains of one as kind, obliging, and of as promising talents as ever started on this journey. The impression made on me that day over the grave when Mr. Thibault was putting up a prayer to the Giver of all goodness, will never be forgotten by me. . . . Tears were running down the cheeks of some who I believe never shed a tear before.

35. Henry Keatts and a man by the name of Hunt helped Brownlee bury Thibault's slave, Jordan, according to Brownlee (1849: September 16).
36. The Gila Pimas lived in extended farming villages scattered along the Gila River in the vicinity of modern Casa Grande, Arizona. Emigrants familiar with Emory's *Notes* (1848:80–89) were assured that the Pima farmers would give them a friendly reception, and, for the most part, this was true. John E. Durivage (1937:v:218) found them "peaceable, quiet, and honest Indians, and possessing considerable intelligence. The men are well formed and athletic, the women bright-eyed, talkative and symmetrical. They have an extraordinary partiality for shirts of all colors, and in fact it is the only current coin in the place." But Alden Woodruff (1850:February 6) of the Little Rock Company, complained that almost every wagon lost some article while encamped, and added that "they might have been honest when Lt. Emory was among them, but they have learnt bad manners since."
37. On leaving the Pima villages, emigrants would short cut a bend in the Gila River in order to reduce travel time to four or five days (Dumke 1945:155). No doubt, many questioned the merits of this decision, for they faced a scorching, waterless desert as they trudged through clouds of windblown sand on a trail marked by discarded wagons and paraphernalia and carcasses of oxen and mules (Couts 1961:72, Durivage 1937:v:213, Pancoast 1930:247). The cacti was particularly irksome. Many a desert sojourner has come to terms with one variety, the many branched *Opuntia bigelovii*, commonly called the teddy bear cholla or jumping cactus. At the merest touch, a portion of the plant appears to "jump" towards its unsuspecting victim, imbedding razor sharp needles deep into the skin.
38. According to reports, Major H. Haralson was a traveling and drinking companion to Sam Houston and accompanied him when he left Ten-

nessee in 1829 to take up life at Fort Gibson in the Cherokee Nation (Gregory 1967:6–7). While Houston was at Fort Gibson, President Andrew Jackson was looking into a number of rumored reports that Houston was masterminding a plot to create an Indian empire in Texas outside U.S. control, and with him as its head of state. There is some evidence to suggest that Haralson was one of Jackson's spies since he regularly reported Houston's plans to the War Department (ibid 137–154). Haralson replaced James McVicar as warden of the Little Rock penitentiary when the latter left for the Mexican War, and was serving in that capacity when the building burned down on July 4, 1846 (Pope: 1895–284).

39. The Yuma Indians occupied territory for about 15 miles north and 60 miles south of the confluence of the Gila and Colorado Rivers but lived chiefly on the west side of the Colorado, where they grew corn, beans, and squash on the flood plain (Kroeber 1953:782). Until a ferry was established in October, the Forty Niners were particularly dependent on the fine Yuma swimmers to help ferry boats and livestock across the river. They were left to their own devices in dealing with what Harris called the "rascally Yumas" (1960:87). Brownlee (1849: September 16) was a little more forthright in a letter to his brother:

> One and a half miles above the mouth of the Gila for three days, we were every minute expecting an attack from the Yaumas Indians about 75 strong, armed with bows and arrows, spears and knives. Our train consisted of 4 wagons and 17 men. We closely guarded our stock and property and showed the *horse-eaters* that we were as ready to fight as they were to attack. I can assure you that we were in a tight place. They were as stout, able bodied men as I ever saw or more so, and as straight as a rush.

F. J. Thibault (1851: May 9) called them "pests of the Colorado" and said that they showed "cool audacity as well as cunning" as he related a friend's adventure:

> It appears that whilst he and a companion were descending . . . a fine athletic Indian waded to his raft, and commenced amusing himself by inspecting the many (to his sight) wonders of the white man. He appeared to be more particularly struck with the usefulness of one of Collins' axes, and tried hard to purchase it. Finding all attempts [thwarted] to become possessed of its usefulness, he laid it down and recommenced his examination of the different articles, paying no more attention to the axe, having apparently forgotten it. So things remained until the raft arrived at a deep and swift part of the stream, when he stepped up to the gun (the only one on the raft), slung it into the water, and with one bound, seized the axe, dove with it like a duck, swam under water out of harm's way, reached the bank, and hailed them at the top of his voice with *how de do*.

40. A group of Cherokees from Oklahoma also caught gold fever and formed a party called the Cherokee and Mississippi Emigrating Company. The good Samaritan was apparently one Dr. G. W. Wilson, who signed the *Record Book* at Rancho Santa Ana del Chino on October 3, 1849. Wilson wrote that he was from Fort Gibson in the Cherokee Nation. Two other emigrants had cause to be grateful to this gentleman. Back in April, several hundred miles out of Fort Smith, Wilson befriended Dr. J. S. Candee and the Rev. Ira Allen, who had become separated from their company, the Knickerbockers, out of New York (Foreman 1968:169–174). Candee and Allen continued their journey with the Cherokees. Allen, unfortunately, never reached the goldfields as he died on August 30 and was buried on the banks of the Gila River (Bynum 1934:25, 27).

CHAPTER V

Ho! California!

INTRODUCTION

The Little Rock Company (and many others as well) had split into small straggling units by the time it reached the Colorado River. Ahead, the men faced a 142-mile trek across soft sand, inhospitable badlands, and rock-strewn hills before reaching California's first settlement at Warner's Ranch. Many had had enough overland travel by this time and turned west at the ranch, hiking the 60-odd miles to San Diego, and then boarding a steamer for San Francisco. Brownlee and company, however, continued their journey along California's coast and across the great San Joaquin Valley to mines near Agua Fria in Mariposa County.

Brownlee's memoirs offer a glimpse of pastoral California during her waning Rancho days. He recalls meeting rancheros Isaac Williams, John Reed, William Workman, and John Gilroy shortly before the California gold rush changed their lives forever. Until that time, California's economy had been based on cattle, and most contact with U.S. citizens had involved concern with the hide and tallow trade. Hides were called the "California Banknote" because they were the main form of exchange. Steeped culturally in a pastoral life, rancheros did not exploit other resources in California during the Mexican regime. Gold discovery changed this; goods would subsequently be exchanged for a "pinch of dust."

The gold rush also contributed to the decline of the native Ameri-

A FORTY NINER'S CALIFORNIA TRAIL

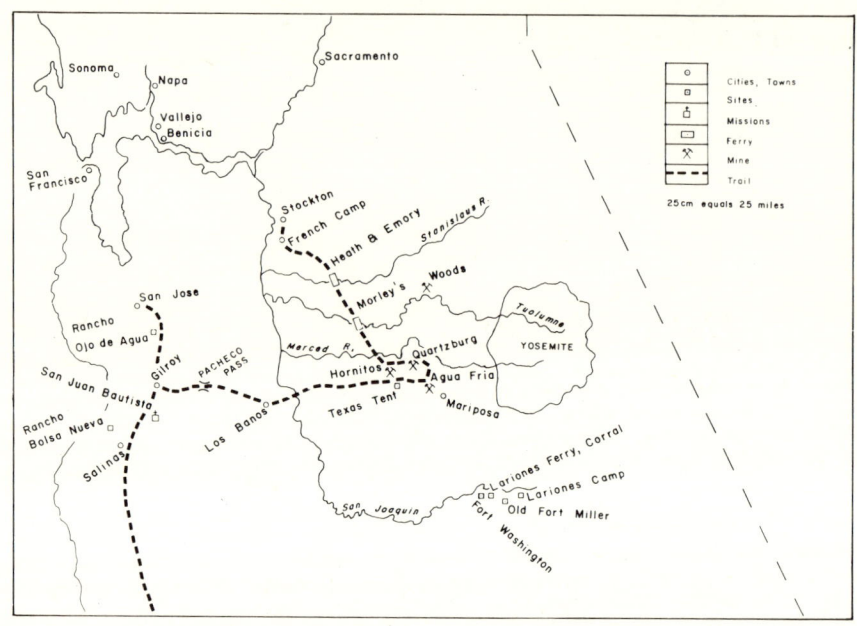

Maps showing portions of northern and southern California.

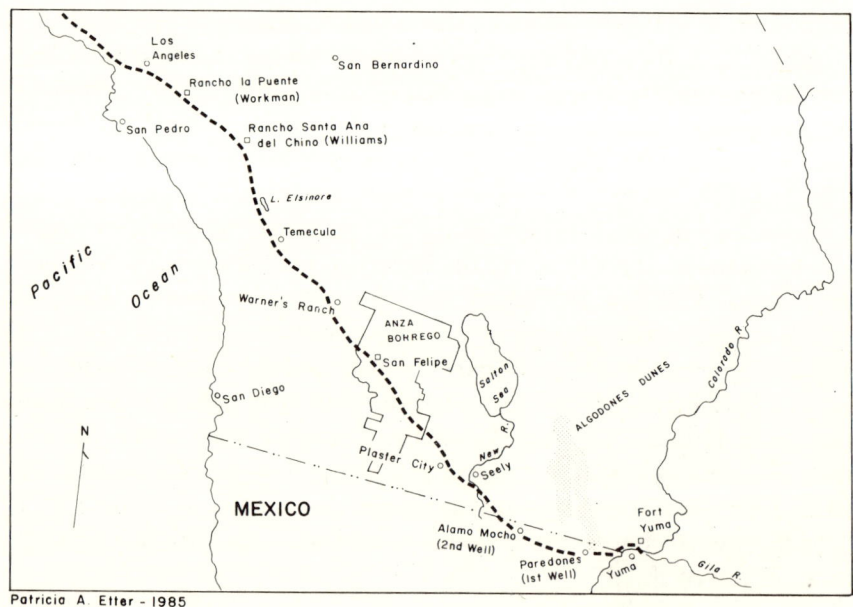

cans in California, their numbers already becoming drastically reduced during the Spanish and Mexican eras. This was true of the small group of Cupeño, Indians, who were still attempting to retain their traditions near Warner's Ranch. Brownlee witnessed one of the last puberty ceremonies before the Cupeño were confined to a reservation.

The San Joaquin Valley was still tranquil and untamed when Brownlee passed through. Spawning salmon filled the rivers, and bands of Tule Elk roamed freely. Thousands of horses, descended from the Conquistadores' Arabian stock, presented a magnificent sight as they ran wild through the valley. It would not be long before incoming settlers turned the valley into one of the most productive agricultural areas in the state.

California had been in gradual transition since conquest in 1846. As Brownlee and his fellow goldseekers traveled toward the mines, lawmakers in San Jose were working on a new constitution and contemplating statehood. San Francisco was a raucous boom town filled with spectators and entrepreneurs. Other towns were springing to life. But attention was focused mainly on the mines, where thousands of emigrants were grubbing along rivers in the Sierra Nevada foothills and recovering the gold that had lain hidden for millenia.

As soon as the men from Little Rock arrived, they settled down with the others and began to work in earnest to realize their dream; some were successful, others not. A few, like Brownlee and McVicar, found gold in other ways.

THE JOURNAL

For the first twelve miles on crossing the desert there is nothing but coarse sand, and in walking one goes nearly as far backward as forward. We had to help the teams, by pushing, as they were very weak. We finally made the twelve miles and reached the first well.[1] At the second Wells the water was not fit for use, being full of dead oxen, showing that some one ahead of us had seen hard times, for there were good wagons, good carpenter and blacksmith tools, rifles, shot, and powder; everything that was needed for an outfit.[2] In crossing the desert, we fared better than when coming down the Gila; for on New river, we found plenty of water and grass, with mesquite beans, of which horses are very fond. The land in the desert is of the best quality, being of black loam, and I predict that some day, when properly reclaimed, it will be the garden spot of California for tropical fruit. All it needs is irrigation, and plenty of it.[3]

We have crossed the desert, and are ascending a small rise with but little, but [have] good water and plenty of feed. You must remember, we have been in California since crossing the Colorado river, which was in the last of July, or first of August, so you see I am prepared to give [praise to] California for fine feed and water from the start, for we never suffered any more for either, and took advantage of both and improved our teams.[4] While staying there [San Felipe], we met a company of Uncle Sam's men, who were returning to San Diego; so I grasped the opportunity to mail, and sent a letter back to my brothers in Arkansas; stating our whereabouts, also the death of Mr. Fagan and the colored man, and of the supposed cause. This was the first they had heard of us.[5] Our route was over rolling land, some good for pasture, some good for nothing. We were passing the country where there are now tin mines.[6]

The first settlement we came to was Warner's Ranch containing lots of Mexicans and Indians. Here the natives cook their beans in a wonderful spring of boiling water.[7] It was here we saw a sight, not soon to be forgotten. A young girl is not marriageable, until purified in the sweating bath in which she has to stay seven days and nights, and I think the ordeal a very severe one. They dig a pit, keep a fire burning with hot stones, and when all is hot they fill the pit with green weeds, and the steam arising from these is supposed to purify her and she can marry in seven days. We were camped close by and on hearing them shouting and singing went up and looked on; the girl was all covered, save her head, and the old women were giving her a drink of something which resembled gruel. Then both women and men would dance and sing. This was during the warm season, and the oppressive heat and disagreeable odor of the weeds made her lot a severe one.[8]

After leaving here we went through another pass, which although not so wonderful as the other two, is very noticeable, and we now struck the first large tract of good land in Temescal Valley, in the center of which is a settlement having a large water mill. In fact, the land seems to improve so fast, and has such a wide scope of country as far as the eye could see. [It] seemed to be all of the best quality, covered with cattle and horses, the latter so fat [they] were out of shape. We could now see the town of San Bernardino away at the foot of the mountain of the same name.

After a day's travel we arrived at [Colonel Isaac] Williams' Ranch where [there] was a water mill and thousands of cattle and horses feeding on a nice level country. Williams wanted to trade for our mules, and in pay would give us passage on a schooner up to San Francisco, but he failed to fool us. He wanted us also to sign a register, merely to show who passed, he said. We wouldn't do this either, for he was a Yankee of the most grabbing kind. After years had passed [he submitted] a relief Bill to Congress for the aid he had given different emigrants, which was all bosh. If he assisted any he was fully paid in some way at the time, and in my opinion his schooner trip was a sell. He said he would haul them 150 miles, and feed them for so much. [He also] had men out to meet emigrants, trying to sell potatoes, flour and corn meal, for which he asked enormous prices.[9]

Farther on we camped at Mr. Rollins' [John Rowland] Ranch. He was a very fine man and said we did well not to have had anything to do with Williams. Mr. [John] Reed, a son-in-law, lived near Mr. Rollins, also Mr. [William] Workman who I think was an Englishman, and a fine man. Our company traded largely with them both; exchanged our broken down animals for fresh ones, which were as fat as butter, only very wild, and we had to break them. His men would catch them and put the harness on, help hitch them to the wagon, when we would start them bucking and kicking, pulling the wagons by their mouths, and as the country was level and our loads getting light, we went over the ground very rapidly. I traded both of my animals, I think. Besides, we bought beef and dried it, and lived fine, for if you wanted a piece of "jerky," all you had to do was to go and help yourself, as it was strung along the outside of the wagon covers. This luxury was not all, for the horse feed was extra good. The land [was] covered with burr clover seed, and in four days our animals improved so fast that we soon made up the four days loss of time. What a fine country, [with] everything in good order. Mr. Rollins had a vineyard and told us to help ourselves, and gave us all the onions we needed, and some eggs, [although] he did not farm much.[10]

I forget how far we were from the ocean, but at night for a distance of ten miles we could hear its ceaseless murmur. We passed through fine country and came to San Pedro, the seaport of Los Angeles, which is situated on a bluff overlooking the ocean. This was [a] considerable town occupied entirely by Spanish. The next place was Los Angeles,[11] where we did not stop, but passed on about four miles and camped, where we were told we could get plenty of fuel out of what was apparently stone, but proved to be tar. It made a splendid fire, of which we stood in great need, as we had just arrived from a warm climate and the sea air was very cold. In coming along the coast we passed several tar springs, and filled our kegs afresh as ours was given out, and we found this far superior to what we had, as it never got dry.[12] We traveled some days on the wet sand, as the teams could make better time, and often passed the remains of whales, which had been washed ashore. Some were quite fresh, and the bones of the neck were so large that it was all a man could do to roll one over. We could also hear large sea lions bellowing.

We passed Ventura, Santa Barbara, and San Louis Obispo, the latter being an inland town. Here we commenced to climb the mountain pass up a canyon having a gorge with large boulders in the bed of the creek, where we would have to unload and pack our goods some way, unhitch the mules, and lift the wagons past the bad places to where we could load and start again. This was the roughest road we had passed so far, and the mountains so very high that we had to follow the bed of the creek. Horsemen could get along, but a wagon is another thing. We reached the top at last, and found very fair land, with oak timber, and maple. From here we had a fine view and it was splendid. The sea on one side, with hills and valleys alternating, made it a grand sight to behold.

On coming down we passed some hot springs, which had been used by some one, as they were in good condition. A hole about six feet deep had been dug and divided in[to] four compartments, making bathing vats about six feet square, the whole being walled up with hewn logs, about ten inches in diameter. We camped near the springs, and had the finest kind of bathing. The water made one feel stronger when you stayed in any length of time, any other water having the opposite effect. I believe these springs are now called Paso Robles.[13] [They] are about ten miles from San Miguel Mission, at one time so extensive, and surrounded by an adobe wall having but one gate. There was no one living there when we passed, but we found two skeletons of men lying along side of the road. The Mission is on the upper end of Salinas Plains.[14] The [Salinas] river here is not very large, but farther down forms a good stream, even in September.

We followed the river down on the left side, until we could see Monterey. We then forded it and went across the valley where lived an Irishman with a Spanish family. Close by his place we passed a tannery of no small pretentions; there was lime, hides, and two or three large-sized vats, all of which showed signs of civilization. The Irishman spoke just as though he had left Ireland that morning.[15] Salinas Plains is a large country, and if I am not much mistaken we came down some eighty miles from San Miguel Mission.

Our road was generally through a hilly country. We passed a wide dry bed of a stream [San Benito River], which is I suppose, full of water in the winter. I remember where we came down a very high hill which was not far from St. John's Mission [San Juan Bautista], where there wasn't any timber but was covered with wild oats. Here a bundle jumped or fell out of a wagon and started down the hill on its own motion, and I can assure you it made some high and lofty tumbling before it reached the bottom, which must have been half a mile off. But as it kept in a direct course, we found it safe. We next passed some Sulphur Springs, where the water was almost black, and we could not use coffee made from it.

We left St. John's Mission half a mile to our right and came to Gilroy, where a Scotchman lived. He was just like the Irishman, and spoke Scotch as broad as I have ever heard, and he too had a Spanish family. Mr. Clark had bought a California mare for twenty dollars, and I was riding her when the Scotchman claimed her as his, as she was not vented. I gave my countryman to understand—the best man could have her, and he admitted I had come honestly by her.[16] The next place we passed was Murphy's Ranch, where several of us went to buy anything that was fresh, and here we saw some Mexicans and a young lady milking cows, and I thought she was the prettiest girl I had ever seen. Her dress was of Scotch tartan, with a scarf thrown over her shoulder, she being about eighteen years of age. On making our business known, she smiled, and said they did not have anything that would suit us, but if we could drink new milk, there was plenty of that. So we accepted, and drank as men never drank before.[17]

Some five miles from San Jose, McVicar's wagon wheel gave way, so we laid by until it could be repaired. The Negro man cut down a dead tree and made spokes, but failed to make the wheels, so I took hold and succeeded first rate, as the job was to make the wheel fit the tire. Next day, as we were going towards San Jose, we met a Mexican who wanted to buy a wagon, so McVicar sold his for two hundred dollars. Then we had to make pack saddles, which took us another day.

In San Jose, we met a white store keeper, who had just returned from the Mariposa mines, which was from there a three days' journey on horse back, and as these mines were as good as any, we decided to go there. San Jose was then a small town of five or six adobe houses, containing two stores, one of which was kept by a white man. We invested all our money in buying provisions, flour, beans, salt pork, etc.[18] In order to reach the mines we had to retrace our steps for sixty or seventy miles, but we didn't mind that as we were assured there was plenty of gold there. I may as well state here, that we knew there was gold, but how much, was the question. We had met small bands of Mexicans returning to their territory who had shown us their gold, probably in a goose quill, as that was a favorite way of carrying it.[19] We could not speak Spanish, therefore were unable to find out how hard it was to get, where it was to be found, or if [it was] confined to a small section of country. Our new acquaintances had posted us, and we were in high spirits, and could now talk with some certainty, that our journey was not to be in vain, and that we would be amply repaid for all [the] hardships suffered in coming down the Gila.[20] As I stated, we had to return as far back as Gilroy. Here we turned up a valley called Clark's Valley [which was] named for a settler. In front of his house was a small lake, where we camped, and as I had killed four white geese, we had two for supper, baked in French Style in a Dutch Oven. Clark and myself cleaned the bones of one for supper and of another for breakfast.

From this camp we had to pass over the Pacheco Pass, which mountain was very high [with a] heavy grade, causing us to unload several times, and to carry our goods over the steep places where the mules couldn't go. This was a very hard day's work, as we had to carry for fifty yards in some places. [We] were without water, as we had quit carrying it. When night came on we were perhaps half way up the mountain, and as luck would have it, a heavy fog, common to California, came up. So we spread our India Rubber blankets on the wild oats, and you would have been astonished to have seen how quickly the water gathered in the center of our spreads. So we had supper, having plenty of water for ourselves, and mules too.

We reached the top of the mountain after some hard labor, and could see before us the San Joaquin Valley with all its water courses and timber. Our friends had given us a rough map, drawn from memory, which on examining carefully, we could see in the far distance all the rivers he had named, also the course we were to pursue. This map proved correct in every instance. He even told us where to camp, and we were able to find where he crossed the river, every time. We camped at the foot of the mountain where [there] was a wonderful large spring, [and] where in after years was built a water mill. From this camp to the San Joaquin river was about thirty miles.

When traveling along the plains we could see wild horse, elk and deer by the hundred, but could not get near them as they could hear as well as see.[21] On the river, we camped on a small island, and had to gather the elk horns out of the way in order to find a place on which to pitch our tents. Some of these horns were very large, and when stood on end you could almost walk straight under them. After we had camped, another small pack came along and pitched their tents close by. Their mules were a hard looking set, very poor and had sore backs. When these mules were turned loose at night, wild horses came snorting pretty close by, and every one of those broken down animals raised his head, pricked his ears up, and put as fast as he was able, which was not very fast, for in a short time the men had caught them. We were on an island, and our mare was hobbled, so our mules never left her. Where we crossed the river it was good bottom, about one foot deep, with beautiful clear water in which we could see salmon, although we didn't know what they were then.

When we got out of the river, we came to clover mixed so thickly with tule, that the mules could not make any headway, so the horsemen rode ahead and made way for the wagons. We were detained here a long time, and often times had to stand up on our horses to be able to choose the best way out, as it was supposed to be about thirty miles, before we would reach the waters of the Merced river. Being on up grade, and with very soft sand in places, it was very slow work, and as we hadn't any water along, the men were suffering. Four of us started for the river, and on approaching, [I] heard a singular noise, which I thought was deer mossing; that is eating moss under the water. I crept up carefully looking for deer through the thicket, when the noise was right by me. In looking down I saw a wonderful sight. Right at my feet there were several salmon, with part of their bodies out of the water, busy digging holes in the ground in which to spawn. I raised the gun and killed one, and had to jump in and catch it as it was floating into deep water. We started two men back with oil skins full of water, and to report our success. It was dark when the wagons came into camp, but we had six salmon, and a fire ready on which to cook them, but as yet none of us knew their names. But when cooked, I said they were salmon, as their meat was reddish, and tasted like the one I had in Scotland. We had a fine feast, also a nice time in catching them, and the crowd had twelve to take along.[22]

I think we struck the Merced river somewhere near the present railroad crossing, and followed this until we struck the foot hills, when we left the river and took to the mountain road toward the mines. Our next camping place was what is now called Quartzburg, then known as Burns' Ranch. The owner had come from Oregon and started an eating and accommodation tent, where wayfarers could get something to eat, as all those who came to California by water traveled to these mines on foot. He charged a dollar [for] a meal composed of fried pork, hard bread and coffee, sometimes flap jacks as an extra.[23]

I may here state, that from the time we left Fort Smith till we arrived in Agua Fria was about six months and two weeks. We traveled steadily, always made it a rule to lay by on the sabbath day if water and grass was to be had; if not, that day we would rest just as soon as we found these necessaries. In camp, most of the time was spent in telling yarns, singing and playing the fiddle, and also a flute, clarinet and horn. I suppose very few of my traveling companions are alive. I know of none except Mr. Clark, and he is an invalid.

NOTES TO CHAPTER V

1. For five months the hardy pioneers had been on the road and still faced another tough march across the hot and arid Colorado desert. Most had crossed the Colorado River a few miles below the mouth of the Gila and

turned southwest into Mexico in order to circumvent the shifting sands of the Algodones Dunes. Cooke's Well, the first well, was near Paredones (Bieber 1938:VII:206), a tiny Mexican village some 20 miles west of the Yuma crossing (Marcy 1863:219). Slaking thirsty throats was a slow process here, for according to Alden M. Woodruff (1850:February 6) the well yielded "about a pailful every 15 minutes." This portion of the trail has been drawn incorrectly on many maps, where it is shown crossing the dunes, an impossible traverse for loaded wagons, oxen, mules or men. Moreover, Cooke had marked the location of water holes on his map. The emigrants, and later, the Butterfield stage, kept this a well-worn path. E. I. Edwards' research for *Lost Oasis on the Carrizo* (1961) resulted in a good map of the trail through this area. I have also made my own reconnaissance; there is no doubt that emigrants dipped into Mexico for this part of the journey.

2. A 22-mile dry trail continued to the second well at Alamo Mocho (Edwards 1961:18, Marcy 1863:219) near El Alamo, Baja, California (Bieber 1938:VII:210). Here, hundreds of emigrants lightened their loads to the bare necessities for there was another hard and waterless sledge of 21 miles (Marcy ibid) to New River. J. W. Audubon (1906:167), son of the famous naturalist, and John E. Durivage (1937:V:231) were only two of many emigrants who witnessed the same scene. Brownlee (1849:September 16) described his feelings in a letter to his brother as he rested at San Felipe: "as we are pretty much in advance of the main emigration we know but little of the suffering of them behind, but the bare idea makes my blood chill—some on foot, others with broken-down mules, without provisions are bound to perish."

3. Today the Imperial Valley is one of California's most productive agricultural areas, which has been irrigated by Colorado River water through the All-American Canal system since 1901. New River is a fast-flowing stream and carries this surplus water into the Salton Sea. Before the canal was built, however, New River was intermittent and ran only when the Colorado was in flood. It was flowing in 1849 and offered blessed relief to the overlanders. B. B. Harris (1960:93) was told that the river had not run in 90 years, and he quoted the Mexicans as saying that the "miracle was especially designed for American emigrants on whose side Providence had arranged itself." Lt. Cave Couts was encamped on New River on September 25, 1849, as tired Arkansans filed in after the rigorous desert crossing. He wrote (1932:20) that he met his old friend, Major H. Haralson here. Additionally, Couts observed that "if any are left in Arkansas it is more numerously populated than I had anticipated. I am now writing and answering the questions of five or six at the same time.

Night before last, last night, all day yesterday, all day today, and to this moment, I have had the multitude around me."

4. Crossing the Colorado signified Brownlee's arrival in California, and perhaps attainment of his goal, even though it was still many miles to the mines. This may be why he dismissed this particular portion of the journey in a couple of paragraphs. Or, they may have traveled at night. In reality, however, the Forty Niners faced a tough and hot journey—some 70 miles—over rolling, sandy hills and through desert washes. There would be rocky mounds to climb and narrow arroyos to traverse. After leaving New River, travelers would pass close to present-day Plaster City and continue in a northwest direction through the Carrizo Corridor. This part of the trail had earned the name, *jornada del muerto*—journey of death (Lindsay 1973:153)—because it was marked by carcasses of animals that had dropped from thirst, starvation, and exhaustion. The trail snaked northward through the area now known as Anza-Borrego Desert State Park. Long sections of this trail may be seen where men would be required to push their heavy wagons up steep grades and switchbacks: on Campbell grade, for example, wheels have carved deep ruts on a boulder-studded trail; and in the Box Canyon area a sandy, narrow wash follows the contours of the hills. It was here that Col. Philip St. George Cooke's men chiseled the hard rock walls to widen the trail so their wagons could pass through. The last hard climb was made over a steep granite ridge between Blair and Earthquake Valleys. Again, passengers would have to help push wagons up the incline. The well-worn grooves made by the wagons of emigrants, and later, the Butterfield Stage, allow one to imagine a cacophony of sounds disturbing the desert silence as men urged tired mules and oxen along; the calls of the teamsters and the crack of their whips; the screech of metal wagon tires across the rocks. Once over these hurdles though, the wanderer would find a good road to San Felipe Indian Village, where he could rest in the cool shade of cottonwoods near a running stream. The worst part of the journey was over.

5. San Felipe was at the junction of modern highways 78 and S-2 near the northern perimeter of Anza-Borrego Desert State Park, a major resting place for both north and southbound travelers in the 1800s. Writing to his brother from this spot on September 16, Brownlee's letter was published in the *Arkansas State Democrat*, on November 30, 1849. In it, he said that they had "met 40 United States soldiers under the command of Major [William Hensley] Emory who [joined with the emigrants] at the mouth of the Gila to run the line from that point to San Diego."

Emory had been appointed Chief Astronomer of the 1849 Boundary Survey, and on September 15 was in Camp Riley, California (Emory

1857:6). Camp Riley's location cannot be determined. However, it is possible that it was close enough so that Emory was able to take emigrant letters back to San Diego where he was stationed. Lt. Cave Couts and Lt. A. W. Whipple (also of the boundary survey) were in San Felipe on September 18 (Couts 1932:20, Whipple 1961:31), but they were going in the opposite direction, toward the Colorado River.

6. Little is changed in this area today except for the presence of a modern freeway. Many acres are devoted to raising thoroughbred horses.

    The emigrant trail continued in a northwest direction, alongside the Santa Ana Mountains, past Lake Elsinore and into the Temescal Valley, then on to Chino, where Isaac Williams' Rancho Santa Ana del Chino was located. Though tin was discovered in the area in 1856 (Hoover 1962:35), or 1859 (Elliott 1883:109), little was done to exploit the resource until 1890. At that time, two English companies enjoyed a short heyday of tin mining but closed only two years later.

7. The Southern Emigrant Trail bisected Jonathan Trumbull Warner's extensive rancho, and the Forty Niners often stopped at his ranch house and trading post four miles south of the famous Agua Caliente hot springs. Many a tired and aching emigrant welcomed the long soak in the springs, which were nestled in a grove of oak, pine, and sycamore, before continuing his way.

    The Cupeño village of Kupa was located here and the Indians had long used the springs for bathing, leaching acorns, or softening basket fibre (Strong 1929:185). Eventually these native Americans were relocated on the Pala Reservation. In the meantime, however, they labored for Warner on his ranch. Capt. Abraham Johnston observed in 1846 that they were "stimulated [to work] by three dollars per month and repeated floggings" (Bieber 1937:V:275). Whether or not this was true, Warner was well-liked and respected by emigrants and other travelers for he was always generous in dispensing aid and hospitality. Today the decaying house and trading post are a few feet from Highway 71 and the walls sag under sheets of corrugated tin. Over the years, pelting rains have reduced the adobe to small heaps. A chain link fence protects the ruins from vandals, and a bronze plaque informs passersby that this is State Landmark 311. A corral is alongside the old trading post, and while men load and unload horses, little notice is taken of this historic site which was once a vital part of California's rancho days.

8. The Arkansas travelers had a rare opportunity to witness the yearly *auluninil* ceremony, a fall rite performed for the purpose of initiating adolescent Cupeño Indian girls into their society (Strong 1929:255). In addition to being a significant rite for all members of the group, it was also an

important social occasion during which various clans gathered to exchange gifts and food, to sing and dance.

Brownlee's observations were correct although he may not have known that the songs passed on the society's traditions and stressed the importance of the girls' roles as adults. Usually a group of girls were initiated together and were allowed out of their steamy chamber from time to time so the stones could be reheated. They drank warm acorn gruel; this was not only an important dietary staple in aboriginal California, but a favorite dish as well.

9. Isaac Williams (1799–1856) arrived in California in 1832, and later married a daughter of an old Spanish settler, Antonio Mario Lugo, who subsequently deeded the Rancho Santa Ana del Chino to his son-in-law. Like other rancheros of the day, Williams engaged in the hide and tallow trade. Many of the Forty Niners who came off one of the southern route trails and went on to the mines by foot invariably stopped to rest and obtain supplies at Williams' ranch. We learn from diaries that emigrants who followed the Southern Trail out of Mexico began to arrive at the rancho as early as June. After greeting a steady stream of emigrants over two months, Williams began asking the men to sign his "guest book." (This is now known as the Record Book of the Rancho Santa Ana del Chino, transcribed and edited by Lynley Bynum in 1934, from the original in the Huntington Library archives.) Well over 500 emigrants wrote in the book during the three months between August 12 and November 16. A closer look at this interesting register shows that the first large contingent to sign in consisted of men who had packed on Kearny's Gila Trail. Those who had come by way of the Southern Trail began to straggle in by September. Brownlee's friends, William Garritty, Seneca Brownfield and John W. Clark, signed the register on September 29, 1849. Only a small percentage of the total left a record of their passing. Some emigrants merely signed in, while others left notes for companions yet to arrive, or made remarks about the just completed journey. In contrast to Brownlee's feelings, many praised Williams for his hospitality and generosity. A number of them even stayed on until the following spring. Most wrote that they experienced no difficulty on the trip. One wrote that he and his group arrived "fat, ragged and saucy." It is possible to identify about 80% of these men and 38 of the companies they traveled with. By far the greatest number (65%) came from eleven southern states, mainly Texas and Arkansas. About 20% were from northern states such as New York and Ohio, with 15% as yet unidentified. The number of names began to decrease perceptibly in November with few signatures in De-

cember. This does not indicate a decline of emigrants, but according to Bynum (1934:3), a government store had been established on the rancho and fewer and fewer emigrants stopped to visit with Williams.

10. William Workman and John Rowland arrived in Los Angeles in 1841 (Bancroft 1886:v:705, says the Mormon community referred to Rowland as Rollins). They both applied for Mexican citizenship and thus became eligible to petition for land grants. The two men subsequently took joint ownership of Rancho La Puente (near the modern city of Industry) and built adobe houses within a mile of each other (Hoover 1962:20). Emigrants B. B. Harris (1960:98) and Robert B. Green (1955:16) mentioned meeting a Mr. Reed, but they were not able to identify him beyond his surname. John Reed came to California from Missouri in 1837, and later married John Rowland's daughter (Thompson and West 1880:36).

11. Brownlee and company would have had to pass Los Angeles before striking toward the coast. It is unlikely that the men went out of their way to present-day San Pedro. However, they would have crossed the 43,000-acre Rancho San Pedro, which extended half way to Los Angeles and some miles up the California coastline (Hoover 1962:16). Brownlee did stop briefly in Los Angeles. According to an interview in the *Los Angeles Herald* on January 4, 1889, he visited the city after leaving Warner's Ranch and later recalled:

> ... then we struck for Los Angeles, for in those days the lightly equipped parties went through the Angel City and the heavy pedestrian [traffic] by way of the Cajon. The sun was lighting up the western sky with the glories of his setting rays as from an eminence we caught our first glimpses of the pueblo of La Reina de los Angeles, and before night had fallen we had reached the settlement. If I remember there were just six adobe houses and one two-storied building of the same material, which stood somewhere about where Wells Fargo office is located. The large building was a store and was run by two white men whose names I forget. We asked them where there was a good camping-place, and they directed us to a place over by the river, so bidding them goodnight we pulled over to the point indicated and there passed the night. We were up bright and early and pursued our journey northward, and until today I never saw Los Angeles since.

12. Early travelers were able to gather natural asphalt and tar from seeps that dotted wide areas of Southern California. Angelenos often used this material for roofing. Brownlee and his friends may have stopped at the Rancho La Brea tar pits, now a tourist attraction located adjacent to the Los Angeles County Museum of Art, and where prehistoric fossils are preserved in still bubbling sludge.

13. According to H. M. T. Powell (1931:218) there was a warm sulphur spring about three miles from Paso Robles and another to the right of the road, about a half mile farther on.
14. Between 1769 and 1823, Spanish padres established twenty-one missions between San Diego and Sonoma, each one a day's journey or about 30 miles apart. Brownlee added his footsteps to the connecting road called El Camino Real, the King's Highway. Like other missions in the chain, San Miguel Archangel had lain neglected since secularization in 1834. Many immigrants commented on this extensive mission, no doubt because they had heard about the brutal murder of the William Reed family there in 1848. J. Ross Browne witnessed the tragedy and related his version in *A Dangerous Journey* (1972). Phineas Blunt also commented on the event (1849:78) and noted that blood stains were still very much in evidence. He added that all of the inhabitants had left the area due to superstition and fear of ghosts. Brownlee was the only diarist to mention the skeletons.
15. Those crossing the Salinas plains would follow a path through Rancho Bolsa Nueva y moro Cojo (Hoover 1962:269, Beck 1974:31) once owned by John Milligan who had taught weaving at San Juan Bautista Mission (Hoover ibid). According to Phineas Blunt (1849:80), the Irishman also kept a tavern. Blunt had observed tanning vats at this location.
16. When John Gilroy jumped a Hudson Bay Company ship in 1814 he became California's first permanent foreign settler (Foote 1888:37). He later married the daughter of the owner of Rancho San Ysidro and built a three-room adobe on the Pacheco Pass road (Hoover 1962:335). Numerous emigrants and travelers, therefore, encountered the old pioneer while enroute to the Southern Mines. According to Bancroft (1886:III:757), Gilroy was honest and good-natured, but improvident, and died penniless twenty years later. The modern town of Gilroy is situated on the old rancho.
17. One of California's busiest roads ran through the senior Martin Murphy's Rancho Ojo de Agua de la Coche in Santa Clara County. Murphy was respected by all who knew him, and a wayfarer could always count on receiving generous hospitality and friendship (Foote 1888:53–54, Hoover 1962:339). Murphy and his large family achieved fame in 1844 as members of one of the first wagon trains to successfully cross the northern plains into California.
18. Erected in 1777, San Jose was California's first civic pueblo and by November 1849, it consisted of three stores and several adobe buildings, which were built around a large and treeless plaza (Sawyer 1922:57–58). California was not yet part of the Union, but two months after Brownlee's arrival, the small village became the state's first capital and hosted the

initial meeting of the California legislature and the swearing-in of its governor. San Jose had changed considerably in the intervening time, and by December was bursting at the seams, and crowded with hastily built wood and canvas shanties in order to house the increasing numbers of legislators, immigrants, and miners (Eldredge c. 1915:III:361).

19. A number of Mexicans from the states of Sinaloa, Sonora, Chihuahua, and Durango were among the first miners to arrive in the goldfields. Normally they traveled in bands of fifty or so, going to the mines each spring, then returning home in the fall with their gold (Guinn 1909–1910:31–32).

20. Bayard Taylor (1857:130–131) was on this same road in late October 1849, and described meeting a number of Arkansans and Texans fresh from the Southern Route. It is entirely possible that Brownlee and McVicar were part of this group. Taylor described them as being:

> ... wild, sun-burned, dilapidated men, but with strong and hardy frames that were little affected by the toils of their journey. Some were mounted on mules which had carried them from Texas and Arkansas. . . . The companies made great inroads on my progress by questioning me about the gold region. None of them seemed to have any very definite plan in their heads. It was curious to note their eagerness to hear 'golden reports' of the country, every one of them betraying, by his questioning, the amount of the fortune he secretly expected to make. "Where would you advise me to go?" was the first question. I evaded the responsibility of a direct answer, and gave them the general report of the yield on all the rivers. "How much can I dig in a day?" This question was so absurd, as I could know nothing of the physical strength, endurance or geological knowledge of the emigrant, that I invariably refused to make a random answer, telling them it depended entirely on themselves. But there was no escaping in this manner. "Well, how much do you *think* I can dig in a day?" was sure to follow, and I was obliged to satisfy them by replying: "Perhaps a dollar's worth, perhaps five pounds, perhaps nothing!"

21. California's San Joaquin Valley at one time contained more wild horses than any other place in the world. The mustangs ran in herds of hundreds and continued to range the valley well into the 1860s. Originally reintroduced into America by Spanish Conquistadores, the horse adapted well to the California climate and multiplied rapidly. So much so that rancheros were put under orders to kill the surplus stock yearly. In spite of this, a number of horses escaped to the hills to be joined by others that had been hidden by horse thieves (Mitchell 1941:28–40). Additionally, large herds of Tule elk (*Cervus nannodes*) ranged the valley. Eventually these animals became almost extinct as more and more settlers arrived, but in December 1849, the great herds must have presented a magnificent sight. John Woodhouse Audubon (1906:184–185) told of meeting up with "a herd of about a thousand elk; so close . . . that I could see their

eyes perfectly. . . . There is no trail but that of wild horses and elk, all terminating at some water-hole, not a sign of civilization, not the track of a white man to be seen, and sometimes the loneliness and solitude seem unending."

22. Audubon was also impressed by the salmon (1906:185). Unfortunately, he went away hungry for although he too tried shooting the fish, his bullets missed their mark. The Northern Valley Yokuts counted heavily on the King and Chinook salmon as a major part of their subsistence, and killed them easily with antler-tipped harpoons. The San Joaquin River and its tributaries during both fall and spring provided major spawning sites, and with luck one could catch a fish that weighed at least 20 pounds. After 1849, dam construction and silting from mining and farming contributed to a drastic and steady decline in their numbers (Heizer 1978:337–464).

23. John and Robert Burns, and Amos and Resin Widener were co-owners of the 2000-acre Burns Ranch until February 14, 1850, when they sold the property to Swift Barton and Company (Mariposa County *Records Book 1*:221). About this time, miners discovered a number of major quartz-bearing veins, and the hamlet of Quartzburg soon became the center of mining activity. The property changed hands again before it was sold to the stockholders of the Burns Ranch Union Mining Company on March 31, 1851 (ibid). Thomas Thorn early became a driving force in the area and as a partner in the Quartzburg Mining Company, had located nine veins by September 1850 (Collins 1949:43–44). He was also a shareholder in the Washington Vein, a mine which would produce more than two million dollars in gold before the end of the 19th century (Collins 1949:29). It too changed hands a number of times, but in the early 1850s records show that James McVicar and [Alden?] E. Woodruff were among those who offered Sam Ward (brother of Julia Ward Howe) a one-half interest in the mine for $14,000 (ibid 149:31).

CHAPTER VI

All That Glitters . . .

INTRODUCTION

The bearded, red-shirted prospector symbolized California's gold rush days. He and his compatriots swarmed over the Sierra Nevada foothills and in two years time had doggedly turned every rock, sifted, tunnelled, built dams, diverted or dredged rivers, and hosed down hillsides. Effects of this mass intrusion are still very much in evidence all the way from Downieville in the north to Mariposa in the south. Hundreds of weather-worn structures dating to the early 1850s can still be found in towns and hamlets scattered along the 200-mile stretch of ore-rich land known as the Mother Lode, drained by the Feather, Yuba, American, Cosumnes, Mokulumne, Stanislaus, Tuolumne, Merced, Mariposa, and Fresno rivers. With each discovery of gold made along these rivers and their tributaries, miners rushed in and built a settlement, thus adding a new name to the California map. Chinese Camp, Arkansas Flat, French Camp, Chili Gulch, Cherokee Flat, Dutch Flat, Kanaka Bar, Mormon Bar, and Texas Camp, attest to the international flavor of the gold camps. Bed Bug, Poison Spring, Drunken Gulch, Poverty Flat, Grizzly Flat, Loafer Hill, Git-up-and-git, Hangtown, Rough and Ready, Rattlesnake Gulch, or Agua Fria reflect a certain character of life in the diggings.

Mexican miners gave Agua Fria (cold water) its name and Robert Brownlee watched it grow from a camp of twenty to a town of thousands almost overnight. It was predominantly a male society, since few women came to California during its early days. The town grew so rapidly it soon became the seat of Mariposa County. Brownlee's colorful vignettes about the men and mines at the height of their prosperity reflect the prevalent spirit of '49 as Agua Fria reached its boom period.

Brownlee quickly learned that it took time to wash a couple of ounces of gold. Instead, he discovered he could rent his tools or sell items of necessity to turn a quick profit. The miners needed supplies. Thus Brownlee and Clark were able to exploit a new opportunity and soon went into business by establishing a store together with a gambling and boarding house.

Merchants were among the big winners in mining towns, but were often maligned. Miners' diaries and letters are filled with complaints that it took just about every ounce of a week's hard earned dust to buy provisions. Brownlee's books confirm that he was indeed successful during his sojourn in Agua Fria and left the mines a wealthy man. Nevertheless, he also had to pay high prices for an inventory of supplies and goods that required weeks of privation, exposure, and hard labor to bring back into his store.

Like so many other camps, Agua Fria declined as gold gave out, and by the spring of '52 mining activities were on the wane. As placers dwindled, miners began to return home with their profits or, more likely, with empty pockets. Some, like Brownlee and Clark, decided to remain in California and pursue new endeavors. Brownlee even thought of settling down. Eventually Agua Fria disappeared altogether, and is remembered today by only an occasional reference in a history book or in the journal of a gold seeker.

Brownlee also mentions some of the Indian affairs taking place at the time. Until gold rush days, Miwok and Yokuts had lived a peaceful hunting-gathering existence on scattered rancherias in the area. When mining activities began to interrupt their way of life, the tribes began to retaliate by stealing horses and mules, and committing a number of brutal murders. This led to the Mariposa Indian War, a conflict recorded by Brownlee, who recalls some of the events that eventually culminated in the demise of these two groups of native Americans.

THE JOURNAL

We came into camp when the roads were dusty, but it commenced to rain that night, and rained for three days, off and on. One wagon was mired down to the hubs before the storm was over. We had to make a ditch around our tent, and lay bunch grass on the ground to keep us off the wet. After the first rain in California roads are always the softest, and mire the quickest. Anyhow we had to leave our wagon and pack our stores into the mine some thirty miles.

There were four of us in our mess, for when McVicar's wagon broke down at San Jose, two of his men joined us. So our mining company was composed of Seneca Brownfield, William Garrity, John W. Clark and myself.[1] The two former men hadn't anything but the bundles which made such high and lofty tumbling coming down the St. John mountain. Mr. Clark packed "Buck" Garrity's and my tent and provisions into the mines and he and Brownfield were going to bring the balance. They then took the mules back where there was plenty of good food, for at the mines there was nothing but chamise brush, and animals would not eat it.[2] "Buck" and myself were prospecting with a butcher knife and a pan in the bed of the creek. I struck a small pocket containing eighty dollars. I hadn't any water with which to wash the dirt, but the gold was coarse and I picked it out. "Buck" was working a little farther up and found some six dollars. He came down to show me his success, and his eyes were as large again as common, and how he puffed and blowed; but when I showed him my luck, he acted like a crazy man.

During this time Clark came in with our outfit, which came in good place; it consisted of picks, shovels, Russian Sheet Iron to make cradles for washing the gold out of the dirt, some quick silver, and plenty of provisions. He also brought a small grind stone, a draw knife, jack plane, an axe, some nails, a frow [froe] for splitting shakes. After this was all in, we took the mules back to good pasture with wagons and harness and left them in care of Burns.

All hands went to work, but without a cradle [rocker] it was slow work, as you could not wash dirt fast enough; so I got "Buck" to fell a tree and split it up. As I was handiest with tools I made a cradle, like one I had seen, resembling in shape a common cradle, with this difference—

a sheet of iron say twenty inches square punched with the square end of a pick [with] as many holes as the iron could stand. This was fastened on top of the cradle, and the one who worked it had a dipper and dipped water into the dirt which was placed on this iron, all the time giving a gentle steady rocking motion till the dirt was all washed off the slate or stone, as the case might be. In the bottom of the cradle were three cleats of wood nailed to catch the gild, and if it was very fine, quick silver was put above the cleats, which would catch all the fine stuff. Some used a blanket for this purpose. As there was water in the creek and our cradle was ready, we now commenced in good earnest, but did not succeed very well. Clark and myself mined only six days and averaged some eight dollars a day.[3] The first cradle I made was sold for two ounces or thirty-two dollars, it being too small for us.[4] I was a long time in enlarging our tent, which was too small for all hands and supplies. We had a fly for our tent, so we added that to the length. Then we made the walls some four feet high with logs and built a temporary chimney, so we could cook and warm ourselves during rainy weather. We were better fixed than any in the fault. There were about twenty men who arrived in Agua Fria, the name of the mine, and in three weeks afterwards there were about two hundred making from one half an ounce to an ounce and upwards.[5]

The winter of 1849 was wetter than any I have ever seen since. It seemed to rain all the time, snowed sometimes too, yet men slept outside, with say one pair of blankets, on the wet ground. The rain prevented them making a fire to cook or warm by, so they would often come and boil their coffee pot at our fire, on a cold wet morning, and at the same time just as wet themselves as water could make them. Still I never heard of any bad effect from the exposure.[6]

By this time provisions were getting scarce. As so many men came on foot and could not carry much, this class of miners was getting short. Mr. Burns sent us word that our mules had strayed away from his place, so Clark, McVicar, a Negro and I started back to where we left them, a distance of thirty miles. We found they had been gone a week, but finally got them at what is now called Hornitos, about ten miles toward Stockton.[7] Being so near we concluded to go to Stockton for provisions, as the mules were fat and well rested.

We had six mules and a California mare; McVicar also had six. We went and bought flour and salt pork. I really forget what we paid

Row houses on Church Road, Bonkle, Scotland. House on far left was Robert Brownlee's birthplace, built in 1792. House, far right, built in 1785.

Alcath Cottage (1817), Allanton Road, Bonkle, Scotland.

Whitebank (circa 1870), Allanton Road, Bonkle, Scotland.

Old State House, c. 1875. *Courtesy Old State House, Little Rock, Arkansas.*

The Brownlee House (1847) at Territorial Restoration, Little Rock, Arkansas.

Capped Rock and terrain in Guadalupe Canyon, New Mexico, one of the most significant landmarks on the Southern Trail.

Agua Fria Valley, circa 1850. *Courtesy, California Historical Society, San Francisco.*

The Brownlee family home, Sunnyside Farm (prior to 1881). *Courtesy, Sacramento Area State Parks, California.*

Annie Brownlee. *Courtesy, the Bancroft Library.*

Sunnyside Farm (1959). *Courtesy, Mrs. Thelma Halterman Bachelor.*

The Robert Brownlee Family. Front Row, seated (l to r): Annie Lamont Brownlee, Robert Brownlee, Grace Annie Brownlee. Back Row, standing (l to r): Margaret Russell Brownlee, Robert A. Brownlee, George Lamont Brownlee, Mary Jane Brownlee, Frederick James Brownlee. Courtesy, *California Historical Society, San Francisco.*

for it, but it was not so very high, as there was so much shipped around the Horn and unloaded in San Francisco and then reshipped to Stockton and Sacramento. So both places had plenty, but there wasn't any way of getting provisions into the mines. Flour came in barrels and had to be repacked in hundred and fifty pound sacks, so it could be packed handy. Whiskey and liquors of all kinds could be left out doors, as no man would think of touching [that] which was left exposed.

We reached Stockton in good season, which place is situated on low flat adoby soil, and the mud was knee deep, and around the steam boat landing much deeper. We were there several days hunting saddles for packing. As there wasn't any market from which we could buy anything we wanted, we had to pick up whatever we could get. After a while we were ready to start. As this was our first attempt at packing and we were badly prepared, had we ever known how, it took us a long time. There is a system in packing which is easy when you know how. The Spaniards are well prepared for this and can do it in such a way that the packs will remain so all day, and their mules are so trained that they will come up and stand by their loads until you are ready. Let me here state how it is done. It takes two men, one on each side of the mule. They place a lariat on the *aparejos* [pack saddles], which are made of leather and stuffed with hair, in such a shape so that each man lifts a sack of flour and with a quick motion of the rope, is fastened and holds it in place. They then lift the third sack and lay it on the center, fasten the rope, and all is done. We hadn't any system, so the first night out of Stockton we hired a Spaniard to show us how, and it was money well spent, as we could never have otherwise made the trip.

This was our first trip, and the roads were very soft, raining and snowing all the time pretty much, and bear in mind, we hadn't any blankets or tent. Every night we camped was full of adventure. I will try to describe things as they really were, as it can hardly be over drawn of our trip from Stockton to Agua Fria. We left Stockton about noon to go as far as the French Camp, a distance of five miles.[8] We out traveled a Spanish pack train, which was ahead of us, and overtook them. Let me describe the road. It is genuine doby. There was but one path where the mules went, stepping out of one foot mark and on lifting up to pass to the second, which was divided by a ridge perhaps fifteen inches high. You may judge that the short legged mules could not make the rise but would fall down. The Spaniards just left them and went on with the main train till they would get to some firm land. Then they would return and get the mired ones. As we were traveling we came to a mule which was down, not mired, but only down. Our mules had to pass the best they could, and I think we found six that were left behind. You may say, "why don't they go outside on new ground?" Well, that's out of the question. They would mire right away and knew it. When ours passed those that were down, they would almost step on the animal before they would step outside of the beaten path. We made camp and had to stay three days, as it rained all the time.

While we were camped, there was another party, like ourselves, situated on a knoll, say about fifty yards away on the edge of the timber. One night we heard in the water, where the timber land is flooded close to our camp, a whistling noise and concluded it must be ducks after acorns. We could hear the splashing in the water late at night. Next morning just at day light there passed between the two camps two hundred elk, perhaps. The last ones were nearly mired, as we could see them plunging they came so close. We hadn't any firearms, therefore we didn't have any elk meat.

We now moved camp ahead about eight miles, to what is called Point of Timbers.[9] We stopped here, as there was plenty of good wood and the weather was very stormy. The other party was camped close by. They managed to get a rifle, the stock of which had been broken, and lashed it together with rawhide. One of them had this under his pillow to keep it dry, when the coyotes came, stole the gun from under his head, dragged it some distance, ate the rawhide off and left the balance. Next morning as we were packing up, four elk came right through our camp. I jumped on a mule bare back and kept in the road while he, being off it a little, was miring at every jump, the ground was so very soft.

Next night we camped on the banks of the Stanislaus River. We had a bar of yellow soap for washing shirts, etc. When through with the frying pan the night before, it was set back from the fire and the soap left in it. We had a piece of rawhide for carrying or tying up. Anyhow, the coyotes came, stole the frying pan and soap, and licked the pan clean. This was not all. We had bought a junk of salt beef, and had taken a hair rope we had, and gone out on a leaning willow, and sunk the beef down for at least four feet. While we were sleeping within ten feet, the coyotes cut the rope above the water and must have gone down those four feet and gotten the beef, as we could never find either rope or meat. The river was pretty full, and how we ever crossed I now forget.[10]

Next day, when out about five miles, we came to a wagon mired the worst kind. On the wagon was a boiler, and I think three mules were dead, sticking in the mud, with their harness still on, and our mules had to walk over the animals. This was the hardest day I ever experienced. We used to call it twenty-five miles between the two rivers [Stanislaus and Tuolumne]. After passing the wagon it commenced to rain and snow, and the ground was so soft that our mules were miring all the time. We could not stop and lift one up, as the balance would bunch up and they would all go down. I used to ride the mare ahead and look out for the best place. As each mule would step exactly in the same place as the mare would, you could not go ahead to look for the best place, as they would climb up on the top of one another in order to get close to the mare. So you see a great deal depended on the judgment of the person on horseback. If he came upon a piece of ground stiff enough to hold them up, he had to stop, go back and unpack, carry his load to where the mules could stand, put on the load again, and then maybe go one hundred yards, when they would mire again, then just go through the same motion again. Between Dry Creek and the mired wagon, a distance of fifteen miles,[11] we must have unpacked forty or fifty mules, lifted and carried the loads, often a hundred yards, sometimes twenty feet, it raining and snowing all the time, we being as wet and muddy as was possible all day.

When we reached Dry Creek, it was dark, and not a stick of wood with which to make a fire, and the creek running full of water. We were compelled to camp right there in the mud and hadn't any time to spare, as it was getting dark, also snowing for our benefit. We took the fifty-pound flour sacks and placed them so we could sleep on them. Even then they would sink half out of sight. When we laid down, we had sacks and pieces of old blanket, which were used under the saddles, for cover. We had worked hard all day and were very hungry, so we mixed flour with cold water and drank as much as our stomachs would hold. We tried to eat raw pork, but this would not stay down. I had to heave it up. Then we prepared for bed, took off our boots and lay down as close as we could get side by side, this being the only way to keep at all warm. Perkins was on the outside, I next, then Clark and McVicar last. And I may safely say, that was the coldest and perhaps longest night I ever experienced.

The snow stopped falling at midnight, when it began to freeze. When day light came, Perkins got up and tried to put on his boots, when he found them half full of ice, he having left them standing upright. What rain fell turned into ice, and he had to take them to the water and thaw the ice out. It was freezing, still the sun was shining, and we could see that there wasn't any wood near us, but there were plenty of soap-weed tops about three feet high. So all hands broke an armful while I prepared a hole for the frying pan. By making fagots and holding them under the pan, we managed to make a large pile of flap-jacks, hot coffee, and fried salt pork, and had a glorious feast. I remember, as though it happened yesterday, Clark's remark—"Oh, Bob, just cut them into quarter sections, so every fellow can swallow as fast as he wants."

After breakfast, having warmed ourselves, we felt as though nothing had ever troubled us, but in lifting and packing flour out of the mud, it looked a little damp, as we did ourselves. What stared us in the face now, was where and how were we going to cross Dry Creek; it being some forty or fifty feet wide and ten feet deep, with high bluffs and banks. I could see the old crossing and road straight toward. It came out all right with the exception of a small mule, which belonged to McVicar. This mule tried to land in his own way, and was half out of the water when he fell backward on his back and went clean out of sight. But he soon came to the surface, right side up, and with care landed when the rest did. As the mules entered the water, each man grabbed one by the tail and swam over, which did not matter much as we were wet anyway, but the water was very cold. Now we were five miles from the Tuolumne River, where we had another adventure.

We had built a large fire by rolling four logs together, and had spread some old sacks to keep the snow off, which was falling very fast. We had a square meal, as we had bought beef at the Fairy Tent,[12] and were smoking and remarking what a nice time we were having, all warm and dry, feasting as only epicures can. But we had built our fire on the river bottom, in a washout, somewhat lower than the land on either side, when all of a sudden the river overflowed its banks and came down that washout some four feet deep, floating away our fire as though it had been a common match. In five minutes the water was knee deep. Here we were in a critical condition, as we did not know how high the river would rise, and here we were with our mules and cargo about half a mile from high land. We hadn't any idea what we were going to do next, everything looked blue, and at the same time it was very dark.

So we took our hand axe and concluded to fell a tree and place our saddles and such things on it as would float away. After much chopping with our dull hatchet, the tree fell. We made it fast to the stump, made a scaffold in the top for our plunder, and then took our positions as best suited our ease and comfort. At first it was easy to hold on and balance one's self, but after a while sleep would come without any courting on our part and when on the eve of falling [asleep] we would waken with a jerk, which would keep our eyes open for a while. Then we would dose off and pass through the same motion again, that of jerking and grabbing. That night was the longest, as we had to sit on one limb and hold on to another, which in itself was very tiring, but, brace up as we would, we would catch ourselves snoozing and nodding to Morpheus. Just about day light the water began to fall. As soon as we could see dry land, and it was only a knoll covered with young rose bushes, we descended from our perches. Like young quail, we stuck our heads into the bush, and although on our hands and knees, went soundly to sleep. Many times we laughed when we told of our position and of how we must have looked.

A party of three emigrants were camped close by, and then the [Tuolumne] River rose so fast, one of them commenced to holler that he was so badly hurt by a grizzly bear that he could not help himself. So Mr. Clark caught his mule, Jack, and got the lame man on behind and took him where there was a great many packers and left him, having to swim and wade to get there.

Next day we started up the river, say one mile, to where there was a ferry, which was a White Haul boat, which could carry pack loads and people. We bargained for our passage and to carry our cargoes over. As we had not enough money to pay the cost, which was $18, they trusted us until we returned. But the third partner came up and began abusing us for not paying, but we were now all across so went our own way.[13] We called the distance twenty-five miles to Merced River, and as the land was of firmer nature, we got on pretty well and reached there before dark. There were a great many campers who had been there some two weeks, waiting for the river to fall so they could ford it. Next morning Clark walked a way up the river for several miles, looking at the prospect for getting across. Below the falls, he found a long riffle and thought he could with good management, cross. On reporting our discovery, the other packers laughed us to scorn, but we didn't mind, but packed up and started off. On reaching the place, we looked for a place to cross. I went on the mare, and the mules followed. We kept well up on the brake of the riffle and found bottom all the way and came out safely with the exception of that same little mule, Herman, who had to swim some way. The reason for all his trouble was in his anxiety to keep close to the mare, but he would always be whipped back by the larger ones.

We had crossed all the rivers and now commenced to climb the mountain road. Our next camping place was Burns' Ranch.[14] This was New Year's Eve. It had been snowing and raining all day, and we had had a very hard time, and it was now getting dark, but after a while we got a fire started and put our different capitals together, which amounted in all to about $8. Got a bottle of brandy, had a "Here's to your very good health," had supper of flap jacks, fried pork and coffee, and I suppose enjoyed that New Year's Eve as much and as loyally as any one else. You must understand that we had not been under a tent for the last three weeks but had made the trip sleeping on wet ground. It hardly seems possible that men could endure what we did. I had wakened up in the morning half side up in water and wet the whole time. It was wonderful that none of us had even a cold, never sick. We were so full of excitement, it pulled us through, and our crowd was none of the whining sort. Was there a river to ford, Clark was the first to try it, and he couldn't swim a lick. If water was scarce, he never complained. If meals were missed, he seemed only to enjoy them the more when he got the chance. McVicar used to find fault with our luck, but it was only for a minute. Perkins, the colored man, was a strong, kind hearted, fine specimen of humanity. Did I have another journey of privations, I would not want better men to join me than these three men.[15]

Next camp brought us to Agua Fria, on a beautiful clear day. We found on going down the stream three or four miles, a great many more men than when we started, and on passing, the miners would ask, "Is the flour for sale?" and would put their mark on the sack and follow us down. When we unpacked, they would hand us their gold sack to pay and never once parted with the flour. A great many were short of provisions, as there wasn't any store to buy from, and we were the first packers that had gotten through since the rain commenced, so we disposed of most of our load that same day. Next day Garrity and I started back to Stockton, for more goods, leaving Clark to start a store on a small scale, as we had the best tent in the flat. The mules had had nothing to eat since yesterday, but we started with $800 for another load of different stuff, more costly, consisting of boots, shovels, picks, with a variety of liquors, as they were in demand, tobacco, cards, in fact, we had a general assortment. I think the first trip took us three weeks, from Stockton to Agua Fria, but the roads had been improved, so we made the trip in ten days.

We made several other trips that winter to Agua Fria and one to Woods' Diggings in Stanislaus County.[16] I packed ten or fifteen miners over to San Joaquin, to what was then called Lariones Camp, where it was reported they were making one and two ounces a day; the camp was situated where the river comes out of the mountains.[17] We stayed three days. As they found nothing, I carried them back for one-half fare, and they helped pack and care for the mules. This was in February 1850, and by this time we were better prepared for packing and could carry three ten gallon barrels or kegs on one mule, with long handled shovels tied on, and most anything that was necessary.[18] The main thing was to know how and be prepared, as the white man is superior to the Mexican any time.

I have given a long account of our first trip, as it was the hardest, with the stormiest weather. But the pen picture of our journey is not overdrawn, as all those things are so firmly impressed on my mind that I will never forget them. I may forget distances, names of places, and mis-spell a great deal, yet the facts are still there; and I have often wondered how we ever stood it. You must remember, that when we first commenced packing, I could not use my arm, and I do verily believe, if I had not exercised my arm, it would be stiff today, for often I had to use it or else make a failure. It would often times hurt so that I would cry with pain, still I have always given the packing credit for curing me.

I have finished with our overland trip and have given an account of our first trip packing. The weather was very fine and as goods were in demand and Stockton was the place where we purchased our stores, Mr. Clark was to take the lines and haul while I was detailed to take charge of the store and to build a regular substantial good tent. The size, I think, was sixty feet by forty. We split logs and set them on end so as to make the inner walls eight feet high, chinked the cracks with mud, built a good chimney, and covered the building with drilling. Over that we put a fly so as to prevent the beating rains from coming through, and also to make the tent cooler in summer.

I could sell goods faster than Clark could haul, so he bought another team. Even then, we had to hire another team to help him. We were selling lots of goods and trying to store a supply away for winter, such as flour and sugar. We must have had about five tons of the latter stored in another tent. As winter was coming on, Mr. Clark concluded to stay in San Francisco and attend auctions. As the consignees hadn't any place to store goods when vessels were discharging, they had to sell them. Clark bought at one time seven ten-pin alleys. One he sent to me, which I put up and covered with brush until we had time to recover it with cloth. It was in great demand, as everybody wanted amusement, and this seemed to fill the bill.[19]

Gambling was going on: monte, faro and poker. I got $8 a night for the use of two small tables with blankets. Both tables were in full blast mostly all the time, till about ten o'clock, when the miners would leave. The Mexicans were great for gambling and drinking light wines, while Americans would take whiskey or brandy with cigars. The Mexicans are fond of cigarettes. Everything was paid for in gold dust, which had to be weighed, twelve and a half cents was the smallest. When the dealer of a game would call out to take a drink, to all those who stood around, no one would be backward in saying what he wanted. When all were served, I would call out how many, and he never disputed but would hand over the money. Often fifty would drink and smoke three or four times in an evening. I had a Spanish boy who could speak English, to help me. I weighed their dust and gave them silver, as it was then at a premium and suited them better for gambling purposes. To show how it was done—if a party hadn't any silver, he would place his bag of dust on the table and bet on it. If he continued to lose, the dealer would send up the bag and sing out, take out three ounces or ten, as the case might be, then I would hand him the amount.[20] Our place was crowded every night with all nationalities.[21] and pretty much everybody had his Colts revolver of the large size in his belt or sash. There was but little quarreling and not any stealing, as that was sure death according to miners' law.

All those in a certain district would call a meeting to regulate and make mining laws, such as making the size of a surface claim or quartz claim, and if not worked for so many days, would be forfeited. Also regulated and put in force was the Civil law, and if any one was found stealing or tampering with sluice boxes, for washing gold, or of taking anything that didn't belong to him, he was adjudged by a called meeting of miners, who after hearing the complaint and defense, would give their decision, which was in most cases strictly obeyed. For instance—a surface claim was sixteen feet square. Supposing another man had a claim joining yours and the paying dirt passed from one to the other. Such cases had to be settled by outsiders whose decision was law; therefore the weak man or party was protected from the grasp of the stronger. You must bear in mind the courts of Common Law had not as yet been established in the different mining camps. Therefore, it was highly necessary to have a substitute for the protection of the camp.[22]

In 1850 I want it to be understood that California, according to her population, possessed more intelligence, more industry and law abiding principles than any other portion of the world. You may ask why. It is easily answered. In 1849 none but the better class of citizens could manage to raise funds to get here—the wealthy man or the preacher's son. The slums of Australia had not as yet sent her convicts, and the Evil world from the East had not arrived, as it took money and lots of it to come round the Horn, besides the length of time it consumed. The Panama route was under contemplation but had not started.[23] Miners could leave their wallets of dust in their tents under their blankets and [they] would be safe.

In the winters of 1850 and '51, those who came were of the lower order of men. Convicts from Australia were coming into San Francisco on sail vessels in great numbers, and as they were of course head-ing for the mines, it became necessary to be more careful of your worldly goods. Every few days some miner's camp would be robbed, or his provisions taken, perhaps his pistol. Yet no man could be caught in the act. The miners became more vigilant and careful about leaving things to tempt the weak kneed, or the men of weak morals. There was a "Sydney Duck" as they were called, caught in the act of taking a watch out of a miner's tent. On being caught, their judgment was so many lashes (as hanging was too severe) with a black-snake. This happened in the town of Mariposa, two and a half miles from Agua Fria. He was told to leave the country or to take the consequences, also to move as fast as was possible.

I was in the store all by myself when a good looking stout young man came in and called for crackers and cheese and some beer. There wasn't anything queer about this, but to my surprise three men dismounted and came in, and without saying a word, all three of them commenced lashing him with their black-snakes. I knew all of the men and begged of them to stop, but when they told me what he had done I could see they were only doing their duty, after which they told him to put, and to move quickly, or they would send a deadly messenger after him. He started on a run, and we could see him running for about four hundred yards. He traveled some four miles and went into another tent and stole gold dust, and I think a gun. I forget what was then done to him, but he got to San Francisco and there was again caught. The Vigilance Committee was in full blast, so they concluded to hang him. I was in San Francisco at the time buying goods. In the forenoon, I was down looking at them dumping sand where they were filling in part of the bay. I was sitting on a pile of lumber, when the City bell commenced to toll in a peculiar way. I asked the cause of so many men running towards where I sat and was told that the Vigilance Committee was about to hang a "Sydney Duck," and sure enough, it was the same man I had seen get the benefit of the black-snake.[24]

I will tell you something which happened. Clark bought two large hogsheads, one of porter, the other ale. I opened them and this being the first of the kind here, was in great demand. The tent was crowded all day, I didn't have any rest, and was handing out porter and ale by the glass. I had no one to help me as I had to weigh the gold dust and was in the habit of taking it out of the scales and emptying it into a tin cup. When this got full I would dump it in a leather purse. In the afternoon I emptied all into my purse and put it behind a bundle of socks. Of course, any one in the house could see me do it as there were four men, two of whom were teamsters, sitting at the end of the room talking and having a time to themselves, when "Liverpool Harry," a Sydney Duck, and a fighting one at that, stepped up and reached over those men and took the purse which contained $800 in gold dust, and some large specimens which I could swear to. I never missed it until the closing of the store, when I discovered it was gone. I put on my thinking cap for some time but could not make anything out of it, so I took the two teamsters into my confidence, and we compared notes. I had a French cook and they had observed him going back and forth towards the bush several times that afternoon, and of course suspicioned him. I could not entertain the idea that he was the man, and the teamsters started out for Stockton in the morning.

There was a mess of four men, two Englishmen and two Irishmen and this "Liverpool Harry," and I had my eye on him for this reason. He sent one of the mess up next morning for whiskey, porter, and a quart bottle of pickled English walnuts, and sent the gold dust to pay for all. I knew he hadn't any dust the day before so at once suspected him. I was forced to take two of his mess into my confidence and when I told them all I knew, they were much surprised, still did not doubt but that I might be right. So both went back to camp to find out what they could before letting it be known. There was an English family who lived a quarter of a mile below them. They went and saw the woman and she told them about him paying for what he got and what he owed her, and that there was some large pieces in his bag and it was nearly full. This satisfied them, but as he was on the fight, they didn't want to get it in that way. On returning to camp, he was found dead drunk, and now was their chance. They kept rolling him about as though making fun, but could see no signs of the lost bag, but when they unfastened his pants found it, and hurried up and told me and gave me the purse.

I called out to some miners who were close by and when they had heard the story, all exclaimed, hang him. We started to his camp with that intention, but Providence had forestalled us, as he was found dead in his bunk, while one of his mess was drunk in the corner. I gave two men half an ounce or eight dollars to bury him, and was never so glad before as when we found him dead in bed. The other one was very drunk, but when we aroused him and informed him how things were, he looked much astonished. After a while he told us how he had acted about the walnut pickles, wouldn't give him but one or two, but would gobble them down and laugh cause he couldn't do the same. He kept on drinking and mixing porter, whiskey and pickles, which was too much for his stomach, as he had eaten nothing for two days, and when the men were rolling him he must have been far gone as all he could do was to grunt a little.[25]

In the fall of 1850 when the first snow fell we turned our mules out to pasture, close by Burns' ranch, and left a teamster to watch and take care of them. We now had plenty of provisions and dry goods, men's wearing apparel, boots, shoes, potatoes and onions, and about twenty and a half barrels of sauer kraut, for which there was great demand, it being a sure cure for scurvy. I can prove this for I think twenty or sixty men were cured who were not able to walk, by giving them raw potatoes, pins leaf tea and sauer kraut. Many were able to get about but there wasn't any money in such customers as they hadn't any, and all this was done simply for charity's sake.

I used to advance to emigrants an outfit of pick, pan and shovel, with provisions amounting in all to about twenty dollars worth and by trusting them I never lost a cent on the first purchase. But when they bought the second time, look out, for a great many would skip the country. Often an overland emigrant would come in and report some family sick, and their mules given out. All I had to do then was to call a meeting, and we would soon raise money right then and there, and send some one out to bring them in. There was a young man from Arkansas who was attacked in the Four Creek Country, now Tulare County, and was shot through the shoulder and had to have his arm cut off at the shoulder. So I called a meeting and I think $800 was raised for him and a relief party paid to go back and bring the others into camp. A great many gamblers boarded with me and were very free with their money, if they had any, their motto being, come easy, go easy. Unless events impressed themselves distinctly on my mind I cannot remember things which have passed so long ago.

The White men around Agua Fria mines, who were out prospecting were having some adventures with Indians, who forced them to return to camp where they were safe. Two men generally went out together with pick, pan and shovel, more following up some canyon with provisions. They often camped in a dense thicket, and as they were often gone two or three weeks, no doubt many never returned, as the grizzly bear was even more to be dreaded than the Indians. Let me mention what happened to a Frenchman while we were working about eleven o'clock in the morning. He was rocking the gold cradle under a small bluff near a pool of water, when all of a sudden a black bear which had been frightened, jumped from that bluff almost on top of the man, and a more scared Frenchman I never saw to have lived after such a shock. Every one was hollering bear, but he made his escape across the flat, for some four hundred yards, then [ran] up the chamise mountain, taking long steady jumps, never looking behind him.

Four men were prospecting, when one shot a young grizzly bear and another cub ran up a tree. The old mother bear came along, knocked one man down, grabbed his head in her mouth and scalped him as completely as though an Indian had done it. He used to come to me to have it dressed, as I had plenty of clean dry goods which could not be found everywhere. After a while he got well, but never a hair appeared again on his head.[26]

In front of our store was a round hill, and after a fall of snow a bear was tracked by two old bear hunters and a Negro to an overhanging rock, a sort of a cove, where they saw the bear lying. They shot but it did not prove fatal so the bear went after the Negro, who climbed a small pine tree, with the bear close behind him. As the tree could not support both, but bent over, the Negro fell on the lower side and rolled over and over with the bear still close to him, and not until the Negro had run across the face of the mountain downwards to a miner's camp where he was safe, did the bear retreat when forced by so many men. This Negro had killed many a bear in Arkansas but had no show with a grizzly.

Grizzlys were very plentiful in '49, there being plenty of acorns and chamise berries of which they are very fond. In the summer at a large Mexican camp, they butchered numbers of beeves, and in the morning tracks of grizzlys of all sizes could be traced where they had been busy with the off-falls. The Indian and grizzly were much dreaded by the prospectors as in every gulch, where was the place to find gold, where it had been washed from decayed rock, was a thicket of chamise brush. So much for the grizzly bear.

Mariposa County contains some very profitable surface mines, also any amount of quartz, but they have never been worked to any extent for General [John Charles] Fremont, to whom the mines belong, asks such high Royalty that no company cares to invest so much money, as is required to put up a first class quartz mill. Clark and myself owned a large interest in two quartz mines, and where the rock was exposed to the weather gold could be seen sticking out, but like many others, we failed to do the necessary work upon the claims and hold them from being jumped by other persons, so all went by default. We were more fortunate than some others who spent thousands of dollars in prospecting, and whenever they found anything valuable Fremont's Agents would be on hand, to demand the lion's share, which would result in their leaving the claim to some other party.[27] In some instances the mines would be so rich, that men could make good wages by working the Mexican Erastus [arastra], which is done in this way. They have a small sweep fastened to an upright stake, and to this sweep a stone is tied and the Jack Ass goes round and round in a circle, dragging this large stone which grinds the gold bearing quartz to a pulp. Then by the aid of quick silver the fine gold is taken up.

In 1850 and '51 there was very little rain and snow and we had a very large supply of goods on hand. Our mules, you will remember, were out on pasture at the "Texan Tent" [Texas Tent, Texas Ranch], some fifteen miles from Agua Fria, in charge of a teamster named McGrath. I forget just how many, but either twelve or eighteen mules and a California mare, the latter being kept hobbled, so the mules never left her. In fact, you could not drive them from her they were so attached to her. But Mr. Indian was as well aware of the fact as we were, for in the night they came, caught the mare, took off the hobble, mounted and rode to the mountains passing about two miles from Agua Fria. McGrath came to let us know what happened, so I started with him and struck the trail and followed it some six miles, when night fall forced us to return as we had still six miles to travel to reach camp, and this was not a pleasant position to be in in a hostile country.

On reaching home, we called a meeting of the miners and had the sheriff present. On making the facts known, the sheriff proposed if he could have eighty volunteers to follow the Indians, and to start right off if I would furnish provisions and ammunition, also go security for the men who loaned rifles or pistols. This I readily did and those who furnished mules were all mounted. Perhaps this company was not as fine in appearance as Uncle Sam's troops, but I can assure you were a much more determined set of men, knew nothing of what fear was, and as they had in crossing the continent, seen much danger, and many had grievances of their own to settle with the Indians, made them more determined than ever.[28]

I think it was the afternoon after the mules had been taken that the posse started, with pack mules and supplies. On the second day they came up with the Indians and had a fight for some four hours, killing some of the latter. Some of our boys were wounded also by the arrows. The battle ground was across a ravine and the Indians had the advantage of ground, as the large rocks afforded them good shelter from the rifles. Our men took their positions behind trees when convenient and would put their hats on the ramrods and expose them. Then the arrows could be seen coming thick, thus allowing our men to see where to shoot. In this way we succeeded in making the red men retreat, carrying their dead with them. This was a hard fought battle as there were five Indians to one White man. They found the heads of all the mules and the mare, with lots of half dried meat.[29]

When they returned to camp, the Sheriff, Major James Burney, called another meeting of miners. It was decided to send to San Jose to the Governor, asking him to authorize three companies of volunteers to be paid by the State, which he accordingly did. He sent his Lieutenant Governor to Agua Fria to fully organize and equip the number and to appoint the different officers, putting Major [James] Savage in command. Mr. Burney was pay-master, Brownlee and Clark, sutlers and quarter-masters, and all were in the field as soon as was possible.[30] This body of men did active service as that summer's trouble ended the war, although they had many a bitter encounter.

[The Indians] were at last forced into their mountain fastness where they lived in their snow houses, living on acorns which were stowed away in wicker baskets. They were finally mastered and made to sign a treaty of peace. I went in person where ever the volunteers were camped and furnished goods of all kinds, such as clothing, canned goods, assorted liquors, boots and shoes, and ammunition. Clark sent all that was needed direct from San Francisco, and we sold any amount of goods, having to take Indian War Scrip in pay which was then worth forty cents on the dollar.[31]

We were camped six weeks on the Fresno River, and entreating with the Indians who had come in from the mountains and camped near us and could see how they lived and cooked. For instance—the acorns were hulled, put into a small mortar, and pounded into a coarse meal. Then they would scoop a hole out of the soil about the size of a milk basin and fill the hole with water after it had been plastered with mud all around with the hand so it was pretty smooth. Then they put hot rocks in the water till it boiled. Then with two sticks would lift them out and put the acorn meal in, and stirred it around with a stick. All this time some fifty Indians were sitting around waiting for it to cook. When not so hot, a big buck Indian would slip up and dip his hand into the mess, go a little way off and sit down and eat it off his hand, after which he'd lick his fingers. So did the balance, each one getting a handful and doing as the first had done.[32]

I saw a new way of cooking grasshoppers which was done in an open basket made of willow, which by the by, was very neat, and twas said to hold water, which I don't doubt. Well, the basket was half full of grasshoppers which a young squaw was roasting over a bed of coals, giving them a gentle flip, burning them partly over from the bottom to the top, with great judgment and much ease. She offered me a handful but I modestly declined, while she at the same time, put some in her mouth.

This tribe is called "Digger Indians," and lives on roots, acorns, pine nuts and grass seed which they gather very fast, considering how scattered the grass stand. They use two-bushel baskets and something like a pan, and when they find anything that suits them they hold the basket in a slanting position under the bush and strike the seeds with the pan, causing them to fall into the basket. When this mixture is eaten, it is served in a manner similar to the acorns, being made into a mush. I don't understand how these poor creatures can possibly exist among the snow of the mountains without any cover or clothing except a small piece of bark of some kind as a breech clout, this being all I ever saw them wear. In summer they are entirely naked. This was a very warm day to be sure. They would work a little while, step to one side and lie down on their backs, close their eyes as if sleeping and enjoy it immensely.[33]

Before the war, Major Savage who commanded the battalion, lived with the Indians just as much as any of the bucks, even though Indiana was his native state. When I first saw him, he was traveling in a very unbecoming manner. All he had on was a coarse cotton shirt, which came to his knees, was bare headed and bare footed, with three wives following him, one after the other a little distance apart, and he an equal distance in advance of the oldest of the three, who was about sixteen years of age. The other two being about twelve or fourteen as near as I could judge. When he came to the store first, I thought him crazy; but soon found out different as his address was good when he asked for something to eat as his squaws were hungry. He bought the best I had, and gave them plenty of it. It was mid-day and my place empty, so they remained for several hours, he buying largely of clothing for himself and squaws. I had on hand a great many bolts of prints, some good, others not so much so, also some red blankets which took their eyes. All they fancied he bought for them; his bill I think was $75. I could not see that he had any place to carry gold dust as all I could see was his cotton shirt, but sure enough, when he put his hand in his bosom, out came a well filled purse, and he never disputed one item. When they started each girl must have been carrying fifty pounds apiece, and I gave each a bolt of cheap but highly colored print, which pleased them very much. When they started I thought of the old maxim, "the last straw broke the camel's back."

    He invited me kindly to make him a visit to his camp which I did, as at this place was reported good diggings could be found. He treated me kindly and I slept in his tent, the sleeping apartments of which I will describe. I was very "green" as [to how] a man could get along with three wives but he showed me. Two large logs formed two sides of his bed, two more the ends, and as he had those red blankets and a sheet, this was cover enough for [five] of us. Of course my modesty made me shut my eyes and look through my fingers. He called out, "Brownlee, here's the way," when he turned in among them, all seemingly happy.

    His camp was very rich in surface diggings, but the war with the Indians had commenced and caused Savage to leave his tent and become a civilized citizen once more when he was elected Major of the Battalion. He could speak Spanish and Indian. After the war he got into a difficulty with Mr. [Walter H.] Harvey who shot him dead. He could have been a rich man while on the Merced River keeping store as he used to give a pound of sugar for equal weight in gold. But like all other Californians he was fond of gambling, would go to Stockton and lose a fortune, would then return and get the Indians to dig more for him; for so far they did not know the true value of gold. He at that time was working a bar on the river. As yet the White miners had not found out that there was gold on the river, but shortly afterwards miners were forced to go to the different rivers as it was scarce. There they then discovered the gold.[34]

The Indian war was now ended, a Treaty was concluded, and the troops returned to Agua Fria. There were three companies, each sixty strong besides officers, and all had to be legally disbanded, each man receiving his Scrip, and to settle with the Sutler. Major Burney was Paymaster, and a particular friend, and had given me the privilege of presenting our bill and of receiving our Scrip from the different men and thus secured an easy settlement for us. All or very near all, were camped in our store for two weeks while things were all settled up.

In connection with the store, we had an eating house, a ten-pin alley and cards, as the men were spending their Scrip which was selling in the market at 40¢ on the dollar. So we had to give as much as anybody else or lose their custom. I think we had some $40,000, and all troops disbanded, our mules stolen, and a very dry winter. As miners could not do anything without water, Clark and myself concluded to wind up and sell out our large store and its contents. We both intended to form a new partnership for life before we returned again, so we sold out very well considering the prospects.[35]

Mr. Clark was appointed Deputy Sheriff under Major Burney. I built a small tent, say ten by twenty feet and sold liquor and clothing, which enabled me to collect old bills from different miners, as I am sure we had over $20,000 on the books. So I was on hand to receive anything I could get, and must admit I am a very poor hand to collect money, always was, and so continue to be at this late day. It was very hard to get money from men who gambled and drank, as they hadn't any worldly effects which could be attached; only a pair of blankets, a frying pan, pick and shovel, with a wash pan, constituted their outfit. But if you happened to meet them when they had dust you would be paid without a murmur.

Mr. Clark as [Deputy] Sheriff, was busy collecting foreign poll tax which amounted to $8 a month. It was a very unpleasant but perhaps profitable job as he got a certain per cent. Even that did not make it pleasant. Often he would take their boots when they refused to pay, bring them to my store and after a few days offer them for sale, very likely to the very person to whom they formerly belonged, selling them for less than the tax of $8. My memory fails me here as there wasn't anything that happened which made a lasting impression on my mind so I will pass it by. Every now and then reports would come in that on such a creek they had struck it rich making from two to four ounces per day. Then there would be a stampede for the new diggings and often those who left were the very men who owed you.

In 1851 Vallejo was the Government seat. State officers resided there and those who held Mariposa Indian War Scrip were very anxious to have [it] bonded. So Major Burney, myself and ten others came to Vallejo and remained six weeks during April and part of June, getting things in shape to present to the Legislature to act upon, so the general Government would assume the debt. The bonds also would be of some commercial value. While staying in Vallejo, a party of us hired two sailors with a White Hall boat to take us to Napa and back. This was in April 1851 and I think there were but three houses. We stopped at what is now called the American Hotel. The other house was not far from where the Napa Hotel now stands for I remember some of our party proposed to buy land, leave the mines and settle down. So we passed over Coombs Creek[36] at about where the stone bridge now stands and I remember of passing a house to the right. On returning to our hotel we were told there wasn't any title to the land, so we gave it up.

Major Burney bought two kittens and two half grown chickens from the land lady for 2 ounces or $32. You may think he was crazy, but not so, as he made quite a nice thing off them. When he arrived in Agua Fria they were a curiosity and each young one, kittens and chickens, were sold for $16 apiece. He had given me two chickens and when I left Agua Fria I sold my first litter for $16; for to hear a chicken [rooster] crow was talked of all over.[37]

When we returned to Agua Fria, Major Burney and I were selected to attend a whig party which was to be held in Sacramento. So we started in a stage to Stockton, then in the same way to Sacramento. I can remember of passing the Cosumnes River where there was a field of fine barley, which to us was something new. How we got back from Sacramento I now forget, possibly by way of San Francisco and Stockton. About this time the State Government was on "Wheels" as we used to say, hauling the archives from San Jose to Vallejo, from there to Benicia, and then to Sacramento.[38] I think it came perhaps from Sacramento to Vallejo, for I can remember of being in Sacramento eight weeks in 1851 and '52, with many other Scrip holders, lobbying the strongest kind with the different members, to try and get our War Scrip in proper shape.

In '52 the river overflowed its banks on J and K streets, the water being from four to five feet deep, and the only dry ground was where what is now the plaza, then used as a horse market. We boarded at the Queen City Hotel, one block from the State House, now the Court House, and had to pay fifty cents to be ferried to the State House. As there was a saloon opposite, the different members had to be taken across the street very often, and had to pay twenty-five cents for each man. You must remember that lobbying was then very expensive, for to go to a theatre, one had to go by water and return the same way. I now forget how long the water remained but t'was for several weeks. Near the steam boat landing, El Dorado saloon and Orleans Hotel, was the only dry ground to be seen.

On returning to Agua Fria, Clark and I commenced setting up in the spring of '52, and we proposed to leave in April for Panama. Therefore I had another [sale] to make, of tent and the remainder of the goods which were unsold, such as clothing, canned goods, tobacco and cigars. I think we left Agua Fria for San Francisco in April '52, where we learned that the Panama steamer had just left the day before our arrival. So we returned to Vallejo and stayed with Major Burney as he had removed from the mines and had invested in Real Estate. Here we remained for three weeks, when the Major, Mr. Clark and some others from Agua Fria went to look at land across the bay, belonging to the heirs of Doctor [Archibald] Tenant and originally part of the Martinez estate; the land which now belongs to John Toomey.[39] Major Burney went to Martinez and examined the Records, found them all right, but that it was owned by ten or twelve minor heirs, and he knew it would take a long time before any distribution could be made. I remember in going around Vallejo that the clover and wild oats were very tall, and very fine pasture was to be had. The Major was authorized to contract for the place during our absence, but failed to make any headway, for reasons above stated. He went to Oregon and bought cattle, which he brought to Vallejo. We had left with the Major some $30,000 in Scrip to be bonded during our absence. You must think we had great confidence in him. So we had, and on our return found him straight. You must also bear in mind there were not any banks, or any safe place to deposit it, and every man was his own banker. Adams & Co's express was the only safe place, and their quarters was nothing but a tent.

Vallejo had been elected the Government seat of the State. Then property was of some value for they were building a State House and hotels to accommodate the legislators. When they would assemble in the fall of '52 at Vallejo, it would make things lively. An Englishman and a Yankee were building what was then called the Union Hotel, the roofs and walls were of corrugated iron, said to have cost $5,000. This came in sections already to be built and Captain Myriat [Frank Marryat], son of the great novelist, brought a ship load of iron houses from England to San Francisco, several of which were built in Vallejo. After returning from Scotland I bought the Union Hotel for $1300, including furniture and bar fixtures. The Legislators had met in Vallejo where they remained a few weeks, then moved to Benicia, stayed a short time, then on to Sacramento where they now meet. I find I am getting ahead of my story, so will go back to Vallejo and start for San Francisco, from where the next steamer for Panama would start in a few days.

NOTES TO CHAPTER VI

1. Seneca Brownfield eventually moved to nearby Hornitos and became an active member in that small community. Records show that he served as Inspector of Elections for a number of years and was also named Judge of the Hornitos Precinct in 1858 (Mariposa County *Supervisors' Minutes Book A*:68, 75, 210). It appears that he owned a local store; in 1858 the Board of Equalization assessed him $1000 for merchandise and improvements (ibid). He was listed as a saloon-keeper in the 1870 California census. We also learn that he had married a *señorita* from Mexico. Brownfield was born in Illinois in 1828. Less is known of William Garrity (also Garratty), but according to the 1850 California Census, he was born in Kentucky in 1822. Agua Fria was still his home in 1851 when he agreed to buy the Brownlee and Clark store. John W. Clark was 21 years old when

he arrived in California (*Census* 1850) and was born in Montpelier, Vermont (DAR 1936:IV:75). In 1859, he was listed as owning Mariposa County property with an assessed value of $2000 (Mariposa County *Supervisors' Minutes Book A*:241). It has been difficult to trace his later movements, but a chance reference in the *Napa County Reporter* (May 29, 1869) suggests that a J. W. Clark was a justice of the peace and land agent near St. Helena in Napa County. The *Napa Register* (August 25, 1866) included the name of John Warren Clark in a list of registered voters from St. Helena. Ransom Drew was 20 years old (California *Census* 1850) and the son of Governor Thomas S. Drew of Arkansas. Jesup McHenry was the youngest brother of John McHenry. He returned to Arkansas in 1851 to marry Sarah A. Douglass, daughter of Thomas G. Douglass (Ross 1955:7).

2. Often referred to as greasewood (*Adenostoma fasciculatum*), this shrub is prominent in the Sierra Nevada foothills. It was a popular medicinal herb among both the Spanish Californios and Indians, who called it *Yerba del Pasmo*, convulsion herb.

3. The would-be prospector held great expectations of recovering at least one ounce of gold per day (about $16 in 1849), and with luck, two. The majority barely made expenses, but they doggedly pursued the golden dream in spite of the fact that talents could be utilized in well-paying jobs elsewhere (The going rate for laborers was $8 – $12 per day, according to Alden M. Woodruff (1849: November 18). The Little Rock men were no exception: Henry Crease, Linus Armstrong, James Murphy, Bun Low, A. Cellars, Ransom Drew, William Pennington, George Henry, a man known as Lavenberg, and Woodruff himself, established the Arkansas Damming Company and worked diligently for many months near Indian Bar on the Tuolumne River. They planned to construct a race to divert the river so they could extract the gold with greater ease (*Arkansas State Gazette & Democrat*, March 22, April 19, May 17, 1850). James McVicar also went to the Tuolumne, and Woodruff (1850: August 6) reported that McVicar had "put up a large trading establishment, eating house, bakery and *rummery*, and [was] doing a very fair business, *on a credit*. If the Damming Co.'s fail, he will be a *broken merchant*" (ibid October 11, 1850). A month later, all hopes were shattered as heavy rains and rising water washed away the almost completed dam. Thibault (1850: September 30) wrote the denouement: "hundreds of men are completely ruined, deeply in debt and out of funds." He sailed out of San Francisco on the *Powhattan* nine days after the flooding disaster (1851: January 31). Presumably, a number of other members of the Arkansas Damming Company had also

had enough of the mines by this time and, like Thibault, returned home in 1850, their dreams shattered.
4. Brownlee found other ways to supplement his income. On December 1, 1849, he told his brother that he was "getting $1 per day for the loan of my jack-plane. This is the usual price for a day's hire of almost any sort of tool. I was offered an ounce of gold for my chopping axe, but I concluded it was best to hire it out for a dollar per day." At the same time, he made some observations on the Agua Fria placers: "The Mexican gold-seekers had preceeded us at these diggings, and therefore we are hunting for their leavings. The gold is found in ravines leading to this stream, the *Aqua Fra*, which is about the size of that well known rivulet in your city, known as the 'Town Branch'. The gold appears to have accumulated here during the lapse of ages, by being washed down from the hills, and lodged in the crevices of the slate rock, and amongst the gravel at the bottom of the creeks." A placer claim along Agua Fria Creek ran for 50 feet and to high water mark on each side (Coffey 1972:16). Placer mining required washing the stream and river gravel in order to isolate the heavier gold particles and Forty Niners devised a wide range of devices to help them do this: the rocker; the long tom and the sluice box; waterwheels, or flumes (panning was universal but used primarily as a prospecting tool). Along streams and rivers miners shoveled and sifted through literally tons of rock and gravel. For deep rivers, some equipped barges and boats in order to dredge gold-bearing gravel from riverbeds. More often, men attempted to dam and divert rivers so as to expose the riverbed. Not even the passage of almost a century and a half has camouflaged the millions of tons of rock tailings still piled high against riverbanks. Hydraulic mining, a radical and ultimately devastating approach, involved aiming powerful jets of water against entire hillsides and then diverting loosened material through sluice boxes. The effect of this operation ultimately turned large areas into desert. In contrast to placer mining, quartz or lode mining did not require the use of water since gold was lodged in underground veins of quartz. Mining these deposits, therefore, required sinking shafts, tunnelling, and blasting in order to get at the gold-bearing quartz. The ore was processed in a stamp mill and gold was separated out using a breaking, grinding process. Like some of the placer mining methods, quartz mining required a great deal of equipment and labor in addition to a heavy outlay of capital.
5. Alex Godey first discovered gold on Agua Fria Creek in the summer of '49, on John Charles Fremont's 44,386-acre grant, Las Mariposas. The mining camp of Agua Fria was subsequently established in the area and

soon became one of the main centers of activity in the southern mining region. When Robert Brownlee and his friends arrived on November 15, 1849 (Brownlee 1849: December 1), they were among the first overlanders to reach the camp. One year after their arrival, the settlement had taken on the appearance of a busy town and was comprised of "but one street of flimsy wooden buildings, laid out roughly in a line alongside Agua Fria Creek, while the hillsides in the vicinity were dotted with tents and shacks of gold miners" (Derbec 1964:223). In December 1850, young Robert Eccleston (Volume 4:n.p.) remembered that "amusements to be had are the Monte and Faro Banks, a billiard Table and Bowling Alley interspersed now & then with a foot and Jackass race & a Knock down." He added that there was "a hotel near the Court House where for money persons are well fed for the Mines, Board $3 pr. day." The combined court house and jail, of course, comprised Sheriff James Burney's log cabin (Chamberlin 1936:35), and the "hotel" could very well have been Brownlee and Clark's log boarding, gambling, eating place, and store. An 1850 sketch of Agua Fria (see illustrations) shows three log cabins. Wood (1954:32) speculates that one may have belonged to Burney. Because Brownlee supplied the jail and courthouse (Brownlee Clark & Company 1851a), it is just as possible to speculate that Brownlee and Clark built and occupied another. They also appear to match Brownlee's description. It is certain that Brownlee and Clark established the first store in Agua Fria early in 1850. There were, however, a number of other stores in town by 1851. Eccleston (Volume 4:n.p) says twelve although this may be an exaggeration. Agua Fria became the seat of Mariposa County on February 18, 1850, and remained so until 1854, when county business was removed to a new court house in the town of Mariposa. In spite of this, and unlike many mining camps that sprang up one day and disappeared the next, Agua Fria continued to grow and was a center for quartz mining until 1866. In mid-June of that year, all but one of its seventy-five buildings were totally destroyed by fire (*Mariposa Gazette*, June 23, 1866), after which the town never recovered. Today its building foundations lie concealed in gently waving grasses that cover oak-studded hillsides. Historic marker #518 is the sole evidence of a once lively and thriving town.

6. Numerous emigrants agreed that their health had never been better since arrival in California. For example, young Alden M. Woodruff from Arkansas had probably been used to the service of slaves, but nevertheless seemed to adapt well to the miner's hard life. Three weeks after his arrival in California, he wrote to his father (1849: November 18) and said he was in the very best of health, adding: "I believe I am more fleshy than

I ever was in my life. I think hard work agrees with me amazingly. . . . I have just dined on venison steak, pork and biscuit, and dessert of apple pie, which I made myself." Woodruff was the son of William E. Woodruff, founder and editor of the *Arkansas Gazette*. He became the newspaper's editor after returning from California in 1851 (*Arkansas State Gazette & Democrat*, October 10, 1851).

7. Brownlee probably used the name to identify his location; Hornitos (little ovens) was settled in 1852 (Gudde 1969:145). It eventually became a boisterous Mexican camp located on Burns Creek, some twelve miles west of Agua Fria. The *Mariposa Democrat* (June 18, 1857) stated that the name came from the outdoor, adobe, dome-shaped ovens (*hornos*) in which the Mexicans baked their bread. On the other hand, Gudde (ibid) suggests the name derived from the town Los Hornitos in the Mexican state of Durango. Other writers, Miller (1978:87) and Hoover (1962:110–111), promote the popular legend that the town was named after the tombs on the nearby hillside graveyard, which they say resembled a Mexican oven.

   Typically, Sonorans interred their dead and built rectangular-shaped vaults (*tumba, sepulchro*) above the graves. These were usually of stone and were covered with a rock slab or stones. The crumbling crypts at Hornitos are of this type and bear no resemblance to the Mexican oven. Legend also says that the famed Mexican bandit, Joaquin Murieta, often hid in the underground passage of the town's dance hall whenever the sheriff was on his trail.

8. There were several roads to the Southern Mines from Stockton, but according to Hoover (1962:152) most took the French Camp road in the rainy season because it had a sandy loam base instead of adobe. This did not seem to make too much difference to travelers during the unusually heavy rains of '49, however, when all roads became quagmire (*Memorial and Biographical History of the Counties of Fresno, Tulare, and Kern*, 1891:42). After leaving French Camp, travelers would continue in a southeast direction toward Heath & Emory's Ferry on the Stanislaus River (Hoover 1962:152, 156). The map on page 90 indicates this route as clearly as possible. Additionally, it locates the various places that Brownlee mentions during his residence in California.

9. Point of Timbers is not identified in any of the major source material on California place names and gold camps (Gudde 1969, Hoover 1962, Miller 1978) and may have been only a locally known landmark in 1849. If Brownlee is correct in his distances, it would have been about thirteen miles southeast of Stockton on the French Camp Road.

10. Three ferries were in operation on the Stanislaus River by the winter of

1849: Knight's; Keeler's (Hoover 1962:152, 156, 179); and Taylor's (Collins 1949:76). Brownlee could have used any of the three, but if he had remained on the French Camp Road, he probably crossed on Taylor's Ferry in the vicinity of modern Riverbank. According to Collins (ibid), Taylor's Ferry was taken over in 1850 by two partners, and from that time was known as Heath & Emory's Ferry.

11. After crossing the Stanislaus, the men would continue in a southeasterly direction toward today's Waterford. There is a Dry Creek in the area, not far from the Tuolumne River.

12. During this time, a number of tent taverns sprang up at intervals on various roads leading from Stockton, where travelers could find a bed or a hot meal. Fairy Tent was not listed in either Gudde (1975) or Hoover (1962), however, it must have been on the French Camp Road at some point north of the Tuolumne River. When Brownlee wrote to his brother Thomas on January 27, 1850, he suggested that a person could make a great deal of money by establishing boarding houses and taverns along these roads. He added that "any person who could have vegetables on his table could have just as many boarders as he could accommodate, as the scurvy is very bad in the mines above. The only places of accommodation now to be had are tents scattered here and there along the roads. For one meal they charge two dollars."

13. Five ferrys eventually served settlers and miners crossing the Tuolumne River (Hoover 1962:179–180). By a process of elimination, however, the ferry that was probably in place by late '49 was the one kept by Calvin Salter and I. D. Morley, nine miles east of today's Waterford.

14. The road from the Merced River climbs gradually, circulating around low, undulating Sierra Nevada foothills, often following streambeds. No traces of the old trail remain, but it followed in part along today's Bear Valley Road.

15. The California Constitution prohibited slavery, and a number of owners freed their slaves upon arrival in the state. Perkins is an example of one who achieved freedom and "struck it rich" several years later. The probabilities are high that he was one-half of the team of "two colored men named Perkins and Oscar [who] made a rich strike in a small ravine a short distance from Mariposa . . . [and] struck a lead or vein of decomposed slate, out of which they took in two days the sum of $1300" (Lapp 1977:55). It is also possible that this was one 'Beltis' or 'Bettis' Perkins who is listed as owning $500 in real estate and $300 in personal property in the 1870 California Census for Mariposa County. Perkins was born in Missouri in 1813; his wife Catherine was born in Arkansas in 1838. The census further stated that there were seven children in the Perkins family

ranging from two to fifteen, all of whom were born in California, and reported the 15-year-old could read but not write. Thomas Thorn was one example of a slaveowner who brought his Negroes to California to work in the mines for him. He was still in Los Angeles in February 1850 when two of his slaves made a dash for freedom. Some "unknown parties" (Thompson & West 1880:90) shot at one and beat the other. The two men were eventually able to run away, but at the same time, the police officer who wrote the complaint against the perpetrators of the crime was also forced to leave town. A letter was published in the *Pennsylvania Freeman* on June 27, 1850, which suggests there was good reason for the men's actions:

> Several emigrants have slaves there now [Los Angeles], and flog them as they did in the states. A man called Col. Thorn administered to two colored men, whom he called slaves, three hundred lashes each one night. On the same night another colored man was decoyed into the hands of a mob. Believing they intended to flog him, he ran. Six pistol shots were fired after him, three of which hit him, though without doing him much injury. He escaped by leaping a wall some ten feet high. In all these cases, the name of the offenders and witnesses were reported to the Alcalde by the Chief of Police, but no warrant was ever issued for their arrest.

Thorn freed his remaining slaves a number of years later (Chamberlin 1936:143, Corcoran, Lapp 1977:285).

Feelings ran high in 1849 because of a technicality in the law which protected travelers with slaves (Lapp 1977:285). As a result, slave owners took an unknown number of Negroes back into bondage when they returned home; others returned willingly because of wives and families. Some Negroes made a successful run for freedom. Others were apprehended and taken to trial—their hope for freedom depending on the judge's point of view. There are also a number of records where slaves eventually purchased their own freedom with mined gold dust. Having done this, they then spent years working to buy freedom for wives and children back home.

Charles Davis was a miner from Massachusetts, who briefly discussed the situation in Quartzburg in letters to friends and family:

> I allow that slavery is a great evil, but I think it a greater, for one million, two hundred and sixty thousand professed Christians to split up and denounce each other in a question that (in all probability) will never be decided in the present generation's day.—At Quartzburg we have one sermon every two weeks,—Brother Gridley of the Church South—Brother Bateman of the Church North. Southern men know they are denounced by Northern Preachers at home, therefore they don't care to hear them preach" (January 6, 1853).

In addition, he said that

> ... everybody here knows I am a friend to the slave—but for all this—his master is a friend to me. I can say, and do just as I wish with the slaves around

me, and their masters have no suspicions of my injuring them, and every black man that knows me, manifests the greatest respect toward me, wherever he meets me. A certain gentleman [Thorn] now holding some ten or twelve slaves not very far from my residence, will sit down with me, and tell of the ignorance and inconsistance of the Abolitionists and represent them as being contemptible (June 16, 1853).

16. Wood's Diggings (Creek, Crossing) is a few miles north of Chinese Camp on a tributary of the Tuolumne River. Gold was first discovered there in 1848 (Hoover 1962:19, Gudde 1975:375) and the surface mines in the area continued to produce very well for a number of years. James Savage ran a trading post at this location until 1849 (Wood 1954:41), where he employed a number of neighboring Indians to mine for him.

17. This is one of the rare references to Larione's and the first that refers to Larione's "Camp." Brownlee described the place as being on the San Joaquin "where the river comes out of the mountain." This would have been near Fort Miller, which was established in May 1851 on the site of old Camp Barbour (Hoover 1962:95, Crampton 1941:149), and built in 1850 to protect miners in the region. Fort Miller was high on the San Joaquin, one mile above Rootville, later Millerton (Vandor 1919:I:85, Edgar 1893: III:25–26), and Vandor said it was situated "at the highest practical point on the river. . . . Above it and Fine Gold Creek, the stream is impassable, rushing out of a mountainous precipitous gorge." This would appear to agree with Brownlee's version above. Larione also established a corral, and according to W. T. Ramble (Elliott 1882:178): "the corral known as and called Lariones was built in '49, [and] was situated on the south side of the San Joaquin River and about one mile north of the place now known as Old Fort Washington. It was built by Larione and his Mexican vaqueros for capturing wild mustang horses and was admirably located for the purpose being directly under the steepest bluff, and was very large and strong." Fort Washington, built by W. B. Cassidy (Cassity, Cassady), was on the San Joaquin River below Rootville. There has been much conjecture about the site of Fort Washington in order to locate the corral and a ferry that Larione also operated. C. Gregory Crampton cites the San Francisco *Herald* of April 19, 1852, when he places Fort Washington some nine miles below Rootville. Crampton (1975:78) suggested that the corral and ferry might both have been one mile north of Fort Washington. Robert Eccleston (Volume 5:n.p.) wrote that he camped at "Larion's old ferry" with Company C of the Mariposa Battalion on May 1, 1851. He did not give its location. Nor did James Savage, when he mentioned the corral in the general orders of the Mariposa Battalion (Elliott 1882:178). One other reference to Larione's Ferry is found in the *Court of*

Sessions Minutes (Volume I) for Mariposa County, when the Court Clerk was ordered on August 12, 1850, to issue Samuel Forkner a license to run ferries at both Larione's and Washington City. Forkner was a Mariposa County Deputy Sheriff. Brownlee was probably quite familiar with the area as he apparently made more than one visit. Robert Eccleston wrote on May 3, 1851, that "Mr. Brownlee arrived & is acting as Sutler to the Battalion." What this seems to indicate is that a mining camp known as Lariones' may have been located high on the San Joaquin before Camp Barbour and Fort Miller were built, whereas the ferry and corral operated a number of miles south of this point. The area is now inundated by the waters of Millerton Lake.

18. Brownlee wrote on January 4, 1850, that he charged $75 per hundred pounds to carry freight and had eight mules worth $150 each to do the job. He added that he and Clark were planning to substantially increase their stock in the near future.

19. Hundreds of ships landed in the Port of San Francisco in 1849, filled with hopeful prospectors and loaded to the brim with miners' supplies. No sooner had these ships docked, than even their crew members took off for the mines, leaving both ship and cargo stranded. There had been no time to organize such things as storage facilities or methods of transfer to the mines in the hectic and crazy days of '49. Clark, therefore, may have been able to make some good buys for the store, taking advantage of an anxious ship's Captain happy to get rid of goods at any price.

20. On March 4, 1851, it was ordered by the court that Brownlee Clark & Company receive a business license, and it was taxed $8 a month for "vending goods, wares and merchandise," $8 a month for retailing liquor, $6 a month for the ten-pin alley, $5 a month for the eating house, and $8 a month for the monte table (Mariposa County *Court of Sessions Minutes I*:24). Brownlee and Clark kept two ledgers that have survived (*Brownlee Clark & Company*, 1851). They recorded transactions with the individual members of the Mariposa Battalion in one volume. The second contains accounts for the general and daily business of the store and gambling house. The number of names confirm that there was a good deal of activity in the card room as Brownlee kept a running tab for each customer. McVicar was a frequent visitor and like the others, paid 25 cents for each glass of whiskey. A miner with more refined taste might risk $2.25 for a bottle of brandy. The men also smoked quantities of cigars or chewed tobacco. Brownlee's store was well stocked with mustard and molasses, no doubt used to flavor the dietary mainstay—beans, but a miner flush with money could treat himself to sardines at $2 a can, or gooseberries at

$3.50 a tin. Shoes went for $6 a pair, and the miner's "uniform," a red flannel shirt, was a popular item at $4. It also appears that some miners became concerned with appearances—one day Brownlee sold a number of "looking-glasses" at 75 cents each. Brownlee Clark & Company also supplied Sheriff Burney's jail and Court House. In addition to such things as paper and ink, they sold clothing, beef, ham, pepper sauce, bread, and other items for the prisoners. A curious entry under J. W. Clark was presumably made during the time he was serving as Deputy Sheriff:

To furnishing prisoners with food at $5 per day for 4 days	$20.00
To 8 meals for self	8.00
To 8 meals for *Uncle Sam*	8.00
To food for prisoners 4 days	20.00
To 8 meals for *Uncle Sam*	8.00
To 8 meals for self	8.00

21. It is evident that pioneer miners developed a unique spirit, and writers have commented on the honesty, generosity, kindness and camaraderie found at mining camps in their beginning years (Taylor 1857:102, Derbec 1964:99–100). There is no doubt that it took men of courage and strength to risk the rigors and hardships of a sea voyage or an overland journey, where survival often depended upon cool heads and cooperation. Too, there was a cosmopolitan air about the mining camps as men of all nationalities learned to live and work together. Etienne Derbec, describing the way he saw things at Agua Fria, said that "All the miners in a placer know each other, associate together in the evening around a roaring fire in one of these houses that they know so well how to build with the trunks of magnificent pines which abound in these mountains. Drunkenness is, so to speak, unknown, and gambling is rare. On my arrival there were only two gambling houses here and they were little frequented. As for the sanitary condition, it is comparable to the state of morals. Not a single man has yet died of illness at Agua Frio."

22. In this case, Brownlee referred to a convention of quartz miners held in Quartzburg on June 25, 1851. Colonel Thomas Thorn was elected president, and James Burney, Sheriff of Mariposa County, became chairman of a seven-man committee. These men believed that protection of quartz mining interests in the county was "essential to the peace of said county" (*Mariposa Quartz Convention*, 1851). The committee regulated the size of a claim, required that each discovery be recorded with the County Clerk within thirty days, should be clearly marked by its owner, and worked within six months. Lands adjoining the vein (necessary for its successful operation: tunnelling; ditching; etc.) were also to be considered property

of the owner. A board of seven referees was to be appointed to settle each conflict. According to Collins (1949:34), the Mariposa Convention framed one of California's first miners' codes and served as mining law in Mariposa County for many years thereafter.

23. The Isthmus of Panama had been a major thoroughfare since Spanish conquest and its popularity increased immensely with the discovery of gold in California. Transportation was by mule. Brownlee was referring to the fact that a railroad was being contemplated, construction of which would actually begin in August 1850.

24. At 11 A.M. on July 11, 1851, two taps on the San Francisco firehouse bell announced an impending hanging. Brownlee was watching when the Vigilance Committee led 31-year-old "English Jim" Stuart to the Market Street wharf, threw a rope around his neck and hung him high on a derrick. Two hours earlier, the San Francisco Vigilance Committee had found him guilty of numerous crimes—apparently this man had committed more murders and burglaries to date than any other criminal in California (Smith 1883:13). Stuart had been convicted of forgery when he was sixteen and subsequently was sent to a British penal colony in Australia. He somehow escaped to South America and made his way to California in '49 (Monoghan 1966:192). Stuart was one among a number of prisoners who had found their way to San Francisco from Great Britain's penal colonies in Australia and Tasmania, then settled in an enclave called Sydney Town. These men proceeded to perpetrate crimes throughout the country in order to support themselves. Frustrated at the lack of justice during this period, some 700 San Franciscans organized a Vigilance Committee to try, apprehend, and punish wrongdoers.

    Stuart's was one of four lynchings that summer. John Jenkins went to his death at 2 a.m., June 11, from the veranda of the old City Hotel, and Robert McKenzie and Samuel Whittaker shared the same fate on August 24 (Smith 1883:9–13). Correspondent G. W. P. from Little Rock, wrote that 15,000 people witnessed the latter execution, adding that "it was truly a day of terror" (*Arkansas State Gazette & Democrat*, October 17, 1851). It must be emphasized that hundreds of honest, hardworking, and law-abiding Australians came to California and some suffered needlessly, including false arrest by Vigilante committeemen, as a result of crimes committed by the Sydney Ducks (Monaghan 1966:191).

25. When law and order came to Agua Fria, court records indicated that Brownlee took an early interest for he frequently accepted jury duty. His first case took place in December 1850, when he and his fellow jurors found the defendant guilty of grand larceny (Mariposa County *District Court Minutes* I:5). The prisoner received six years in the penitentiary. In

August 1851, Brownlee was foreman of the jury which found the defendant not guilty of the charge (Mariposa County *Court of Sessions Minutes* I:49). The following December, Brownlee appeared as witness in a case in which the jury found the defendant guilty and levied a $1000 fine (ibid I:75). The day after this trial, the court ordered Brownlee to examine the facilities for prisoners in Agua Fria, and he reported that they were adequate (ibid I:78–79). Presumably these were located in Sheriff Burney's log cabin. Brownlee was also appointed County Auctioneer about this time, along with Benjamin F. Whittier and John Sylvester (ibid I:16). Miners very often left some of their property behind when they traveled on to new diggings, and auctioneers made money for the county by auctioning off abandoned equipment, according to Bertha Schroeder (1979).

26. Robert R. Givens described this same scene in *Letters to Family from Agua Frio Mines* (1849–1859). The accident happened on October 11, 1850, and Givens, on December 8, 1850, told how his brother, Lazer, was hurt and described a most serious wound:

> The scalp being entirely removed in a circular form of near six inches, beginning at the upper part of the forehead and projecting back. A portion of the bone was entirely bare, but that portion has already scaled off and granulations have entirely covered it supplying the place of the original muscle. His wounds with this exception are all well, and it is doing extremely well. He has concluded to stay in California a little longer, but I judge he will never be engaged in another bear hunt.

In January 1851, Givens reported that Lazer's head was nearly well, and in October, he wrote that his brother had returned home to Kentucky. Givens subsequently decided to remain in California, and on April 5, 1852, he told his family that he had purchased one-half of the Texas Ranch for $4000. This property is a few miles from Hornitos, near the junction of Hornitos and Indian Gulch roads, and is still owned by descendents. Givens apparently had success in the mines, for when he had first arrived in California in '49 and signed the Rancho Santa Ana del Chino *Record Book* (Bynum 1934:32), he had said: "R. R. Givens arrived here October 28th. *Broke.*"

27. Fremont did not, however, collect from the placers (Crampton 1941:56).
28. Miwok and Yokuts Indians had long clustered along watercourses in the Sierra Nevada foothills, subsisting on an abundance of acorns, game, and fish. Their peaceful life-style ended abruptly as thousands of miners crowded the countryside to scan every rock in search of gold, to fell trees for firewood and housing, and pollute the streams by sifting and dredging. Moreover, hundreds of farmers began coming into the San Joaquin Valley between November 1850 and January 1851. According to J. Muñoz

(1980:65), these activities further aggravated the Indians as farmers began turning the soil and fencing large tracts of tribal lands. The California natives began to retaliate by stealing horses and mules all over the county. The incident Brownlee describes was one of the last in a series which helped provoke war. The Mariposa Indian War began on December 17, 1850, when a group of Indians raided James Savage's Fresno River trading post and brutally murdered three of the men stationed there. Indians also began to attack other camps and outposts, and as raids and massacres increased, the men in the Mariposa mines came to realize that their situation was very serious. Directly after the massacre on the Fresno, Sheriff James Burney (1851:603–605) asked for a posse to pursue and punish the Indians. Seventy-four men gathered in Agua Fria on January 7, 1851, and elected Burney to lead. That day, Burney sent James Savage ahead with a small spy force, the rest of the volunteers bringing up the rear. The men left with eight day's provisions (Crampton 1975:21), presumably those that Brownlee supplied. The small army soon struck the trail of stolen mules and followed it up the mountain slopes until they found the animals in an Indian village. Seventy-two mules, according to Robert Eccleston (Volume 4:n.p.), belonged to the Hon. W. J. Howard, and had been stolen from his ranch near Burn's Creek a few miles south of Hornitos, not far from where Brownlee's mules were out to pasture. This happened on January 7, 1851. Burney recapitulated the sequence of events in a letter he later wrote to Howard (Hutchings 1888:36):

> The first night out you came into my camp and reported that the Indians had stolen all your horses and mules—a very large number—that you had followed their trail into the hill country, but deeming it imprudent to go there alone, had turned northward, hoping to strike my trail, having heard that I had gone out after Indians. I immediately, at sunset, sent ten men (yourself among the number) under Lieutenant Skeane—who was killed in the fight next day—to look out for the trail, and report, which was very promptly carried out.

There is no reason to doubt Brownlee's version, and though his and the Howard reports are similar, they may recount two separate and coincidental situations. It is also possible since Brownlee's mules were pastured at nearby Texas Ranch, that the Indians took mules belonging to both Howard and Brownlee. It is even possible that Brownlee and Howard went out together on the first search. Too, the timing is similar, the animals being stolen about the 5th or 6th of January. These notes are intended only to amplify or to put Brownlee's statements into perspective. For in-depth reading on the Mariposa and Indian War, the reader should consult the Robert Eccleston diary, the only known day-to-day record of the sequence of events. It has been expertly edited by C. Gregory Crampton. Other sources include: L. H. Bunnell (*Discovery of the Yosemite and the Indian War of 1851*); Annie R. Mitchell (*King of the Tulares*); Paul Vandor (*History of Fresno County*); Wallace W. Elliott (*History of Fresno County*); and Raymund Wood (*California's Aqua Fria*). Additionally, the *Journals of the Legislature of the State of California* (1851) contain correspondence on events leading to the conflict.

29. C. Gregory Crampton (1975:22) wrote that there were only four eyewitness accounts to this campaign in the war. Brownlee's version might add a fifth, although he does not clearly state that he accompanied the men to the Indian rancheria. At the same time, no participant (including Brownlee) described a locale for the battle that could be pinpointed with any degree of certainty, though Crampton suggests the battleground could have been in the Oakhurst region some fifty miles from Agua Fria. Brownlee was the first to describe how the men tricked the Indians by exposing their hats, only one eyewitness told about finding the mules, and T. G. Palmer (1851:30–33) told how the men found, then burned, several tons of dried horse and mule meat. Eccleston (Volume 4:n.p.) later wrote that the fight lasted three and a half hours. During that time six men were wounded and one was killed (Burney 1851:603–605, Palmer ibid). The little army returned to Agua Fria on January 13, 1851.

30. The Mariposa Battalion replaced Sheriff Burney's volunteer group and mustered in at Whittier's Hotel in Agua Fria on February 10, 1851, to form into three companies of 204 men (Bunnell 1911:33). The volunteers elected James W. Savage to command. Sheriff James Burney was appointed paymaster (Burney 1853). Robert Eccleston (Volume 5:n.p.) kept a record of the proceedings which tell that two days later, the company elected Francis W. Lauermeister Commissary and Quartermaster. This is confirmed in Elliott's *History of Fresno County*, which also contains a roster of the men who served. In the meantime, Col. Neely Johnson (1851:375), an aide-de-camp to Governor John McDougal, appointed Judge John G. Marvin to fill the same position. Eccleston wrote that the volunteers agreed to accept both men: Lauermeister as Commissary; Marvin as Quartermaster. Crampton (1975:42) wrote that Judge Marvin subsequently had to use his own credit to obtain supplies for the state. Marvin (Lyons 1852:372–374) was still trying to recover his expenses from the state a number of years after the war. The Brownlee Clark & Company, therefore, was not appointed to act as Quartermaster, but apparently received permission to act as sutler and set up a post exchange wherever the men were stationed. Eccleston (Volume 5:n.p.) confirmed this in his diary, and on May 3, 1851, wrote that "the orders were to move

to the Friesno [Fresno] where the Commissary is Camped . . . I got down to camp about 1 o'clk. Mr. Brownlee had arrived & is acting as Sutler to the Battalion." Brownlee's own records (Brownlee Clark & Company, 1851b) confirm this as Brownlee kept an account of the charges made by each battalion member, Eccleston included. The Mariposa Battalion had a number of skirmishes with Indians that summer. The Government's main objective, however, was to first try and make treaties with the various Indian groups and to settle them peacefully on reservations, and for the most part they were able to do this. The battalion was disbanded when the various groups had come down out of the mountains.

Brownlee did not mention some of the more significant achievements of the Mariposa Battalion. As it ranged through the Sierra Nevada searching for groups of recalcitrant Indians, the men discovered one of the world's greatest natural areas, the Yosemite Valley. Additionally, they explored the Fresno Big Trees area and the High Sierra between the main forks of the Merced and San Joaquin rivers (Crampton 1975:1).

31. As he said, Brownlee settled on the Fresno River with a supply of goods and kept an extensive record of the purchases made by the men of the Mariposa Battalion (Brownlee Clark & Company, 1851b). James Savage, for example, ran up a bill amounting to $579.90 between May 1 and July 5, 1851. He bought a great deal of clothing: 16 pairs of cotton pants; 6 woolen shirts; handkerchiefs; and 2 Panama hats. He also purchased a number of pipes along with tobacco, brandy, whiskey, molasses, cooking utensils, and several bottles of Castor oil. Brownlee billed him $50 for expenses of a barbecue on July 2, 1851.

Brownlee had previously delivered the Governor's letter on June 12, of that year, which ordered disbandment of the battalion (Eccleston Volume 6:n.p.). Two weeks later, on July 1, the men were mustered out and Robert Eccleston wrote about the festivities that followed: "About 4 o'clk we proceeded to partake of a Barbacue, which consisted of Roast Beef, any quantity of bread, Cheese, & Walnuts, besides drinkables. These were a half barrel of wiskey & a barrel of port wine, a sack of loaf sugar to make the Liquors palatable. The viands were discussed in a manner which spoke well of their qualities."

32. Brownlee left out one step: Indians first leeched the acorn meal in the mud basin by sprinkling water over it. Then they stone-boiled water in a basket and added the meal at this time.

33. The Northern Valley Yokuts lived in this area of the lower San Joaquin Valley. Officials gathered them into reservations after the Mariposa War, but mission interference, confinement and disease contributed to a dramatic reduction in their numbers. As a result, there is little ethnographic

information on the group, and no existing account of the type of clothing these California natives wore (Wallace 1978:464). Anthropologists have had to postulate that the major garment was the breechclout. In this case, Brownlee's observations may be useful.

34. James Savage, a native New Yorker, was thirty-four (Wood 1954:39) when he and Brownlee first met. He came to California in 1846, and during the ensuing six years became a major topic of conversation, being acclaimed by some, maligned by others. Brownlee adds to the history of this colorful figure. Soon after arrival in California, Savage joined John Charles Fremont's California Battalion in the Mexican War. After the battalion disbanded, he moved on to Sutter's Fort and helped construct the famous mill where James Marshall first discovered gold in 1848. He next moved south, and before the end of 1848 (Crampton 1975:110), was working Savage's Diggings, later Big Oak Flat, on the Tuolumne River. Savage never stayed long in one place and by 1849–1850 had opened a trading post on the South fork of the Merced River, some fifteen miles below Yosemite (Bunnell 1911:2–3). During this time, he made friends with a number of Indian groups, hiring them to mine for him and giving them goods in exchange for the gold they brought in. He also learned dialects and began marrying women from a number of the principal tribes. As a result, he exercised a great deal of influence, and for a time was chiefly responsible for preventing hostilities between the Indians and the white men. Bunnell said that Savage had five wives and most believe this figure accurate for Bunnell knew the man extremely well.

Robert Eccleston (Volume 6:n.p.) wrote that Savage had:

> 33 wives among the mountain females of California, 5 or 6 only, however, of which are now living with him. They are from the ages of 10 to 22 & are generally sprightly young squaws. They are dressed neatly, their white chemise with low neck & short sleeves, to which is appended either a red or blue skirt. They are mostly low in stature & not unhandsome. They always look clean & sew neatly. The Major has a little house built for their accommodation.

Brownlee could easily have visited Savage at his post on Mariposa Creek near its junction with the Agua Fria, where Savage moved in the spring of 1850 (Bunnell ibid), after hostile Yosemite Indians attacked his store on the Merced. He also opened a post on the Fresno River about this time, where the Mariposa War began. Since Savage had a number of trading posts, one wonders why he was purchasing supplies from Brownlee. However, this could have been after the attack on the Merced establishment when he was in the process of changing his location. No portraits of James Savage have been found, but Robert Eccleston wrote an interesting account in which he described the man as "rather small but very muscular & extremely active. His features are regular, & his hair light brown which hangs in a negligent manner over his shoulders. He, however, generally wears it tied up. His skin is dark tanned by the exposure to the sun." Savage was shot on August 16, 1852, during a scuffle and argument with Judge Walter H. Harvey. Further details about Savage's life and his influence in the Mariposa area between 1846 and 1852, can be found in books by L. H. Bunnell (1911), Annie R. Mitchell (1941), Carl Parcher Russell (1968), C. Gregory Crampton (1975), and Jeanne Muñoz (1980).

35. Brownlee and Clark sold the store and its contents to William Garrity on September 8, 1851 (Mariposa County *Records Book I*: 223), for $3800 plus debts due the firm. Under terms of the agreement the firm would revert to Brownlee if Garrity defaulted on payment which was due on November 1, 1851. Garrity was apparently unable to discharge the debt on time and Brownlee again took possession of the store and was forced to liquidate the goods himself (Mariposa County District Court *Judgments* 1850–1858). This helps clarify Brownlee's inconsistent statement.

36. Coombs Creek preserves the name of Nathan Coombs, who laid out Napa's first streets in 1848 on a large tract of land purchased from General Mariano Guadalupe Vallejo, which had been part of the Soscol Rancho (Leach 1918:61).

37. James Burney initially appears in the historic record in April of 1850 when he was elected Mariposa County's first sheriff (Chamberlin 1936:9). Agua Fria was the county seat at that time and Burney housed prisoners and held court sessions in his log cabin. This appeared to be a lucrative position, for he was not paid a salary as sheriff, but instead was paid piecemeal for his services (Schroeder 1979). In addition, he charged a daily rate to board each prisoner; fees for the arrest and transportation of the same; additional charges for clothing, blankets, etc. (records show that Brownlee Clark & Company supplied many of these items to the court). The *Court of Sessions Minutes* (Mariposa County 1850:2–8) show that Burney billed the county $2673 for a number of services between June 3 and August 12, 1850. On March 17, 1851, the California legislature appointed Sheriff Burney paymaster to both the Mariposa and Monterey Expeditions against the Indians. This was an apparently costly experience for Burney as his repeated requests for reimbursement of expenses appear over and over again in Senate and Assembly journals. He was still attempting to collect some $3000 in 1853 (Burney 1853). Brownlee's is the first-known reference to the fact that Burney spent a few years in Vallejo, and county records (Solano County *Deed Books H & I*) confirm that he owned a fair amount of real estate in the area. Presum-

ably Burney, like others, hoped to reap the benefits when Vallejo became the state capital. Though he was still on Mariposa County records as jailer until 1852 (Wood 1954:77), Burney went to Vallejo in December 1851 to manage the Grand Christmas Ball, which was given to celebrate the opening of the next session of the California legislature (Gregory 1912:87). By 1854, however, Major Burney had become a resident of Camp Washington, near modern Oakdale in Stanislaus County (Solano County *Deed Book H*:305). About this time, he took over nearby Islip's Ferry. He also served as Justice of the Peace and it was said (Brotherton, 1982:11) that Burney would issue warrants to arrest any fisherman who dammed or otherwise obstructed the Stanislaus River during the salmon run. The river changed course during the winter of 1862, and Brotherton reported that Burney relocated a quarter of a mile away (Ibid. 66). There he built a hotel and according to Elias (1924:272) gained fame as a gallant and cordial host. He moved again in the fall of 1867 and constructed a ferry and warehouse on the Stanislaus River north of Riverbank. The small settlement that grew up here became known as Burneyville. The town now lies below the level of a modern concrete bridge over the Stanislaus (Brotherton 1982:62). Burney moved to nearby Modesto in 1871, then during ensuing years ran for a number of elective posts, serving as school superintendent from 1872 through 1875, and as coroner (Branch 1881:230 and 253). California census records (1850) tell us that Burney was born in North Carolina in 1814.

38. Brownlee is correct. For the first few years of its existence, it was hard to keep track of California's fledgling government. The legislature removed from San Jose in 1851 and convened in Vallejo, the new capital, then temporarily moved to Sacramento, but spring flooding there caused early adjournment. Legislators returned to Vallejo for the 4th legislative session in January 1853, stayed for a few weeks, then went to Benicia and named that town its new permanent capital. The 5th session reconvened in Benicia in 1854, but before it was over, legislators decided to move one last time and returned to Sacramento.

39. The town of Martinez is across from Benicia on the side of the Carquinez Strait and honors the name of Ignacio Martinez, who had lived nearby on his Rancho El Pinole (Hoover 1962:235). The Toomey family was also well known in the area and were neighbors and kin of the great pathfinder and frontiersman, Joseph R. Walker (Gilbert 1983:285).

CHAPTER VII

Sentimental Journey

INTRODUCTION

    Gold mania subsided as placers ran out. Miners began to sit back and take stock and no doubt many concluded that the investment in both time and money had cost them dearly. They longed for home and began to make arrangements for the return journey by way of Nicaragua or Panama.
    Conversely, thousands saw future opportunity in California's cities or in her rich and fertile valleys. Some men returned home only long enough to wind up affairs and make arrangements for a permanent return to the state. Brownlee, McVicar, Clark, and Burney were representative of this latter group of pioneers who decided in favor of California.
    Having earned his spot in history as a Forty Niner during the gold rush migration, Brownlee had been toughened and matured by his experiences in the male-oriented, free-wheeling mining society. Almost forty, he decided it was time to settle down. The bride he had in mind was young Annie Lamont, sister of brother Thomas' wife, and he intended to ask her to marry him.
    Brownlee returned to Little Rock by way of Panama. Except for meeting a fierce-looking, sword-bearing native on the Isthmus trail, he had a fairly uneventful trip, which also included pleasant diversion in Cuba. By contrast, most diaries and letters written on the homeward trek are full of the miseries of travel: a tedious voyage, terrible food,

deplorable accommodations. Brownlee, however, had been successful in the mines and was confidently looking forward to new endeavors. Any hardships he encountered must have diminished in importance over time, since few were recorded.

Annie Lamont accepted Brownlee's proposal, and they made arrangements to marry in New York before returning to California. And, like thousands of other ex-miners who saw future potential in California, Brownlee had persuaded his brother Thomas and his wife to emigrate to California after the wedding.

First, Brownlee planned to return to Scotland to visit his family, go sightseeing, and have a holiday. By 1852 travel had improved considerably, though Brownlee must have had to plan his itinerary between Little Rock and New York with great care in order to meet connecting boats and trains. Once in England, Brownlee was surprised by the new custom of tipping.

During this time, he was perhaps thinking about his future and how he planned to make a living when he returned to California. Though he had seen much of the world, his rural background, frontier experience in Arkansas, and years spent in a mining camp precluded any thought of life in a city.

THE JOURNAL

I took passage on the steamer Columbus, and arrived [in Panama] safely after a very slow passage. I then hired a mule to carry me across the Isthmus, and owing to its not being brought up in time, I was left behind the main train. About two miles from town I passed a lot of natives, scrambling in the dust, and was told that they had had words with a returning Californian, had killed and dragged him to one side, and were now gathering up the spoils. On hearing this I hurried very fast and overtook the gold train of Adams & Co's express, composed of some forty pack mules which made it impossible to pass them, the road being just wide enough for one mule. This path in places was worn down from two to six feet according to the soil, and to pass on either side was impossible; it being a perfect thicket of matted vines and underbrush. So I had to remain behind until the train stopped, which it finally did, but I was now farther from our crowd than ever as the passengers traveled much the fastest. I was alone and pushing ahead as fast as things would permit, and was suddenly accosted by a native who carried a short spear in his hand and who demanded tobacco. He was certainly a hard looking case. I made a motion as if to draw my pistol, when much to my delight he stepped out of the path and let me pass. As I hadn't any pistol was glad he did so. I overtook two passengers, and very soon our train.

I think we left our mules at Garzonia [Gorgona] and took a White Hall boat to a point where we got on the railroad cars.[1] On arriving at Aspinwall we took a steamer to New Orleans and Little Rock, Arkansas. The steamer called at Havana, Cuba, which has a fine location for a town, being at the end of a narrow bay some ten miles from the ocean. All along you pass fortifications.[2]

We hired a buggy and drove into the country where we saw quantities of tropical fruit in every stage of advancement, from the blossom to that fully matured. We [later] entered one of the fashionable apartments, which was carried on in a grand scale. There were several fountains, small marble tables and two chairs to each, on which you seat yourselves. The weather being very warm, you are soon asked, "What do you wish brought to you?" And all you can see is very enticing, cakes, wines, fancy drinks of all kinds, and all very cold as ice seems very plentiful, being in everything you see.[3]

After the steamer had done coaling she started for New Orleans, and in going up the "Father of Waters" can be seen some interesting sights. I saw one tug towing eleven ships, each of which did its own steering, as the boats were so far apart and the river was so very crooked in places. We could also see some fine cotton fields, and sugar plantations with sugar houses having tall chimneys, all of which had the appearance of some city. New Orleans is anything but a handsome city, being ten or twelve feet below the levees, which are surrounded by cotton and sugar casks, a great deal of shipping being done there. I had to stay one day and two nights waiting for a boat to take me to Little Rock, where I arrived in June '52 and stayed until after July 4th.

On arriving home, I found brothers and sisters-in-law all well, but not doing anything as they expected me home any day, when we all intended to start for California. Brother Thomas had married Miss Mary Lamont while I was in California.[4] So I now tried to settle up my business and found it hard to sell for cash money, as money was very scarce. All things were arranged for my brothers to go with me to California when I returned from Rising Sun on the Ohio River in Kentucky, where I had gone to see Miss Annie Lamont, to make arrangements of going, or rather forming a partnership for life, as I was tired of being alone in a new country.

After presenting my case as strong as I was able, for I had prepared many fine speeches, [I] found when the time came to use them, they had fled. I think I stayed in Rising Sun some four days and enjoyed it hugely, as I had proposed in good earnest, had presented my case in the most flattering shape, and was waiting patiently for an answer. This was given, and everything arranged for all to meet at her Aunt's house in New York on my return from Scotland, and to be married. Her father and sister were present to see the knot properly tied.[5]

I left Rising Sun for Cincinnati and took the cars from there to Lake Erie, then on to New York. My brother's wife, Mrs. James Brownlee, was with me and I was escorting her home to Scotland from Little Rock, Arkansas. She was in poor health, caused mostly by homesickness, as she was discontented with her home surroundings. This "by the by" was better than she had ever been used to, plenty of everything and a Negro woman to do the house work, having a good brick house with no rent to pay. Still, homesickness had such a hold on her that she would take the sulks, wouldn't speak to any one for weeks and made all around her unhappy, giving vent to her feelings on poor old Tabby, the Negro woman, who poor creature had to bear and suffer from her unbridled passion. She wasn't any company to me on the trip home, her ways and mine being at variance. I was always polite and gave her the best of accommodations in New York, also in Liverpool, yet we were as strangers, having nothing in sympathy one with the other, as she never gave me her confidence in anything. She treated me civilly as I did her, and I landed her safely in her father's house in Scotland, where I am told she treated them in a like manner, but did not live long after reaching home.[6]

From Cincinnati I took the train to Cleveland, then the steamer on Lake Erie to Dunkirk, then to New York on the cars. Names of places which were passed I now forget, but after a while we landed in New Jersey. Here we took the ferry and went to the Astor Hotel, where I think we stayed three days, waiting for a steamer.[7] It took nine days in crossing from New York to Liverpool, while in 1836 I was six and a half weeks, and so you must admit this to be a progressive age. I got acquainted with an Irishman who proposed that we should go to the White Bear Hotel, as his wife would be company for Mrs. Brownlee, and he had stopped there before.

Living at hotels in England is as dear as in San Francisco, if not more so. Besides you have to order what your next meal is to be, which to me was very inconvenient as I had been used to sitting down and eating what was placed before me. The annoying part was when your bill had been settled and you were about to leave. The man servant would say, "please remember the waiter," and so with the servant girl who made your bed. She too wanted a reminder. I told them I had settled my bill and would not stand such nonsense. The custom was a bad one and was in vogue in Scotland also and must be degrading to a servant, causing too much humility and no spirit of independence, in a man who by his dress would be judged every inch a gentleman of the first class, after asking aid from one far more poorly dressed beside him. I condemned the system from what little I saw. With an evil minded person this might mean a good deal, when a pretty, fresh young woman, well dressed, asked to be remembered.

I saw Liverpool Basins prepared and built out of cut granite from immense blocks, and it is a wonderful undertaking. When a ship wants to unload her cargo, she floats into one of these docks at high tide, and when once in there is safe from ebb tide; and while there her cargo is received for next passage. Liverpool tide rises and falls a great many feet, so they have these basins ready for the benefit of the larger ships, as the river Mercy is not deep enough for them at low tide.

I bought tickets to Glasgow in the Express, but forget now what first class passage was worth but I think it was higher than in this country. On leaving Liverpool we traveled through a very long tunnel for when we came out of it there was no city to be seen. The cars travel fastest probably, but are not one half as comfortable being divided into small compartments, each place holding four passengers. On entering, the conductor locks you in and you haven't any accommodation what ever, not even drinking water, or water-closets which I missed very much having contracted a very bad dysentry while on the Isthmus, caused by drinking ice water, and which lasted until I returned to New York. I suffered great inconvenience for I could never get out of the car without assistance from the conductor who passed along on the outside, holding on to a rod of iron for the purpose, and passing very seldom. That is not all. The cars are about one half as long as our passenger coaches. Besides, the ties are laid along on blocks of square stone which cause a very unpleasant sensation, making it impossible by the constant jostling to even read a newspaper.

We arrived at last at Motherwell in the night and hired an Irish jaunting car. The seats are on the outside, both fore and aft, something like those in San Francisco, where you have to step up to your seat and sit with your back to the center of the car. It was a beautiful clear moonlight night when we started for Wishaw, where Mrs. Brownlee's father lived, a distance of three miles. The driver was very talkative and gave us all the news. He knew her father and my brothers, which made it all the more interesting. On coming to a toll house we made him stop, and we had something to drink, and a splendid lot of oat meal cakes and new cheese, all of which we enjoyed very much, as we hadn't had any supper. Everything was beginning to look like the days of boyhood, to hear the driver talking the broadest kind of Scotch, and we eating cheese and bread reminded me of days gone by. We arrived at Mrs. Brownlee's father's house and her sister came to the door, when she got so confused she could not realize anything. So we left them hugging and crying.

I had three miles still to travel to reach Bonkle, where I arrived at midnight. When the driver wakened my Brother "Sandy" [Alexander], he seemed to know me at first, but became so confused that he scarcely knew what he was doing for a few minutes, although he was expecting me every day as I'd written I would be home by August 12th, that being the day the game law was out. And as this was the 11th of August, I was on time to shoot the moor cock among the heather.[8] By the time I got in doors my three nieces were up and dressed but as they were little children when I left, I could not recognize any of them. That was in 1836, now it was 1852. I soon became used to their ways and knew brother Sandy right away, but when brother John called next day to see me I couldn't remember him, as he had aged very much. Sister Grace I knew on sight, as we had met on the road by chance and she did not know I had arrived. Brother Sandy was with me, going to her house. I stopped her and asked if she had any cheese for sale; she stood and looked me square in the face and said, "Let me see your hand," which I did. She remembered that while with me when I was a boy she saw me tear the skin off the back of my hand which had left a great scar, and when she saw this, she cried to brother Sandy, "Why it's brother Rob," and caught me round the neck in a very affectionate manner.

I stayed some two months in Scotland and had a very fine time although for the first two weeks I was at a loss to fully understand and enjoy their conversation. Their mode of living too, was all strange to me. As I was visiting relatives, being feasted and toasted by night, as well as day, it kept me very busy telling about California and the sights I had seen. You must know that I had a great many cousins, nephews and nieces, some of whom had grown to womanhood and manhood, many larger than myself. All had to be entertained in some way, as they were all so very kind and obliging. I traveled around with brother Sandy considerable, but not half as much as I'd like to have done, attended church regularly, was in my own eyes a model young man. And seemingly a curious one, for I told them I was engaged to be married and to whom, which seemed something new. They are accustomed to concealing the intention of getting married until the last moment, when it is then proclaimed in church, before which none are supposed to have known the fact.

It is forty years since I left Scotland, so my memory is not very fresh on many things and prevents me from being more definite about my visit in 1852. But I may say that before I had left them I had become more accustomed to their ways and expressions. My mother, father, brother William and one sister had all died while I was away, so I made my home while there with brother Sandy and William's daughter, Agnes. They were living in a very fine cottage that I helped to build when an apprentice, so I knew where to go to find shelter.[9]

Now in 1892, my sister Grace who lives in Canada, and myself are all that are left of a family of ten. Sister Janet, Mrs. Cassels, who lived in Carluke and was some four years older, had died. Sister Grace is a well preserved woman according to the difference in our ages, she being six years older, and may live some time yet. [On] April 24th I will be 80 years of age and [that] shows how merciful Providence has been to me in carrying me safely through so many different ordeals, mostly by powder, as I have bursted two shot guns, besides was blown up in the mines, and had some close shaves with water at different times, many severe attacks of sickness too, while in Arkansas. All of which should make me pause and consider to whom I should return thanks for His ever protecting care.

I have written all of this without glasses, entirely from memory, without any notes to assist my memory in recalling events which have long passed. No doubt I have forgotten in many instances that which should have interested you more, and I hope you will forgive a bad memory, but you can judge whether or not my mind is in any way affected. Your mother's memory never fails her, and was it she who was writing this, it would be more correct. In fact I think her mind is too retentive on some subjects.

I am about to leave Scotland, in order to keep my appointment with Miss A. Lamont, in New York, half to hasten across the Atlantic with my nephew John Brownlie, son of brother John, as he had started to California with me.[10] The other nephews were taken up with Australia, to which place they went and where they are still I think, but they never write to me, so I never hear from them.

I will mention some of the places visited while in Scotland ere I left there, being determined to see some of them. We went first to Edinburgh, examined the castle and room where Queen Mary gave birth to James I of Scotland. This was a small dingy room, say sixteen feet square, having ceilings about eight feet high, with one small window three feet by two, from where the infant was lowered to the street below, a distance of two or three hundred feet, to be in safety from the English and Tories among the Scotch people who wished to kill the child. The rock on which the castle is built is almost perpendicular, and in some places hangs over. The building itself is of very poor masonry of the commonest kind, being made from what is called "Rubble Work," there being nothing attractive about the place save the view, which is very fine, being so very high there is nothing to obstruct the scene.[11]

In the distance may be seen Fifeshire, Leith, Arthur Seat Mountain, where Ancient works say the Lilliputians lived, Dalkeith, and Sterlingshire. While down the West side may be seen the North Bridge spanning a deep ravine, resembling what a bridge built over our house from the East to the West, to a point above the vineyard would represent. Murray's Crescent, as this is called, cannot be excelled in masonry, being built of the best stone work in the world, and of the best quality, the workmanship being a pleasure to a stone cutter to gaze upon. The street beneath the bridge is a fish market and is one of the main thoroughfares, and from the North leads from the old to the new town, also to Murray's Park and High Street. Upon the latter of which is built Sir Walter Scott's monument, which is a complete bit of masonry. From here you can descend stone steps of great length which may be fifty or sixty in number, which brings you down to the fish market, where all the different railroads terminate. I can remember of going to this place to take the cars for Aberdeen. Where there was a tunnel towards the ferry which crosses the Firth of Forth to Burnt Island, is now the finest kind of a steel bridge. On arriving at Burnt Island I had to call on McVicar's family, as he had sent his sister a nice new gold watch by me, and she was very proud of the gift.

I did not remain long as we had to meet the train. The next town was the long town of Fife, made of a row of houses on either side of the road, all built of "Rubble Work," which hadn't any attraction for me. Next was Perth, beautifully situated on the river Dee, but the buildings were of poor masonry and fishing was the main business. We had passed the finest of farming country which I had seen either in Scotland or England, all under a high state of cultivation, being a large flat country for Scotland, known as the "Carse of Gowrie."[12] We passed Dundee to our right. The road forked here, one going over the long Tay bridge of historical fame,[13] the other direct to Aberdeen, which place we reached in good time, put up at the best hotel, where I was much amused at not only what they said but also, the manner in which it was said. I was told to call for Finn and Haddis, which I did, and can advise any traveling that way to try the same as the fish are fresh and they know how to prepare them. When I left I carried just as many as a young fish girl could tie in a large handkerchief and wherever we stopped had some cooked, and found they helped my Panama dysentry very much, Brother Sandy enjoyed them equally as much as did I.

My real business in Aberdeen was to call on Mr. [Alexander] Lamont's father [James] in old Aberdeen, about one and a half miles distant. I went to see him and found him in bed. When his daughter told him who I was, and that I had come direct from his son's, the old man raised himself up in bed, took my hand and showed he was really glad to hear from his folks. And when I told him I was going to marry one of his son's daughters he seemed very much delighted. He was then upwards of 90 years of age, a hale and hearty old man.[14]

We then walked back to Aberdeen, found good accommodation, also flirted with the Chambermaid, who spoke a mixture of Gaelic and English, and was young and beautiful. We then started for Glasgow by way of Sterling Castle, where we stayed all night and examined everything, for in those places were men sitting around ready to show and explain things of past events. They showed us where the Battle of Bannocksburn was fought, and the stone of Scone, where the Kings of Scotland were crowned. We found the guides very talkative, sometimes too much so. Sterling Castle is not to be compared to that of Edinburgh either in size or situation, as from the former can be had a fine view of the Firth of Forth, winding its way about, being as crooked as one could well imagine.

We arrived in Glasgow and called on a cousin of mine who was about my own age, with whom [as] children I well agreed. I heard the other day that she was still living, and has a family, the number of which I now forget. Am thinking of writing to her, as nearly all of my cousins have passed away leaving her and myself alone.

Bidding good-bye and shaking hands, in themselves [offer] a trying moment, and often the apron is required to dry the overflow of moisture which swells up spontaneously in the eye. And in such occasions I found it very contagious, however strongly you may try to prevent it. In such cases 'tis best to allow nature her own way, as I think it proves the climax of pure affection, also the true interest they take in your well fare even though to outsiders, it may seem weak and childish. When I left Bonkle and had bidden them all good bye, I started to Carluke to meet my nephew, John Brownlie, who joined me on my way to Liverpool where we arrived in good time and engaged passage to New York.[15]

We arrived there in ten days, landed, and on making enquiry, found Mr. Lamont, brother Thomas' wife and baby, and Miss Lamont, all at their Aunt's house, which was a small boarding place of which we soon became guests. And after a short breathing spell, Annie and I were married by her cousin Mr. Hodge.[16] A supper had been prepared at a hotel, the name of which I now forget, where about fifteen or twenty were present and everything passed off fine. Mr. J. W. Clark came from

Vermont to witness the ceremony, and to have him extend his congratulations, also to hear it from others, was entirely new to me; for I want you to understand I had as yet been but little in ladies society since I landed in America in 1836, so you must not expect any gallantry on my part, as I had never studied the many ways of when and how to shine at the right time. I had always laughed at other people when I saw them putting on airs, but have since been told how gallant I was.

We were now ready to start for California and tickets for six had to be bought. I now had a family, which called for two, also those for brother Thomas and wife and John Brownlie. Mr. Johnson who was married to my wife's cousin, and who should have known better, went to procure the tickets, for which I gave him $1200 or $1300. As I was otherwise engaged at the time, I trusted him to attend to it as brother Thomas was with him. Unfortunately they went to a runner's office, gave him the money for six tickets, with the proviso of getting the same next day, so you may guess I was very much vexed that I had not attended to it myself, for when they returned, [the] money was all gone and no tickets. Next morning Johnson and myself started for the office of the runner to get them or to have the money refunded. After parleying sometime, by giving him the commission, which runners were allowed on each ticket sold, he gave the money back. We then went to the general office and bought our tickets.[17]

We had a pleasant trip to Aspinwall but had the usual trouble of having to ride mules across the Isthmus. My wife and Mrs. B. donned bloomers,[18] rode man fashion, which is a great improvement on bad roads which are covered with vines and fallen timber, where we would often have to stoop and in this way pass under. I rode and carried Alick,[19] who was then about one year old, while Thomas and John walked. I was riding a man's saddle, the horn of which was in the way, and made it impossible for the child to sit between the horn and me, and it would have hurt him to sit on the horn, so I had to carry him in my arms, he being at an age when all children are hard to manage, would lean out from me, besides he was a very heavy child. Money could hardly get me to undertake the same trip over again.

The ladies got on much better than I and hadn't any particular adventure, while other women were continually falling off their mules, or their saddles turning, some mishap always taking place. Many men too, were unfortunate, while our party experienced no difficulty, although on each of our saddle horns were hung a variety of articles. It took us two days to cross Panama.

On arriving there found out that the steamer which was coming around the Horn was burnt at sea, thus compelling us to remain there a good many days. This placed me in a bad position as money was giving out, and things looked blue in general. Although expenses were not much, they were constantly accumulating. In a belt around my body I had some $10,000 of Mariposa County Scrip, of the value of which I could not find any one who had any knowledge, nor who would advance money on it. In San Francisco this Scrip was worth eighty cents on the dollar, and if I could reach there could deposit it, and get what money was needed.[20] To cut short, we landed in San Francisco in good time and met Colonel Thorn who gave me $300 in dust, which was enough for my present use.[21] We stayed at the Niantic Hotel.[22]

NOTES TO CHAPTER VII

1. The mule path snaked over hills and valleys through the lush, Isthmian tropical forest to Gorgona, some 24 miles out of Panama. At Gorgona, travelers could hire a native bungo or climb aboard a 15-passenger, flat-bottomed ferryboat for the trip down the Chagres River to Barbacoas (This is probably the best description for the "White Hall" or "Hull" boat that Brownlee refers to in Chapter VI). The Panama Railroad was built as far as Barbacoas that summer, and for the first time passengers could travel the last 25 miles by rail to Aspinwall (today called Colon). Robert Brownlee was a very lucky traveler that summer. Most reminiscences are filled with stories of hardship, misadventure, and tales of sickness: malaria, yellow fever, dysentry, cholera. Ulysses S. Grant crossed Panama only one month later during an extremely serious outbreak of cholera. He said that this July trip was more horrifying than any of his battles—enroute, some 150 fellow passengers died of disease (McCullough 1975:95).
2. A number of fortifications guard the entrance to Havana harbor. The most impressive, however, is the castle-like fortress of El Morro built in 1589, a prominent landmark on the eastern channel.
3. Richard Henry Dana remarked in 1859 that the Cubans "eat ambrosia and drink nectar" (1966:12–14). The islanders had been cooling them-

selves with a medley of iced drinks—*refrescos*—since ice was first introduced to the country in 1806. Brownlee may well have sampled the refreshments at Dominico's, "a huge, stone-floored, Moorish Inn . . . with a spacious bar glittering with decanters, and with marble tables around" (Abbott 1859:44–45). The menu offered a variety of tempting drinks (Hazard 1871:227–230) to please a thirsty traveler: *limonada* (lemonade); *naranjada* (orangeade); *limonada con ron* (lemonade and rum); *orchata* (almond milk and sugar); or *agraz* (juice of the unripe grape). Each was 10 cents.

4. The Reverend J. F. Green married Thomas and Mary on Friday evening, June 29, 1849 (*Arkansas Gazette*, July 5, 1849).
5. Except for the few statements Brownlee has made, and some extant photographs, little can be learned about Annie Brownlee. Some phrases from her 1849 copy book may give insight upon the thoughts of the young Victorian lady: "Youth is the most favorable season for improvement," and, "You walk in beauty, like the light of cloudless climes and starry skies, and all that's best of dark and bright meet in your aspect and in your eyes."
6. Isabelle Brownlee was 16 years old (Pulaski County *Census* 1850) when she and James, 17 years her senior, arrived in Little Rock in 1842. It is possible to sympathize with the young girl from a rural Scottish town. Naive and unsophisticated, it may have been difficult for her to adjust to a different lifestyle in a new country, far from the security of family and friends. Moreover, two years earlier, she had given birth to a daughter Eliza who died when she was just 21 days old, and is buried in Little Rock's Mount Holly Cemetery. Isabelle died on September 8, 1869, and shares a grave with her husband in Cambusnethan Parish Cemetery, Scotland.
7. New York's Astor Hotel was still on its original site at 225 Broadway when Brownlee stayed there in 1852. It moved twice during a long history but finally closed its doors in the 1970s.
8. The red grouse (*Lagopus lagopus*) is also referred to as Moor Fowl or Moor Game. Brownlee and his brothers probably hunted this bird for years, but when the breech-loading shotgun was introduced in the mid-19th century, Scotsmen eagerly turned grouse hunting into a national sport. Since then, Parliament has traditionally adjourned for summer vacation in time for the start of the grouse season on the 'Glorious Twelfth' (*Book of British Birds* 1973).
9. His father, Alexander Brownlee, died in 1843, his mother, Margaret Russell Brownlee, in 1849. William was a widower when he passed away in 1851, leaving an 18-year-old daughter, Agnes. It appears that brother Al-

exander must have gone to live with her at that time. The 1851 Cambusnethan Parish Census records that two of sister Grace's children, 16-year-old Margaret and her 5-year-old brother Robert Russell, were also members of the household. The cottage that Robert helped build before he left Scotland in 1836 has not been identified. It might very well have been the cottage between the row houses his father and grandfather built on Church Road.

10. Evidently Robert Brownlee's brother, John, used the 'ie' spelling in his surname by choice and his sons, John and James, also adopted the same spelling. James Brownlie followed his brother John to California in 1858. Both men settled in Vallejo and founded two separate Brownlie lines. John was employed as a laborer at the Mare Island Navy Yard, later purchasing a livery stable in Vallejo. He also owned a 500-acre farm, which he worked for many years. John was the town's notary public, and served a term as Supervisor for Solano County (Munro Fraser 1879:336–338).

    James, on the other hand, was immediately struck with gold fever when he arrived in California and spent his first year mining unsuccessfully in Humboldt County, soon learning "all he cared to about mining." After a series of misadventures—a shipwreck on the Klamath River—wandering lost in a snowfield—he returned to Vallejo and settled down to operate lucrative grocery businesses there and on Mare Island. He too served the town in the elective office of City Trustee for a number of years (MBH 1891:481–482).

    Both brothers recalled colorful incidents in which they were involved through no fault of their own. John had an adventure in Panama (see Note 20) and James, returning from an 1863 visit to Scotland, witnessed an attempted mutiny aboard the *Ocean King* in 1863. When the vessel was transporting 100 sailors from New York to Aspinwall to serve man-of-war vessels on the Pacific coast, the sailors attempted to capture the ship near the Cuban coast in order to hand it over to Confederate authorities. The Captain restored order after two men were killed, the ringleaders put in irons, and the rest kept under heavy guard (MBH ibid).

11. Better masons used well-finished, good stone in construction—the Bonkle houses are an excellent example. Therefore, Brownlee would naturally criticize rubble-work, where walls were constructed with roughly dressed common field stone or irregularly set small boulders (Lavicka 1977:II:24–30).

12. This fertile tract of land lies along the north bank of the River Tay in Perth and Angus counties. It is a raised beach some fifteen miles long and one to two miles wide.

13. Current residents repeat a story that the Tay Bridge was demolished by a

storm some time in the 1840s and that a trainload of people were killed.
14. James Lamont was then 85 years old and patriarch of a large family of twelve children. He died four years after Brownlee's visit and is buried in the Church and Cathedral of St. Machan, Old Aberdeen (DAR 1936: 73–76).
15. They sailed October 7, 1852, on a Cunard steamer out of Liverpool (Munro Fraser 1879:336).
16. Robert and Annie were married on October 26, 1852, at 338 Hudson Street, New York (DAR 1936:73). Hudson Street may have been an area with rooming houses. James Mason Hutchings, later publisher of *California Magazine*, became innkeeper and promoter of Yosemite Valley, and rented a room at 299 Hudson Street in 1849 for $2.50 a week (Sargent 1980:74).
17. John Brownlie (Munro Fraser 1879:336) said the family sailed on the S.S. *Northern Light*. Built by Briggs Brothers of Boston and launched in 1851, the ship soon earned the reputation of being one of the fastest clippers at sea. In March of 1852 it sailed from San Francisco to Boston in a record-setting time of 76 days (Clark 1911:152).
18. When Annie put on bloomers, the young bride donned the latest fashion rage which had become the subject of derision, jokes, and commentary in London, Paris, New York, and San Francisco. According to Tinling (1982:LXI:18–25), the outfit had become a symbol of feminists and was being worn by those with an independent nature. It was a sensible garment for riding and probably contributed to the ease with which Annie and Mary traveled across the Isthmus. Knowing Brownlee's practical nature, he might have wondered why others spent time criticizing such outfits.
19. Alexander James Brownlee was born to Thomas and Mary on October 3, 1851, in Little Rock. On arrival in Vallejo in December of 1852, he achieved distinction by being the first white child in the city. He later trained as a civil engineer and was employed at the nearby Navy Yard on Mare Island. He was appointed City Clerk in 1878 (Munro Fraser 1879:336). He died in Portland, Oregon, on February 29, 1896 (DAR 1936:IV:74).
20. All did not go well for 19-year-old John Brownlie, and his account of the Panama adventure appeared in 1879 (Munro Fraser:336–338), a story closely following the trials of others on Panama terrain. John recorded that he walked his boots into shreds, became lost at one point, and forded rivers by hanging onto the tail of a mule. To make matters worse, once they arrived in Panama, his family persuaded John to surrender his California ticket to provide subsistence money while the group waited for

a San Francisco steamer. Robert, Thomas, and their wives found accommodation aboard the *New Orleans* on November 24, 1852, which was crowded with passengers from the *City of Pittsburg*, which had burned at Valparaiso (Rasmussen 1965:IV:212). In their absence, young John went to work at the Louisiana Hotel while he waited for the mail and a promised ticket. Luck ran out again when he came down with malaria. However, John met an uncle by chance whom he had not seen for many years who took pity on the young man, and gave him his own newly-purchased ticket to California. The uncle then went back to the island of Taboga, where he had been working to earn his own passage. It is possible this might have been Robert's brother, James Brownlee, who disappeared from Little Rock records about the same time that Robert and Thomas left for California, making his way to Panama about the time Thomas and Mary went to Robert's wedding in New York. Perhaps he fell on hard times and had to go to work for the rest of his passage, or perhaps he had a change of mind after giving John Brownlie his ticket, and after working for a time, decided to return to Scotland. Taboga is a tiny island eleven miles south of Panama City, and in 1849–50 served as the Port of Panama. The Pacific Steam Navigation Company built a number of machine shops here and employed 700 skilled workmen who were almost without exception, Scotsmen (Neimeier 1968:67–90, Tomes 1855:156–194). James did return to his native land later in life, and is buried in Cambusnethan Parish Cemetery.

21. It is conjectured that Brownlee and Thorn became reacquainted during the latter's sojourn at Quartzburg. Brownlee could have journeyed there to collect part of the long-standing debt, or he might have had a chance to meet with Thorn in San Francisco.

22. The Niantic was one of San Francisco's newest and finest hotels in 1852, located on the corner of Clay and Sansome streets. It had been built over the burned ruins of the old whaler, *Niantic*, abandoned by its crew during the gold rush madness of '49. Construction workers recovered part of the ship in 1872 while raising a new Niantic building. In 1976, excavations for a modern highrise exposed the ship's hull, still undisturbed (Delgado 1979/80:LVIII:316–325).

CHAPTER VIII

Forty Years in Napa Valley

INTRODUCTION

  Speculators descended upon the town when they learned General Mariano Guadalupe Vallejo had donated land there for California's second state capital. Among this group was the noted novelist, Frank Marryat, who built a hotel for the legislators utilizing salvaged cargo from a sunken ship. Brownlee and Burney had also spent some time in the area during '51 and '52 and no doubt came away believing that they too could profit by investing in the new town. Accordingly, Brownlee entrusted Burney with money to buy property for him while he was in Europe.
  Brownlee must have been both surprised and frustrated when he learned on his return that his money was gone and there was no property. To make matters worse, the peripatetic lawmakers so disliked their accommodations that they moved to nearby Benicia. Not surprisingly most of Vallejo's residents packed up and followed, leaving the Brownlee families and a dozen others to chance life in a deserted town.
  Frontier conditions in this small community seem to come alive as Brownlee recalls numerous set-backs as the citizens tried to promote business and growth. When Burney proffered land to repay his debt, Brownlee had no choice but to accept it, and wrote that he was suddenly "converted into a California farmer without the least knowledge of how it should be done or managed."
  Like thousands of pioneer farmers who purchased land and ac-

cepted the challenge of transforming California into a productive agricultural state, Brownlee rose to the occasion as his memoirs reflect. Up to this time, there had been no large scale agriculture in California, and farmers had to learn what crops would grow in the state's varying soils and microenvironments. Most of all they had to innovate. If crops could survive disease, pests and the vagaries of the weather, California's rapidly increasing population would provide an excellent market.

The Americanization of California brought these men face to face with a more vexing and long lasting problem as Robert Brownlee discovered. A complex situation arose out of the rancho system and was exacerbated by California's lack of a federal land policy when migrant farmers claimed property that Brownlee and his neighbors had purchased. A squatter war followed which Brownlee remembered as a time of bitter court battles, riots and murder. Nonetheless, many of his fellow Californians—vigorous and optimistic entrepreneurs—overcame such reversals and set the stage for expansion and future opportunity for millions.

THE JOURNAL

We went to Benicia from [San Francisco]. It was raining and continued to do so for three days, and we couldn't get any conveyance to take us to Vallejo as roads were very soft. I was anxious to meet Major Burney, rest, and get what money I wanted for further use. After three days we reached Vallejo and found [the] Major who was keeping a hotel. So we put up there for two or three weeks.[1]

The Legislature was about to assemble, so I rented a small house and went into housekeeping on a very small scale, for as yet I had not decided what I intended to do, as [the] Major and I had not made any settlement concerning money matters. Clark and myself had left with him all of our war Scrip when we had started East, which he was to have bonded while we were away. While we were East, Major went to Oregon, bought a lot of milch cows and brought them to Vallejo by water, using our war bonds with which to pay for them. To make matters worse, in the mean time he had lost some six thousand dollars out of his pocket, for when he arrived in Vallejo it was gone. So you may judge I was at a loss to know what to do. Things looked very blue for a short time, as he had sent Clark in Vermont $10,000 of war bonds which at that time were worth eighty-five cents on the dollar. He hadn't any bonds to give me as he had invested in eighty acres of land.[2]

The land had a picket fence around it, situated about two and a half miles north of Vallejo. In those days—1852—fencing was very expensive and he had the largest part of the field sown in barley. He had also rented what was known as "Bolster," on which land he ran a fence from the cove North of Vallejo, across the tule in front of Mrs. Austin's place taking in Mr. William Carter's ranch.[3] There was perhaps sixty acres in this which had been sown with barley. Besides, he had mules and cattle. He also bought the Vallejo House and had converted the same into a hotel in order to accommodate the legislators.

Such was the state of affairs when I landed in Vallejo—our war bonds gone, with little or no prospect of ever regaining the amount which had been left with him. I felt very blue, for what could be done? No accommodation, and money I expected not forthcoming. It was enough to make me feel badly, for I want you to understand I now had more responsibility, being at the head of a family with others also dependent on me.

I must admit, the Major acted very Honorably, proposed to pay me in land, also his crop of barley, so many cows at $100 apiece, three mules and horses, with his interest in Vallejo. But by this time Vallejo property was not worth much as the Legislature had met and adjourned to Benicia,[4] which left our town very dull. Any who had houses here were moving them to Benicia,[5] so for me to be paid in Vallejo property was not very encouraging. But what could I do, other than accept his proposition and turn farmer although I knew nothing about it, and less about dairying, all of which seemed to puzzle me. As this was the only alternative left, did I expect to save anything from the wreck, I concluded to accept his terms, take the eighty acres, now known as the Brownlee ranch having J. B. Frisbie's deed,[6] also the "Bolster Ranch," which was rented land, and the crop which was on it, the crop of barley, with so many cows, three mules, and one or two saddle horses. This was in 1853. I now forget the exact price paid, as whatever the Major valued them at was allowed.

'Twas here that I was converted into a California farmer without the least knowledge of managing, or how it should be done. Not having any sort of tool or farming utensils, being guided solely by what others told me; as every man would have his own way, so on with the next, each one being of different opinion, so I was forced to adopt what plan seemed best and to go ahead. For instance, there wasn't any wagon with which to haul grain together. So I made a truck out of the top part of a pile which I had found lying on the beach, sawed four pieces some five inches wide for wheels, took four inch scantling and made axel trees, had a box to form the bed to carry grain, put in a tongue, so was now ready for harvest.[7]

I hired men to cradle the grain, hauled it loose and stacked it. After which the puzzle was, how was it now to be threshed? Some one proposed to do so with horses. So we built a corral around the stack, turned in a lot of horses and made them gallop around and around till we were satisfied the grain was all beaten out of the straw.[8] Then we would turn the horses out, take the straw and throw it over the fence. The next process was to clean the grain with a fan mill, put it in sacks, when it was ready for market. One floor full or about 30 sacks was considered as a general thing, a good days work, having four men hired at $60 per month, this being common wages. I had some four or five hundred sacks and sold the same for four cents a pound in Vallejo, all of which went toward purchasing the Union Hotel, as I gave $1200 for house and furniture. The Legislature had gone by this time, so we left our shanty which was then situated on the East end of the present St. Bernard Hotel, and moved into the Union Hotel where we stayed about two years.[9]

On July 4th, 1852, some five or six patriotic spirits met in Vallejo in front of what was then the Vallejo House, to celebrate the 4th by burning tar barrels and by making Public Orators of themselves by making many Patriotic speeches, calling forth frequent applause. It was thought grand by us, although a stranger might have felt differently.[10]

I rented the place [Union Hotel] to Job Dean for $100 a month to accommodate the work men of the Navy Yard which was then in full blast.[11] I then moved down to the corner where the bank now stands, into a house which is now our meat house, and lived there until 1857, when we moved out here to our present home—Creston.[12]

While Mr. Dean occupied the hotel in 1856, on New Year's morning there occurred the heaviest wind I have ever experienced, and I had seen some very severe wind storms. Being awake, I went up to see how the building was standing it. While passing what is now Eureka Hall, the whole roof of the hotel rolled up, as you would do a piece of paper, and it all about sixty feet square and made out of heavy corrugated iron weighing about three tons, was carried over the Vallejo House fence and fell some 150 or 200 yards from where it started and never touched a thing till it fell rolled up.

There was a vacant lot between the hotel and the Vallejo House. I tried three or four times to pass this lot but failed each time as the wind seemed to lift me right off my feet and I had to hold my coat over my mouth to prevent me from being smothered, for the wind seemed to choke me. After taking many roundings I made the trip and found everybody up and scared to death as the rattling of torn paper, canvas, and partitions of loose iron were making a wonderful noise, increased by the whistling of the wind. And they did not know what moment the whole structure might be blown down. I can remember the moon was full, not a cloud in the sky, and five or six ladies were in their night clothes, running around trying to find a place of safety, but one spot was as secure as another. Fortunately by daylight the wind moderated. I hired men on New Year's day to put on a good wooden roof which cost me just $100 and this roof now covers our barn.[13]

You may be wondering what I have been doing with the cows. I hired Mr. Vaness Sanborn to run a milch ranch and to give me one half the proceeds, and would have made money had he attended closely to it, but was too slow at collecting and so continued to be. He sold milk at fifty cents a gallon and with fifteen or twenty cows we should have made big money. Instead we were barely making expenses. But there were entirely too many "'49 Habits" remaining in me, to come down to retailing milk as I had become accustomed to measuring and retailing the spirits. The cattle had a large range from Benicia to Napa, plenty of good pasture, and they increased considerably. They could roam where they liked there not being a fence to stop them.[14]

I farmed the eighty acre track, made a vegetable garden, for the produce of which there was ready sale on Mare Island, there being a great many men at work there. At first the men boarded on Mare Island but the building of Dry Docks was nearly completed and as the Government was taking possession, they were forced to come to Vallejo for bed and board. This place was now a very busy town. During one election there was some twenty-two hundred votes polled and the amount of money spent for provisions, lumber and buildings, cigars and liquor, must have been immense. There was not the convenience to San Francisco as now, the Napa boat ran but once a day and otherwise you had to go by Benicia. When we arrived in Vallejo, all goods were gotten at the latter place, there were not any stores in Vallejo at the time.[15]

We made butter and I tried my hand at cheese making, but can assure you, made a complete failure. And what I did make was sent to Stockton for which I never received a cent for my venture. I did not understand the art and there wasn't any one around who did. I had seen it made when I was a herd boy, but never knew how the cream was saved in the cheese, for I found out when pressing, all the cream would run away, and I knew not how to prevent it. The cream would rise to the top of the whey as it does on milk, but now when too late, I know the cause—I did not scald the first whey when taken off and in order to save the cream it is necessary to scald the curd to a certain degree of heat.

When I first came to Vallejo there were about twenty houses, but after the Legislature moved about eight were left, as all had followed only to be again fooled as the above body soon left Benicia and went to Sacramento, where the seat of Government still remains. There wasn't anything worth noting from 1852 till '57 when I left Vallejo and moved to where we now live.[16]

I had traded places with John B. Frisbie for 696 acres of unimproved land valued at $2800 in 1857, for 80 acres of land near Vallejo, known as the Brownlee Ranch. It was improved having a picket fence around it with a ditch outside two and one half feet wide and two feet deep to prevent wild stock from rubbing the fence down. These eighty acres were valued at $25 an acre, which made $2000, with the privilege of paying the difference in baled hay, to be delivered at the Embarkadero, at ten dollars a ton.[17] In '57 I made hay on this place, hauled enough to make $600 less debt, and paid $200 cash and that made all straight, so far as Mr. Frisbie was concerned.[18]

Peaceable possession had to be bought as there was a Mr. Porter on the place herding sheep, who had built a house and small corral valued at $200, which I had to pay in order to keep his good will. That house was the one Mr. and Mrs. [Alexander] Lamont occupied for so long, now occupied by Joe Babtiste.[19] My memory is not as good as formerly and [I] cannot recall anything since landing in Vallejo which made any lasting impression as it would have done in younger days, and cannot think of anything interesting to relate to you. In trying to do so brings the past up to the present, when many of you are conversant with events since 1852 better perhaps than I.

I will now state the ages and names of our family: Robert A. was born in Vallejo, in the Union Hotel on October 14th, 1853; Mary Jane, in the same house August 1st, 1855; Margaret Russell, June 4th, 1857, in a house built where the Vallejo Bank now stands; A. Grace, July 10th, 1862, at Creston, our present home; George L., born February 23rd, 1864; William, November 25th, 1866—died 1868; Frederick J., August 19th, 1870. And Mrs. Brownlee and myself are not ashamed of any one of them, but are rather proud as all are of steady, industrious habits, each trying to carve out his fortune in his own way. My prayer is; may they all ever continue to be just in all their dealings as, "Honesty is the best policy" in the end. For then a person, when time comes to die, has nothing to fear on that score. I might continue to write, but whether I can make it interesting is doubtful.

When I moved here in 1857 I had to work very hard. In the spring [I] made hay enough for my own use and rode from the home to Vallejo every night. The Union Hotel had been torn down so I could put the same on a two horse wagon, and made a load a day as the team was fed on hay, and on arriving home, gave me but little time to waste in order to re-load for next day's trip.

James Newbert commenced to build us a home, which is now our kitchen. We had it all plastered throughout and when thoroughly dry in the fall we moved into our new house, which I must admit was then considered very fine, as it was something so far ahead of anything I had been accustomed to. In fact, it was the talk of the neighborhood, "Such a fine house, plastered and painted, and the weather boarding all planed and a nice brick chimney." I don't suppose there was a better house in either Napa or Solano counties at that time.[20] All I know is, we were a very happy family, composed of Old Sanborn, [a] servant girl, Kate Lawson, James and George Lamont. Our house was never empty of visitors one night in the year as the wife was as fond of company as I.[21]

Her father, Mr. [Alexander] Lamont, moved to Creston about this time. The boys worked for me and slept in their parents' house.[22] In 1858, hay enough was made to deliver at Embarkadero and to have plenty left for our own use. There was a small stack situated where the barn now stands. We were compelled to cut this stack in two with a hay knife and throw the hay to one side in order to put the sills in their proper position. Sanborn, James Lamont and myself built the barn out of lumber taken from the Union Hotel. The roof was hauled in sections from the old kitchen in Vallejo, and we had to use block and tackle to put it in place. Now, in 1893, that barn is still in full blast. It shows that the workmen must have understood their calling.

James [Lamont] was about 14 years old, George [Lamont] being too young to help at mechanical work. They cut pigeon holes in the ends of the barn, which have been used ever since by both birds and owls. Both hatch in the same place and never quarrel, and we find in cleaning the place, numbers of rat's, squirrel's and snake skins. Therefore the owls are of value and are never disturbed. Jim Lamont was here Sunday and remarked how nice the pigeon rookery looked and how well he remembered when he sawed the holes, having nothing but a saw, an auger and a pocket knife.[23]

I think in 1862 the Vallejo title to the Suscol Rancho was rejected by the Government, containing eighty six thousand acres of good land, and was hence considered nothing more than that much of public land by a certain class of people who were ever ready to jump and claim land as their own, just as though no improvements had ever been made on the eighty six thousand acres. Buildings, fences—in fact peacable homes, where all had been in quiet possession from ten to twenty years. All believed the Vallejo title perfect and felt so much at ease that they continued to improve their places, to build and fence, to buy and sell, never thinking for once that in a few months the whole thing would be rejected and the whole country overrun by squatters staking off their claims and building shanties. The ranches had passed muster by the Board of Commissioners appointed by the Government to examine and report what title General [Mariano Guadalupe] Vallejo had from the Mexican Government. They did so and found his right good which may have been several years after the title was rejected.

Taken as a whole the squatters were a desperate set of men, coming mostly from a distance, who would as soon shoot as not, and were not of the class who could be scared off or in any way intimidated. Such was the state of affairs on the Suscol Rancho and had been for several years. Many men had been killed, and the squatter element was very determined to have the land. While on the other hand, the land owners fought stubbornly for every inch of ground, and with the best organizations of land owners that could be suggested or money could devise. And we had the law on our side as we had been in peaceable possession and had the Sheriff and posse ready to meet any emergency which might arise, and were thereby somewhat comforted. I can assure you that for several months things looked blue.

On one occasion which I remember well, we were summoned, or rather, notified by our business committee from Vallejo to be sure and be on hand on a certain day, as there was going to be a pitch battle. This notice meant for every person who owned Vallejo title to come prepared, as the land owners were going to tear down and remove a squatter's shanty. The latter swore they could not do it, as they were mustered in full force and intended to protect their castle. Right here I must give some of the squatters credit for remaining quiet, making no defiance or effort to protect the shanties from ruin, and as the more lawless were not able to resist, since some of their party had backed out, they left a clear field for the land owners to remove every objectionable shanty or improvement from their lands. So what in the morning looked blue and dark, could now be settled without shedding of blood or loss of lives perhaps, all being diverted by the quiet law-abiding squatters. This gathering had a fine effect as the squatters were not so bold, but went more into Courts, which was just what we wanted, for if we could not hold our lands by law, we could never expect to by force.

The land owners had plenty of the best advice and all agreed to keep the squatters off until they could get a memorial before Congress for our relief. In the meantime we had the whole ranch surveyed by the United States Surveyors, and of course had to pay them. Then every settler bought School Scrip and located it on his own purchase. This cost us [a] dollar and a quarter an acre, which stopped the hue and cry for a short time. We had Agents in Washington presenting our case as a whole—that we had bought and improved the land, and that we must be considered innocent purchasers as the land commissioners had led us to believe. After some time, Congress passed a relief bill for the benefit of the Suscol settlers—that each purchaser should have the privilege of having his land resurveyed, and by having his land resurveyed and by paying a dollar and a quarter to the Government which would issue its patent for the property. Thus ended the long vexed question after several years of anxiety, for in every few months was a new assessment, in order to keep all things moving, as you know money has a great influence, and the more you have of it the more influential you will be. Such are the ways of man.

I never had but one squatter who tried hard to get a foothold. He came very innocent like and wanted to rent some timber land and gave me to understand that he liked the looks of the place and already had two teams on the ground. I was just ready to start for Napa after dinner. I told him, we were now friends, for him to go take those teams away, or our friendship would certainly cease. I spoke earnestly and he must have thought so too for he soon left. Our land trouble was now settled. Farmers commenced making improvements and felt once more as though they owned the land for the second time; and I really believe the second purchase cost more than the first, but the exact amount is now forgotten.[24]

In 1868, when our little boy died, Mrs. Brownlee was very nervous, caused from nursing and loss of sleep, as the child would not go to any one but his mother and she had to carry him most of the time. Poor little fellow suffered great pain most of the time, and it was distressing to look at or hear him, but death relieved him of all suffering on this earth, to go where he will await the coming of the Resurrection, where we may all meet in Eternal Bliss, never more to part. After the funeral my wife was very much out of sorts and was advised to take a trip to Yosemite Valley. My nephew John Brownlie joined us and we made the trip in some ten days in the latter part of May. On our return she proved to be much better, the horseback riding was just the exercise needed to cause her to gain strength, and she rode from Yosemite by Clark's Ranch to Mariposa, a distance of sixty miles, one half in deep snow, all in one day, and I question very much if the same distance was ever made by a lady before or since.[25]

After the land question was finally settled, I commenced to make improvements of a more permanent character, to rebuild fences and keep on planting wheat and raising hay, as shipping quantities of the latter to [the] San Francisco market paid as well as anything could, the ruling price being about ten dollars a ton delivered on Suscol wharf. All the hay was mowed by hand, which made it cost more than now when done by machinery. Still there was money [in] it at that price. We could make two loads a day from any part of the ranch, having little mustang horses which although fed only on hay, were well fitted to endure what our larger and heavier ones of today would have been unable to do.

The hay was always made before July, when the wheat harvest began and I could have it all stacked and put away ready to commence to cut wheat, which was done with a New York Combined Reaper, and all the grain was bound by hand. It took eight men to bind, one man to rake off, besides a driver of eight horses which were hitched with two on the wheel and three on the lead. This machine cut a swath five and a half feet wide, and what there was left on the ground after binding and hauling might be called real waste, but I had always from a hundred to a hundred and fifty head of hogs, which we turned loose to glean the fields as did Ruth in olden times.

We would get about one ton of grain to an acre in ordinary seasons, besides the waste already spoken of. Expenses of running a reaper for one day, with ten men, was $20, and twenty acres a day was considered fair work then which was twenty-five years ago. Now they have combined reapers and threshers, and all is done at the same time by one machine doing 100 acres a day and run by five men, one driver of twenty-eight mules, and a sack sower; the others make themselves generally useful, doing an average day's work of five hundred sacks weighing a hundred and forty pounds apiece.[26] This combined harvester cuts about twenty-eight feet at once, and when cut the grain is elevated into the cylinder and comes out into the sack which is sowed and thrown off on the ground, where teams come and haul it where wanted. The driver sits on a seat high up above the mules, which are hitched eight abreast, and in this position can keep them under good control.[27]

Twenty-five years ago wheat was worth from two to two and a half cents, and now in 1893, brings one and a fourth a hundred pounds. But there was more money made in former days than is now with all the improved machinery, for the land was new, nothing but cheat to bother you, while now we have Canada thistle, mustard and the worst of all, the hessian fly, which for the last fifteen years, in certain seasons, has taken everything. They attack the wheat when it is well sprouted, lay their eggs in the tender plants which soon begin to wilt, and then die entirely. This fly is a very small gnat, and can be seen on the ground all winter whenever the sun shines. It was several years before I found out the cause of the plant dying, but on close examination found in the first joint what were very small white specks at first, but as they matured turned copper colored; soon they burst their shells and came out full fledged hessian flies, ready at once to commence business on their own account. I have stopped sowing wheat as the crop is not certain, as one year all was taken, some three hundred acres totally destroyed by these pests, but as luck had it, I had a fine crop of hay.[28]

The fly being very bad in this locality, I rented some four sections of land in Fresno County, farmed there two years trying to raise wheat, but to my sorrow found that was no country for wheat, for without rain it wouldn't grow, and this fell but little, being only two to four inches a season. Did the rain come early while days were short and the sun not strong, one might raise wheat, with four or five inches of rain. I think it is 17 years since I farmed in Fresno, and those same sections of twenty-five hundred acres are at present in the very highest state of cultivation, containing fruit of all kinds, quantities of grapes, figs, prunes, apricots, peaches and nectarines. It is not only near Fresno City that all is so prosperous, but in the whole of Fresno County fruit of all kinds flourish, and since the irrigating ditches are so well distributed and so well equalized, anything can be raised with water. The beauty of it is when the snow melts in the spring, it is just the time when they need the water most, and had I remained one or two years longer, should have taken a hand no doubt myself, as I am ever ready to try anything new.[29]

The land in this part of Napa County is not well adapted to raising fruit especially grapes, the soil being black adoby, makes it too heavy, but is fine for grain of any sort, and makes good pasture land.[30] Another thing in its favor for a home, it has an even temperature. This winter has been a very cold one, although the thermometer was not down to freezing point but once, while in summer it seldom gets to ninety-five degrees, which will then be for only four or five days, when it will fall to an average of sixty to eighty. The summer I was in Fresno, the thermometer stood a hundred and fourteen degrees in the shade for three days. I cannot endure hot weather, which was one reason why I left Fresno when I did. I had an offer from the party who owned the ranch, to take an interest, but just then I thought the land good for nothing but for raising wheat, as fruit at that time had never been tried. All this goes to show how very short sighted I have always been in looking into the future.

For instance—when the railroad was first built into Vallejo, of course it was plain to be seen that by investing in property there, which was the terminus of the road, a fortune could be realized in the near future. I of course, with plenty of company, invested in such property thinking the railroad would soon build up a town of no mean pretentions. I paid two thousand five hundred dollars in cash for nine acres of water front land and five hundred dollars for one corner lot, on which today I could not realize one fourth of what I paid for it, besides losing the interest on the amount invested in the last twenty years. It is all a mistake to think that a railroad passing through a place will build a town, for trade passes on to the end of the road but does not benefit your desired town [site] farther than to afford traveling accommodations for yourself and neighbors. This is the case with Vallejo. As every passenger and every pound of freight passed on to San Francisco, not even deigning to say, "How do you do," or "By your leave we will continue on our way." I am thoroughly convinced that if I ever made a dollar it must be gotten by hard licks and not by speculation.[31]

I suppose every man sometimes during his life time, either in youth or matured manhood, has had his hobby, a something on which his mind was bent, and of course I was no exception. When young, say of about twenty years of age, I conceived the idea while in Scotland, during the long winter evenings, that I could make money by making curling stones, out of whin stones which are the hardest and toughest stones known. The curling stones weighed about thirty pounds and were used in playing a game on ice. It would take ten or twelve days to finish one, having to be polished very fine and smoothly, the market value being five dollars.[32]

While yet a youth at School I worked during the evening making wooden spoons and toddy ladles, used for lifting or filling glasses, and having a whistle in the end worked like plating of a rope. When I returned home in '52 I saw one I had made and question very much if I could make any better today. My father's family were all supplied with wooden spoons by me, and if disposed to be generous to any friend, I would present him with a spoon made from the thorn bush, as the grain of this wood was very close and fine.

Even today I have my hobby. I once thought I could make incubators and raise poultry, so commenced raising ducks. I had some eight hundred young ones but found out there wasn't any money in them, for when only half grown, it would take two sacks of wheat a day to feed them, which would soon have bankrupted me so I quit the ducks and tried to hatch chickens in the incubator next season. From the first batch of a hundred and sixty eggs I got some thirty young chickens and was very much elated, and thought all I required was a little more practice to be able to make success. So I borrowed another incubator as I could attend to three as well as one, as I had allowed to give them all my time and attention, as to keeping the lamps filled and turning the eggs twice a day. You must bear in mind to turn four hundred and eighty eggs, and to sprinkle them with water was no small job. I would even get up during the night and see that the heat was right, having thermometers in each one to show how the temperature was. But [I] may as well acknowledge here, that instead of making any improvement in the art, I had forgotten the way entirely by which the thirty had been hatched the first time, as I never did so well again. Still I did not give it up, but tried every way; which would take out the rotten eggs, put in fresh ones, but all to no purpose. And I found out when too late, that I was not the proper person at the helm in order to make a successful undertaking. One thing I do know—I could spoil eggs as fast as anybody. So after my failure I let the hens hatch them, and then took the young ones away and put them in a heater where I could raise them easily enough. When they were half grown a disease came among them and killed fifty in one night before the disease could be checked. So that hobby of ducks and chickens was smothered as I thought for all time, but not so, for every once in a while some female member of the family inquires "What are you going to do with the incubators that are in the cellar?" you see, never allowing me to forget my poultry experience.

My latest notion was that of turning wagon and carriage maker, in which I was more successful than in hatching fowls for I filled the wheels of three wagons, one spring cart for the school childrens' use, and one buggy, all the spokes of which I made from blue-gum timber [eucalyptus] which I had planted on the place. Some were made of laurel, the fellies or rims I bought, and taking them all in all, and considering the tools with which I had to work, they would compare favorably with those from a genuine wagon maker's shop.

Judging by the way I feel today, being almost unable to stand with rheumatism, I will have to give up my hobbies, and think of things more spiritual during the remainder of my advanced years. You may say that my writing this account of my life is nothing but another hobby, and I really believe it's nothing else myself, for I'm sure I had no idea when I commenced writing, that I would, or could be prevailed upon to write as much as I have done. My daughter Mary J. and I have been together by ourselves this winter a great deal and I have had her to read some what I had written, so she kept urging me to continue. The weather was so cold and damp that being housed caused me to benefit by her advice and keep scrawling and putting down past events as near correct as I could possibly remember them.

Past events have been so tangled in my brain that I could not get a starting place, which has been the cause of my omitting many things which may have been of interest to my family and friends. But I have had to pass them by, and hope to be forgiven for such omissions, as there is no intention of hurting the feelings of any one. I have tried to write about no one without they were directly concerned with myself, for had I branched off I could never have told my own story. And if this history of one who has battled with different sections and different states be of any interest I may consider myself well repaid.[33] My grandchildren and perhaps great-grandchildren may read this and will know where their ancestor came from and will never have occasion to be ashamed of their forefather, as he was one who never owed a dollar but if justly due, paid it immediately. I never had a law suit nor a quarrel which occasioned blows. I was always able to take my own part, and have no doubt done many things rather to be condemned rather than to be admired, and my advice to you all is to avoid as much as possible—all evil associations and bad company, as from them nothing good nor commendable can be gained. Remember the old maxim— lead us not into temptation, which is well to bear in mind at all times.

Providence has been ever kind to me, keeping me under His protecting care for eighty long years. Have suffered some from sickness, still have been blessed with plenty of the good things of this earth, and since my arrival in California, my family as well as myself, have enjoyed excellent health. I think we are as happy a family as can be found anywhere, and home seems to be a favorite resort, and this I can assure you tends to gladden the heart of both mother and father, and both hope to be able to live and enjoy many more years with them. As I have now about worn out my subject, and have fulfilled a long standing request, will lay aside the pen and leave this little book with you all to remind you of the days of '49 and of the experiences of Him who persevered through many hardships to attain an end, this history of which I hope will be of interest to one and all and a constant reminder of your father.

Rob.T Brownlee

Dated April 1893

NOTES TO CHAPTER VIII

1. The hopes and fortunes of residents in the small hamlet of Vallejo, Solano County, California, were closely tied to those of one of California's outstanding citizens and native sons, the *comandante-general* during the Mexican regime, Mariano Guadalupe Vallejo. Vallejo had been responsible for colonization of the northern part of the state, where he founded the city of Sonoma and built his home. He had openly supported the United States' annexation of California and was a friend to many incoming Americans, in spite of the fact that the Mexican government discouraged foreigners in the territory. When California sought statehood in 1849, the General was among those selected to participate in the Constitutional Convention, and was subsequently elected to California's first Senate. In February 1851, the legislators accepted Vallejo's (1851:709–712) offer of 156 acres on which to build a new capital city. Moreover, he proposed to donate some $370,000 to erect state buildings, schools, hospital, library, asylums, and a penitentiary. The proffered acreage was part of the 84,000-acre Suscol (also known as Soscol) Rancho, which the Mexican government granted him in 1843. The land encompassed acreage in both Napa and Solano counties, north of the Carquinez Straits and on San Pablo Bay. Vallejo's offer prompted a number of men to rush

to the area. Many of them were tired of the mines and looking for new opportunity and sought to get on the bandwagon and find their fortunes in California's new capital. Unfortunately, the General was not able to make good on his magnanimous offer in time, and the legislators, unhappy with meagre and unsatisfactory facilities, pulled out in 1853 to Benicia, the next new state capital. At this time, Vallejo was one of California's wealthiest men and largest landowners. As the years went on, he sustained enormous financial reverses, in part due to years of litigation as he tried to prove title to his considerable holdings. He had also spent freely when he had money to spend and had been a generous donor of land, and provided succor to those in need. However, he had difficulty collecting past-due mortgages and funds he had lent. Though his Petaluma grant had been confirmed, he could not eject squatters who had taken permanent occupation (McKittrick 1944, Emparan 1968). When the General died in 1890, he had lost all but his Sonoma home. The U.S. Park Service has restored and maintains the Vallejo house to honor the man who did so much for California under the flags of two countries.

2. Major Burney was one who expected to capitalize on the government's move to Vallejo. Though he may have lost some money (or even misspent some of Brownlee's money), Burney had invested in a considerable amount of Vallejo's real estate, some of it deeded to him by the General himself. By the time Brownlee arrived home late in 1852, Burney had begun to sell some of his holdings. In October 1852, for example, he and George H. Branham sold two prime Vallejo lots, including a house, to John B. Frisbie. The lots were located on the Southeast corner of Georgia and Sacramento streets. Burney received half of the proceeds of the $3500 selling price (Solano County *Deeds Book J*: 54–55). Frisbie lived in this location on Block 263, lots 9 and 10, for many years.

Old county histories say that there were two buildings on Georgia Street about this time: Frisbie's residence, and the small house where Robert Brownlee ran his milk ranch (Gregory 1912:93, Hunt 1926:87). The St. Bernard Hotel eventually replaced Frisbie's homesite, while Brownlee's house was moved to the east side of Sacramento Street between Georgia and Virginia (Gregory 1912:90). It served the city as Justice of the Peace courtrooms for a number of years before it was torn down or moved. Brownlee sold this same lot to William Aspenall of Vallejo in 1857, when he moved to his ranch (Solano County *Deeds Book L*: 240–241). The commercial Bank and White's stationery store were built on the vacated property (Gregory 1912:90). Burney sold his hotel, the Vallejo House, on June 24, 1853, along with four other Vallejo lots (known as the chicken ranch) to Capt. Charles J. Stewart for $800 (Solano County *Deeds*

Book G: 518). Up to this time, county histories have credited Capt. Stewart as being the hotel's first owner, and Burney's presence and real estate dealings in Vallejo had escaped notice. The records show that Burney claimed he was a resident of Solano County during this period. He had relocated in Stanislaus County when he returned to Vallejo in 1854 to sell two more lots to Charles Stewart. These were also in prime locations, situated on the east side of Sutter Street between Virginia and Georgia. He received $150 (Solano County *Deeds Book I*: 103–104), suggestive, perhaps, of a decline in real estate values after the legislature moved out of town. He also signed over the 50-acre Wallace Ranch to Robert Brownlee (the tract which had previously been deeded to Burney by M. G. Vallejo). Brownlee paid $1000 (Solano County *Deeds Book H*: 305–306) for the acreage, which eventually became known as Brownlee's Field or Brownlee's Ranch.

3. Wife of E. A. Austin, who was a local agent for a "fashionable" and new novelty of the day: celluloid door plates that imitated tortoise shell and marble (*Napa County Reporter*, March 10, 1882).

4. Before he returned to Indiana in February 1852 after his stint in the mines, a man by the name of Stanislaus Lasselle did some sightseeing in California, leaving a colorful description of Vallejo and Benicia as they appeared in 1851:

> A few days ago, I was at the new capital of the state. It is rather a handsome place, but it has not the advantages awarded to it. Instead of a large and safe harbor it has none worth speaking of. I think however, eventually it will be a large city composed of fashionable people. . . . Benicia is a city adjoining the capital, and has some hundred houses. It has a much better harbor and on the direct route to the northern or southern mines. It will always be a rival to Vallejo the capital. Benicia is the only place in California that looks like towns in the states. There are churches and school houses in it. Indeed, it is the only place fit for a family to live in in California. Vallejo the capital has but four or five buildings in it at the present time. It has only been about a month since lots were surveyed. Great preparations are making to build it up. Hank Thomas was with me when I went to the capital. We landed at Benicia off a steamer. From Benicia we walked to the capital, some five miles. On the road we were chased by a wild bull. It was lucky for us that a man on horseback saw the danger we were in. He rode between the bull and us. The bull chased him, and we ran out of sight. There was not a tree in sight for protection. The capital of the state is called after General Vallejo who donated it to the state. He owns some twenty miles square. He also owns thirty thousand head of cattle, among them four thousand bulls. We were informed afterwards by the person who rode between us and the bull, that he and others were employed by General Vallejo to protect persons traveling the road.

5. Since the legislators departed permanently in 1853, this appeared to be a final blow to many who had put down stakes and invested in the hoped-

for bright future of Vallejo. Consequently, a number of residents did, indeed, follow the legislators to Benicia and took their homes with them. Those left in Vallejo included the two Brownlee families, Justice of the Peace James Wyatt and his wife, Capt. Charles J. Stewart (who had purchased Burney's Vallejo House), C. W. and E. H. Rowe, civil engineers, Justice of the Peace Henry Hink, and several single men (Gregory: 1912:90). Hunt (1926:84) added that Mr. and Mrs. Beegor, Mr. and Mrs. Mann, and B. T. Osborne also remained in the town. Osborne has been remembered as the man who built Vallejo's first 10' x 10' structure in 1850 and opened the town's first carpenter shop.

6. John B. Frisbie arrived from New York in 1847 with a contingent of New York volunteers, who were charged with occupation duty after the Mexican war. He later married one of General Vallejo's daughters, moved to Vallejo, and subsequently became a powerful force in that city's future. Frisbie not only managed the General's vast real estate holdings, but actively promoted business in the town. He served in office as a member of the California Legislature, promoted the building of the railroad to Vallejo, and led the court fight for Brownlee and other settlers on the Soscol Ranch. He was also a farmer. Presumably it was from the 80 acres that he exchanged with Brownlee that Frisbie shipped the first cargo of grain to Europe in 1860 (Hunt 1926, Leach 1918, Gregory 1912). Frisbie was president of the Vallejo Savings and Commercial Bank and lost everything when it failed in 1878. The following year, he and his wife moved to Mexico City, where he eventually made a new fortune developing mines. He was 85 years old and still living in that city in 1905, when the *Los Angeles Times* published news of his wife's death. Frisbie himself passed away in 1909 (Emparan 1968:138–143, 270–278).

7. California's economy was based on cattle and horses during the Mexican period and each rancho was a self-sustaining unit. Beef was the dietary mainstay; hides and tallow were the major exports. By 1852, as gold fever abated, many miners looked at California's fertile hills and valleys, settled down and gradually began to transform the state's economy to one of agriculture. Like Brownlee, all of these pioneer farmers faced a unique set of problems. First, they had to cope with the state's numerous micro-environments, each with a different soil that supported some crops better than others. In contrast to the East, farmers in California had to learn to work with two seasons: wet and dry. They had to build much of their own equipment and solve irrigation problems. They also needed to work out systems for transporting their produce. As would be expected, wheat had been mostly imported during the gold rush so as farmers overcame their problems during transition, they found a ready market for their

produce. It was not long before Napa farmers turned their valley into one of the most productive wheat-growing areas in California. And as Brownlee found, the yield was large and the prices were good.

8. Brownlee adopted an age-old method, which Catholic fathers had long practiced at California missions. The mission fathers watered and pounded the surface until it was hard and dry before herding in the horses.

9. The old iron building was located on Main Street, according to Gregory (1912:90). As soon as the state capital was moved from San Jose to Vallejo on February 14, 1851, Frank Marryat, son of Frederick, the English naval commander and novelist, joined other would-be entrepreneurs to invest in and help build the new capital. The "iron" houses had been part of a cargo on a ship that sunk in San Francisco harbor during a storm. Marryat decided to recover the sunken goods and move them to Vallejo. He wrote (1952:177–178):

> Landing my cargo on Vallejo Beach at low water mark . . . I ordered the tide to complete the very dirty work I had set before it, which it did, and, to finish the story here, in the course of six months I erected a very handsome hotel out of the materials. I felt rather pleased when it was finished, and painted, and handsomely furnished, to think what a butterfly I had turned out of the very dirty grub I had found in the hold of the old hulk. But the moral of the story lied in the fact that at this juncture the government altered their minds relative to the site of the capital, and selected Benicia in preference.

The legislature's last sitting in Vallejo was on February 4, 1853, and the Brownlees moved into the hotel shortly after the lawmakers left town. They were occupying the hotel in October 1853, when their eldest son, Robert A., became the first male child to be born in Vallejo (Gregory 1912:92).

10. This was in celebration of Independence Day at Vallejo, and the small group of participants started off festivities with dinner at Capt. Stewart's Vallejo House. Gregory (1912:91) said that Annie and Mary Brownlee were the only ladies present. Other guests included Henry Hook, Edward and West Rowe, and B. F. Osborne. Lemuel Hazelton was there as well (Hunt 1926:84), and it was said that as the proud possessor of a herd of goats, he supplied the townsfolk with their "mutton chops and roasts."

11. Rounded by San Pablo Bay on the west, Carquinez Straits to the south, and the Napa River to the west, Mare Island was considered an ideal site for a U.S. Naval station on the Pacific Coast, and thus, Congress authorized construction on August 31, 1852. Once again, residents of Vallejo looked forward to a needed boost to their town's economy and growth. Commander David G. Farragut (later Admiral and Civil War hero) as-

sumed command of the station in 1854. Workers who had been living on the base were asked to seek quarters in town. Job Dean, who also may have been known as Theodore Dean (Hunt 1926:89), was manager of the Navy Yard and headed one group of mechanics who needed quarters, Brownlee's hotel providing an ideal solution. During his tour of duty on Mare Island, Farragut made considerable investment in Vallejo real estate. He built Farragut Hall, which was used as a theater for many years (Leach 1918:210), and continued to maintain interest in the city. In 1868, while stationed in Austria, Farragut signed a petition asking for the overdue paving of Georgia Street (Hunt 1926:96).

12. The Commercial Bank was eventually built on this property (see Note 2), and Brownlee's house was moved and used as justice of the peace courtrooms. Brownlee may have torn down this building later on as he had done with the Union Hotel, and used lumber from its structure for buildings on his ranch, Sunny Side Farm. Creston Station was to be a stop on the California Pacific Railway just below the section of Brownlee's property that faced on Jamieson Canyon Road.

13. Gregory (1912:92) repeats this story, adding that the roof rolled downhill to Marin Street, to rest near the residence of John Morrison. He further wrote that "it was a memorable 'blow-out' that but few people are living to tell about."

14. This was presumably a site on Georgia Street, where Gregory (1912:93) said Brownlee had his milk ranch. Brownlee purchased the property from John B. Frisbie in 1855; the lots were 10, 11, 12 in block 262 (Solano County *Deed Book H*:482–483).

15. A two-horse stage ran between Vallejo and Benicia in the early days, and one old-timer remembered that whenever an important social event appeared on the horizon, the ladies traveled the five miles for their gloves and laces (Hunt 1926:84).

16. During this time Brownlee was apparently taking an active interest in the town's growth. A small newspaper appeared in 1855 (closing only six weeks later) that reported a 250-foot wharf had been completed at the foot of Maine Street, which could accommodate the largest class of steamer. The report went on to say that "the public are certainly indebted for this valuable improvement to Capt. Charles J. Stewart, W. R. Woods, J. B. Frisbie and the Messrs. Brownlee" (Hunt 1926:92).

It appears that Brownlee was also participating in local social events. For example, the California Historical Society furnished a copy of an invitation to a *National Ball*, which was held at Vallejo's State House on October 9, 1855. The U.S. Flagship *Independence* provided music for guests who paid $5.00 to attend. Among the ball managers from Vallejo, the names of Brownlee, J. B. Frisbie, and B. T. Osborne were listed. Nathan Coombs came from Napa that night. Vallejo was there as well, one of the representatives from Sonoma. E. H. Rowe was a member of the reception committee. Perhaps the ball was organized to celebrate Vallejo's new prosperity at a time when the naval base was in full swing.

17. Brownlee explains that he settled his debt to John B. Frisbie when he exchanged "Brownlee's Field" (two miles north of the town limits) in December 1856, for 692 acres of Frisbie ranchland in Napa County (Napa County *Deeds Book D*: 70–71). This tract had been part of General Vallejo's 84,000-acre Soscol Ranch. It is interesting to note that Frisbie purchased thousands of acres from Vallejo, at 33 to 66 cents an acre, and then resold it at a high profit (Nash 1964:131). This would complicate matters of ownership considerably, when years later Brownlee and other ranchers would suffer anguish and a great deal of expense when squatters questioned the validity of the Vallejo grant and the ranchers' right to own their property.

18. This land was included in the Suscol grant and part of the acreage that Frisbie bought from his father-in-law, General Vallejo. As of 1985, Brownlee's former holdings remain intact (Napa County *Deed Book D*: 70–71, and *Deed Book 231*: 434–435) and are located about 14 miles north of Vallejo, in a pastoral setting of undulating hills in the southern part of Napa County. An ungraded country road—one used by generations of Brownlees—leads to the ranch from Jamieson Canyon Road. The photograph shows the cherry orchard and vineyard planted by Brownlee. The buildings, cherry trees, and vines are gone and some of the hills show slight flattening and reshaping, but the general vista is much the same today. Part of the eucalyptus grove that Brownlee planted is still thriving.

19. The house stood next to the Brownlee family home, Sunnyside Farm.

20. James Newbert was the contractor who built Vallejo's public schoolhouse about 1857 (Gregory 1912:97). The present owner has supplied a photograph of the Brownlees' house, Sunnyside Farm, as it appeared in 1959. It is evident that changes and additions had been made when this photograph is compared with the earlier one. The original house would become the kitchen when the Brownlees built on a large, two-story house. The best estimate for construction of the addition would be at some time prior to 1881. Palmer (1881:406) wrote that Brownlee's residence was "a magnificent two-storied building, having rooms of fine proportions." Its present owner said the house originally measured 40' by 40'. There were four rooms on the main floor with 14' redwood ceilings throughout. A large table surrounded by twelve chairs dominated the dining room.

There was a beautiful marble fireplace, possibly the one Annie Brownlee chose as backdrop for her photograph. An ornate, twelve-foot front door was originally hung in a frame of cut glass panes. Upstairs were five bedrooms, a small nursery, and a bathroom. Brownlee's real and personal property were valued at $20,650 when his will went to probate in 1897 (*Napa County Recorder*, December 3, 1897). Annie and Robert's son, George L. Brownlee, lived alone in the house until it was sold in 1945. Local residents recalled that he then moved to a Napa hotel, where he was often observed by passersby reclining on the front porch. George died in 1952, when he was 88. The old house was destroyed by fire in 1969, while its owners were out of town. (Later, they salvaged the staircase and fireplace and donated them to the Magnolia Hotel in Yountville, whose charming rooms are decorated to celebrate the Victorian era.) The building was razed after the fire, its foundations and Brownlee's stone cellar are today barely discernible under a tangle of grass, a forlorn reminder of a once lively home.

21. This is illustrated by an article appearing in the *Napa County Reporter* on September 15, 1882:

> . . . last Friday evening a sheet and pillow case party was given at the residence of Mr. Robert Brownlee, Republican candidate for Supervisor of Napa Township, under the auspices of some of the young ladies at present residents in the vicinity. The attendance was large, being chiefly from the canyon. A limited number from Vallejo, Napa and Bridgeport, were also among those favored with invitations. About 9:30 the white-robed figures which had been flitting about the house and grounds for the preceeding half hour, took possession of the granary, where they were soon tripping it merrily to the strains of music evoked by the Rice Brothers of Vallejo. This granary was handsomely decorated, festoons of evergreens covering the entire interior, while pendant from the roof were numerous Chinese lanterns which, when lighted, added doubly to the ghostly appearance of the dancers. At 1 o'clock sheets and pillow cases were laid aside, when all repaired to the dining hall where a sumptuous repast had been spread, to which ample justice was done. After supper the granary was again resorted to, and dancing being resumed was kept up till nearly daybreak, when the last of the merrymakers departed, all delighted beyond measure with the night's enjoyment.

Apparently Brownlee had thrown his hat in the ring one more time, since he completed two terms as Supervisor, District #1, Napa County, between 1872 and 1875 (Palmer 1881:140).

22. A reminder of the days in Bonkle, when families lived in close proximity, worked for each other, and helped out.
23. After graduation from Collegiate Institute in Benicia, George Lamont

formed a law partnership in Fairfield, Solano County, with a schoolmate, Joseph McKenna, who later served as an Associate Justice of the Supreme Court. George was elected District Attorney for Solano County in 1869, and again in 1892, in addition to having a distinctive law career. In the meantime, he married Hattie E. Yount in 1877. He died in 1909 (*Solano Republican*, February 12, 1909). His brother, James, also attended law school at Benicia College, and in 1878 married Sarah D. Barry of San Francisco. James passed away in 1907.

24. Brownlee's problems were experienced hundreds of times over by individuals throughout the state who fought to retain property they had purchased in good faith from owners of Mexican land grants. The rancheros, too, suffered more than enough as they sought to prove their own titles. At the time of American conquest, about 14 million acres of prime land, stretching from San Diego to Sonoma, were held by 750 families (Gates 1958:215)—acreage that the Mexican government had awarded to deserving petitioners who were both citizens and practicing Catholics. Many English speaking immigrants also obtained grants by meeting the above requirements. The American government promised to respect these grants in the Treaty of Guadalupe Hidalgo, but thousands of Americans poured into California and began to question rancheros' rights to such vast quantities of the state's most fertile acreage. Moreover, Congress had failed to provide for any survey or distribution of public lands in California during its early years of statehood. According to Gates (1958:214), "in dynamic California in 1849–1853 . . . [this] delay was responsible for some of the worst social disorder and vigilantism in American history," for with no land to claim, immigrants began to homestead on rancheros' property and threatened violence if disturbed or questioned. In the Sacramento Valley and San Francisco Bay area, for example, Gates reported that squatters took over almost every inch of land, even going so far as to build improvements right next to the rancheros' adobe homes. As trouble between squatters and landowners escalated, Congress created a Land Commission in 1851 to review and pass on all Mexican titles (Nash:1964:125). Each time the Commission rejected a title (any number were fraudulent or questionable), the land was declared public and open to the new claim. Years of litigation often followed if a former owner brought suit in efforts to regain his title.

The Land Commission had approved General Vallejo's title to the Suscol grant when Brownlee bought his land in 1857. Of course, by this time Vallejo had given much of the land away or sold it to others including his son-in-law, John B. Frisbie. Frisbie, in turn, resold acreage to people like Brownlee. Such deeds were legally recorded and witnessed, the parcels paid for, and the owners settled down to build and improve their holdings. It soon became evident that the land was fertile and productive and a number of landless people were attracted to the area. Squatters and land sharks began to attack the Vallejo title, and in 1862 the Supreme Court of the United States ruled that under Mexican law, the General could not hold two grants (Petaluma and Suscol) and declared the latter title invalid. As a result, more and more squatters began to arrive and take possession of the now "public lands."

This resulted in what Hunt (1926:81) called a "squatter war." Now armed, squatters and original purchasers confronted each other. As soon as a squatter built a shanty, citizens gathered to tear it down. This sort of retribution soon resulted in violence and murder. Leach (1918:102–105) told the story of a settler called Manuel Vera, who was suspected of shooting and wounding a squatter whom he believed had taken the life of another settler. Vera was apprehended and put under arrest in E. J. Wilson's home since Vallejo had no jail. A band of masked squatters rode into town, broke into the house and murdered the suspect. Some of the gang were pursued, arrested and taken to trial but the case was dismissed with the first verdict of not guilty.

Meanwhile, settlers continued their appeals to Congress. Squatters, too, were represented by lawyers, who called the Vallejo title "a forged and fraudulent grant, intended to disregard the interests of citizens, settlers on the public lands, who have always been the objects of the peculiar care and favor of the government." They also said that when the Supreme Court announced the Vallejo title invalid that "there was no vestige of right or title remaining in any one of the purchasers under that pretended grant. They were nothing more nor less than actual trespassers on the public lands" (Walker and Stanton 1865:6–7). So Brownlee and his neighbors were considered trespassers on their own land! They continued their legal battles through the firm of Halleck, Peachy and Billings which handled much of the legal work, and in Napa, where the acreage was small, claims were treated as a group. Fees were high at fifty cents an acre. However, as Paul Gates pointed out (1958:234), Napa land had higher value because it was well developed. Eventually, Congress ruled that the settlers who could prove purchase of their titles from Vallejo or his assignees should be given a patent for holdings after paying $1.25 an acre for survey. Squatters were still not ready to give in and once again questioned the authority of Congress to deny them the right of preemption. At length the U.S. Supreme Court ended the long contest on March 22, 1870, with a decision stating that squatters had no vested right in land paid for by others.

25. Annie and Robert Brownlee rode along an old Indian trail out of Mariposa into the Yosemite Valley (the first wagon road would not be completed until 1874). Like other visitors in the sixties, their first overnight stop was at Clark's Ranch (now known as Wawona) where, according to C. P. Russell (1968:99–100), the old pioneer, Galen Clark, homesteaded on a site occupied by the Mariposa Battalion back in 1851. Clark was noted for offering guests excellent accommodations in his long and rambling house. It was said that visitors invariably remembered him as a character who spurned civilization, but who had an abiding love and knowledge of the area in which he lived. Unfortunately, Brownlee made no comment on his stay there.

    Annie was by no means the first woman to visit the valley nor the first to ride in. She was, however, among the first to sample the early hotels. There were two hostelries in the valley by the late 1860s, and the Brownlees may have stayed at the first structure erected for Valley visitors, Lower Hotel, which was opposite Yosemite Falls (Bunnell 1911:315). Accommodations were primitive. Lower Hotel was simply a shed divided into stalls. There were no windows, and guests were able to view the stars through the roof (Russell 1968:94). Alternatively, they might have rested at Upper Hotel, where J. M. Hutchings, noted journalist and naturalist, was host. A guest described the quarters by saying that his "door is a sheet, and his partition from the adjoining chamber is also a cotton cloth . . . bed-room conversations conducted under these circumstances, it may be judged, are discreet."

26. Brownlee was apparently among those Napa farmers who continued to handle grain in sacks. Frank Leach (1918:146–147) recalled that in 1867 a Chicago man suggested a grain-elevator system would be a better way to handle Vallejo's production. Easterners had already condemned the sack system as being wasteful and useless. Therefore Frisbie, in 1869, together with the president of the railroad, and a grain king from San Francisco, organized a company to erect an elevator on the Vallejo waterfront. Upon its completion, they waited for farmers to bring their harvest for storage until the grain could be sold and transferred to ships on their way to Europe, but were soon sorely disappointed. The farmers refused to cooperate and continued to sack and store their wheat in local warehouses. For only a short period did the builders use the elevator for a warehouse and finally, in 1872, it tumbled from its foundations, crashed and sank into the mud of the estuary.

27. Frank Leach (1918:56–58) said that everyone thought this first machine for separating the grain from the chaff was a great invention in its day,

but it required an experienced driver with a watchful eye. He described how it worked:

> The motion was derived from a large gear wheel several feet in diameter into which were horizontally fastened six to eight poles. The gear wheel was mounted on a heavy frame which also carried the smaller connecting gears, communicating power to the driving shaft. From two to three horses were attached to each pole, according to the size of the horse-power, and were made to walk around in the circle permitted by the length of the poles. The big gearwheel was covered over by a floor on which the driver took his position—something like a ringmaster in a small circus. However, there was not much fun or amusement in this business, for it was the duty of the driver to keep close watch on the horses and maintain the steady motion required for the proper operation of the separator. . . . Too high speed would send some of the grain out with the chaff, or if too slow some chaff would be retained with the wheat.

According to Leach, there was a wagon that would transport the contraption anywhere it was needed.

28. When Brownlee first came to Napa Valley farmers grew wheat almost exclusively, and the region became one of the most productive wheat growing areas in the state. Realizing this potential, Frank Leach purchased acreage near Sunnyside Farm and contracted with Brownlee to sow a 300-acre field for him. Leach, however, soon suffered the same reverses of the farmer and had his own problems when the Hessian fly made its first appearance in California. He went on to say (1918:246) that the pest was so bad on a neighbor's farm that he did not even harvest that year.

29. Brownlee rented 2563 acres of land on the Banner Ranch, Fresno County in 1875 from Captain A. Y. Easterby, who had come from Surrey, England and had spent fourteen years in the merchant navy. Easterby was Captain of the *Levantine* when it sailed into San Francisco harbor in 1849, but seized an opportunity to purchase abandoned vessels and turn them into store ships. In 1855, Easterby opened a new store in Napa and remained in business until 1872, when he turned his interest to mining, real estate and farming (Menefee 1873:165–166). His agreement (Easterby 1875) with Brownlee read that Brownlee was to pay him one-quarter of all products and one-half of all hay and stubble as rent. In return, Easterby was to provide the necessary tools. An irrigation system was already in place when Brownlee went to the Fresno area. Fancher Creek, which passed through the eastern half of the ranch, was kept filled with water from the Fresno Canal, and according to the *Napa Register* (April 15, 1876), no part of California had better irrigation facilities. The soil was excellent for growing grapes, peaches, figs, apricots, oranges, and

almonds, though wheat was also grown. Brownlee's first efforts appear to have been a great success, according to an article in the *Fresno Republican*, reprinted in the *Napa Register* on May 12, 1877:

> Nearly 1,800 acres were seeded with wheat and barley last season and 7,000 sacks of wheat and 2,000 sacks of barley harvested without any irrigation whatsoever. The crop was profitable and the same parties [Robert Brownlee and his son, Robert] again seeded the place for a grain crop. Although water has been upon the place for several years, extensive irrigation has not been practiced till the present season and the result has been beyond all expectation. What promised to be an absolute failure and total loss has been changed to a year of prosperity and satisfactory harvest. A noticeable feature of this place is the handsome stock. There are 22 head of horses and mules in the small pasture, the finest and fattest to be found in the county, and they have lived the whole winter when not at work upon straw. . . . The place is under the immediate charge of Robert Brownlee, Jr. and everything about it—the crops, machinery and farming implements, the horses, the hogs (weighing 400 pounds each), the buildings and the gentleman himself—indicate the active, intelligent, and prosperous farmer. Our advice is, go and see the farm for yourself, for it will strengthen your faith in this country and irrigation, and will make you feel good natured to meet the good-natured lessee and manager, who takes a laudable pride in his labor and its results.

30. Brownlee may be correct about the soil, for at present the southern part of Napa Valley remains ranchland. He must have given some serious thought to growing grapes, however, for by 1880, the valley was renowned for its wine. Thirty-four hundred acres of vines were under cultivation that year, which produced over two million gallons of wine and sixty thousand gallons of brandy (Hussman 1912:147). Brownlee may have planted vines prior to 1881 since it is believed that his two-story house was built prior to that date, but the photograph showing his first house also shows a vineyard. He did, however, plant another vineyard in 1882. The *Napa County Recorder* (February 3, 1882) reported that "Mr. Robert Brownlee of Creston, was in Vallejo last Friday. He is planting a fifty-acre vineyard on his ranch, and came down to procure the necessary stakes. He says he never saw the crops in the Suscol hills look better at this time of the year than at present." Like some of his other ventures, this too may have been a failure. During the late nineteenth century, the root louse *phylloxera* began to attack valley vines and by 1892 had destroyed 10,000 acres (Hussmann ibid).

31. Hopes ran high in 1867 and 1868, as residents of Napa and Solano counties anticipated the railroad terminus would bring new prosperity, and it is evident that Brownlee hoped to gain as a result. On June 3, 1867, he deeded right of way to the California Pacific Railway (Napa County Deeds Book *K*:474), whose planned route went through his property.

However, the Central Pacific Railroad acquired the California Pacific and other branch lines, and moved railroad shops to Sacramento in 1871. At the same time the Navy Yard reduced its employment, and Vallejo citizens faced a sharp decline in property values.

32. Curling is a popular game in Scotland and Canada. The stones, which are more elliptical than round, are picked up by a handle on the top center and hurled along glassy smooth alleys of ice towards a tee. Two players are positioned on either side of the stone and encourage it along with well coordinated and fast sweeps of household brooms.

33. As he approached his late fifties, Brownlee became actively involved in Napa affairs. Perhaps relying on the road-building experiences in his youth, he was elected roadmaster. Napa County roads turned into quagmire during heavy rains, so in 1866 (*Napa Register*, March 10, 1866) the Board of Supervisors authorized the cost of Macadamizing the roads through the valley. Brownlee was named roadmaster the following June (*Napa Register*, June 30, 1866), a position which, according to the *Register* of February 22, 1876, required "work 10 hours a day as faithfully as a hired man works for a private person." In addition, he was responsible for disbursing road funds, collecting road poll taxes from all (and charge only commission, not per diem), and keeping daily records of all work done. Last, he was not to charge the county for white or Chinese labor more than he actually paid for. Brownlee must have discharged his duties satisfactorily for he was still roadmaster in 1870, when he supervised construction of a bridge spanning the creek near Oak Grove in the lower part of the county (*Napa County Reporter*, August 27, 1870). He was also Trustee for Holly Oak public school in Napa County and was present at its opening ceremonies in 1872 (*Napa County Reporter*, March 30, 1872). Brownlee was elected Supervisor for Napa County for two consecutive terms, serving from 1872–1875.

His 1874 term was not without incident. It seems that an act of the Legislature, February 25, 1874, divided Napa County into four districts and provided for the election of two additional Supervisors. Five new Supervisors were elected two months later and the Board of three in office, Robert Brownlee, F. W. Ellis and Joseph Mecklinberg certified the elections of the new Supervisors. But the three men refused to leave office stating that both boards were elected and qualified to serve at the same time. The Legislature took up the matter and subsequently ruled that both Boards could act as one. Kanaga (1901:88) wrote that following this, "Napa County was then blest (or otherwise) with the largest Board of Supervisors in the state of California, except the City of San Francisco. The meetings of that double-header were marvels of astuteness, so contemporaries state. They agreed to disagree from the start and held firmly to their 'joint resolution.'" It may be imagined that Brownlee, who liked to get to the point and preferred a no-nonsense approach, was a vigorous competitor in discussion! He was 69 years old in 1882 when he again threw his hat in the ring and ran one more time for Napa County Supervisor.

EPILOGUE

Robert Brownlee's story embodies the American spirit. An immigrant arriving with few possessions and little money, he set out with youthful energy and optimism to make his way in the new land. The work ethic, instilled since childhood, together with his practical nature and Scottish thrift, enabled him to cope with frontier realities. He sought citizenship with gusto and confidently set out to make his "fortune" even though things "looked blue" from time to time. Probably the trait that most contributed to his success was his ability to adapt to changing times and situations during his lifetime. He was an adventurer, making his way from one sea coast to another over terrain that was virtually unexplored, with little knowledge of what he might find upon arrival. Brownlee courageously turned farmer despite scant knowledge, but succeeded nonetheless, thus achieving the American dream of prosperity for himself and his family.

He completed his memoirs in his eightieth year. Partially crippled by arthritis, he would spend the years left to him in a wheelchair. (Given Brownlee's nature, it can be assumed that he did not accept that fact with equanimity.) Presumably, frequent visits by members of the growing Brownlee and Lamont clans cheered him, while he regaled them once more with familiar stories of the American frontier. In 1897 Brownlee passed quietly away.

NAPA, CAL., FRIDAY, NOVEMBER 26, 1897.

Passing of a Pioneer.

Death Terminates a Useful Life and Long Illness.

At his home near Creston Station, not far from the dividing line between Napa and Solano counties, ex-Supervisor Robert Brownlee bade farewell to earthly scenes. He died at 9:30 o'clock Friday night, Nov. 19th. He had been an invalid a number of years, a large portion of which time he was in a partially helpless condition and was moved about the house in a wheeled chair. During his young manhood and in his prime he had been a very active man and when old age came the machinery that had given force to his life broke down. But he had a wonderful constitution, a cheerful disposition, and despite suffering and enforced confinement his heart seemed ever light. In his home he was always a most hospitable host and with his wife, children and grandchildren, he was happy and content.

Deceased was born at Bunkle, in the parish of Cambusnethan, in the county of Lanark, Scotland, in 1813. He emigrated to America in 1836, and settled in the City of New York, where he sojourned four months, working at his trade; that of stone-cutter. In September of that year he proceeded to North Carolina, and was employed for thirteen months in the capital of that State, at the expiration of which he moved to Arkansas, arriving in Little Rock on Christmas day, 1837. He there prosecuted his calling for four years, working on the Capitol and State Bank, when he embarked in the cultivation of land. In 1848 he retired from the occupation of farming, and commenced prospecting for lead, getting blown up during this employment. Mr. Brownlee was a resident of the State of Arkansas altogether thirteen years. In 1849 he crossed the plains to California. He arrived in Mariposa county in the first rains. He labored in the mines for six days, in the first hour and a half of which he dug up $40 worth of ore, his only implements being his jack-knife and tin pan. This was in October, 1849. With this sum he entered into partnership with John W. Clarke, of Vermont, who had also been moderately lucky, purchased a team of six pack-mules, and commenced what is known as a "packing" business, between Stockton and Ajuafria, two towns one hundred miles apart. In the Spring of 1850 Mr. Brownlee established a store in Mariposa, having a mule team in connection therewith. The former combined all the mining luxuries of a boarding house, ten pin alley and card room, as well as the agency for Adams' Express. In 1852 he wound up his affairs in Mariposa and sailed from San Francisco for Scotland, visiting *en route* Arkansas and Kentucky, where he met his wife, Miss Annie Lamont. After a short visit to the old country he returned to the United States and was married in New York soon after his arrival. In October, 1852, he came with his bride and his brother back to California, locating in Vallejo. Early in 1853 he commenced farming and a dairy business on a small scale, purchased a tract of fifty acres of land two miles north of the town limits, which he afterwards exchanged with General John B. Frisbie in 1857 for the present home place at Creston Station.

Mr. Brownlee at one time served on the Board of Supervisors of this county and that trust, like all others committed to his keeping, he discharged faithfully and well. His eldest son, Robert A., is Under Sheriff of this county, a second son, Frederick J., is court reporter here and a third son, George, lives on the ranch. He also leaves three married daughters, Mrs. Durbin of Sacramento, Mrs. Urquhart of San Jose and Mrs. Seymour of Sacramento.

The funeral was held from the family residence last Monday at 11 a.m. Interment in Tulocay cemetery.

—Napa *Register*

APPENDIX I

Arkansas Emigrants

There are no published figures to confirm the number of Arkansans who traveled any one of the southern trails to California in 1849. Based on studies of known companies, together with letters, diaries, and newspaper accounts, a conservative estimate would total 12% or 1440 individuals. This figure includes slaves and women, who usually were not included on printed lists of emigrants.

A number of men are listed in Grant Foreman's *Marcy and the Goldseekers* and Francile Oakley's *Arkansas' Golden Army of '49*, so they will not be repeated here. The following roster includes 50 individuals (names marked with an asterisk) known to have traveled with the Little Rock Company. Many names are taken from the register of the Rancho Santa Ana del Chino (See note 9, Chapter V), which has not been studied since Lynley Bynum transcribed it from the original in 1934.

Little known is the fact that 115 Arkansans added their names to this register—almost 20% of the total. In many cases, the traveler left a few lines to describe his condition and experiences on the trail. Punctuation and obvious spelling errors have been corrected when quoting their words. Most of the men would have remained anonymous. Except for a few signatures by members of the Batesville and Clarksville Companies, they have not appeared previously on a published list of emigrants, and should be on permanent record as part of "Arkansas' Golden Army." The following sources have been used: *Arkansas Gazette* (referenced AG); *Arkansas State Democrat* (ASD); *Arkansas Banner* (AB); the Rancho Santa Ana del Chino *Record Book* (RB); Arkansas History Commission Bulletin #13 (AHC); William F. Pope's *Early Days in Arkansas* (POPE); and the Brownlee memoirs.

*ARMSTRONG, Linus. From Johnson County. He had made $4000 by November 1850, and said that he had seen as much of California as he wanted. He returned to Little Rock (Thibault letter AG: 11/22/1850).

BENTLEY, George H. Captain William's Company of Fort Smith. From Lewisburg. Arrived at Rancho Santa Ana del Chino, California on October 4, 1849, "six months and 3 days out all well" (RB: 27).

BRADFORD, W. H. Dr. Tucker's Company. From Jefferson County. Signed in at Rancho Santa Ana del Chino on September 6, 1849 (RB: 14).

*BRALLY, John. Scott County. Signed in at Rancho Santa Ana del Chino on October 8, 1849 (RB: 28).

*BROWNFIELD, Seneca. Signed in at Rancho Santa Ana del Chino on September 29, 1849 (RB: 24), and went to Agua Fria in the Southern mines. Remained in California. See Brownlee. Also mentioned in CAC letter (AG: 5/17/1850).

*BROWNLEE, Robert. Wrote letters of experiences from San Felipe, Ca.: (AG: 11/30/1849); Agua Fria (AG: 2/22/1850); Stockton (AG: 3/22 & 3/29/1850). Mentioned in ANON letter (AD: 9/28/1849); CAC letter (AG: 5/17/1850); Parcell and Woodruff letters (AG: 10/11/1850).

*CAGLE, William. From Pope County. Arrived at Rancho Santa Ana del Chino on October 16, 1849, "in Good Health" (RB: 29).

CATES, William. Arrived at Rancho Santa Ana del Chino on October 22, 1849, from Creek Nation, Arkansas, with J. R. Davis and Leroy Jobe. Davis wrote that he was in good health but Cates and Jobe were "in most pitiful situation . . . taken in by Col. Williams. Sheltered and provided for." The men left for Stockton and the mines on April 23 (RB: 38–39).

*CELLARS, C. A. From Washington, Arkansas. Age 22 (CC). Served in Mexican War (AHC). Cellars, Murphy, Robbins, Lowe, and Quigley took steamer to mines from San Diego (CAC letter AD: 12/21/1850). Worked in the mines at Indian Bar on the Tuolumne River (CAC letter AG: 5/17/1850). Also mentioned in Robins letter (AD: 1/25/1850); Thibault letter (AG: 4/19/1850); and Parcell letter (AG: 10/11/1850).

*CLARK, John W. Born in Montpelier, Vt. Age 21 (CC). Signed in at Rancho Santa Ana del Chino on September 29, 1849 (RB: 24). Went to Agua Fria mines. Became a California resident. See Brownlee. Also mentioned in CAC letter (AG: 5/17/1850) and Parcell letter (AG: 10/11/1850).

COOPER, S. H. Signed *Record Book* on October 9, 1849, along with some members of the Clarksville Company (RB: 29).

*COUNTS, George F. From Clinton, Arkansas. Signed in at Rancho Santa Ana del Chino on October 16, 1849, "in Good health" (RB: 29).

*CREASE, Henry. Age 25. Served in Mexican Army (AHC). Mined at Indian Bar on the Tuolumne River and was treasurer of an association formed to dam the river (CAC letter AG: 5/17/1850). Also mentioned in Woodruff and Thibault letters (AG: 11/21/1849); Woodruff letter (AD: 1/25/1850); Galloway letter (AG: 3/22/1850); Thibault letter (AG: 4/19/1850); CAC letter (AG: 5/17/1850); Parcell letter (AG: 11/22/1850).

CREATH, Albert G. Arrived at Rancho Santa Ana del Chino on August 17, 1849 (RB:7). Traveled the Gila Trail with the Knickerbocker Company.

DAVIS, H. H. Captain of a company from Washington, Arkansas. Arrived at Rancho Santa Ana del Chino on October 18, 1849. He reported that he had lost two horses near Temecula, California, "one a bright sorrell 6 years old, Star in his forehead a scar on his right shoulder . . . The other a bay, 17 years old, star in his forehead. Saddle mark no brands, heavy made. Short body steep rump" (RB:29).

DAVIS, James A. With Captain Davis' Washington, Arkansas Company. Signed in at Rancho Santa Ana del Chino on September 29, 1849 (RB:24).

DAVIS, J. R. See William Cates

*DONAHOO (DUNAHOO), Calvin. From Saline County. Age 31 and a native of Alabama (CC). Signed in at Rancho Santa Ana del Chino on October 17, 1849 (RB:30), and went on to the Agua Fria mines (Wills letter AG:3/29/1850).

*DREW, Ransom. Age 20 (CC). Son of Governor Thomas S. Drew of Arkansas. Mined at Indian Bar on the Tuolumne River (Parsell letter AG:3/22/1850). Also mentioned in Brownlee letter (AG:3/22/1850) and CAC letter (AG:5/17/1850).

*EATON, NATHANIEL. Signed *Record Book* on October 8, 1849 (RB:28).

*FAGAN, Dr. James. One of the youngest soldiers to serve in the Arkansas Regiment in the Mexican War (POPE). Wrote letter from the plains (AD:8/18/1849) and read the Declaration of Independence during July 4th celebration at Socorro, New Mexico (ANON letter AD:9/28/1849). Died on the trail outside of Tucson. See Brownlee.

FORBES, N. Signed *Record Book* with members of the Clarksville Company on October 9, 1849. A member of the company wrote that "Forbes remained with Col. Williams" (RB:29).

FORT, Dr. James L. From Washington, Arkansas and member of Capt. Davis' Company. Signed in at Rancho Santa Ana del Chino on September 9, 1849 (RB:24). Attended Dr. Fagan during his illness.

*GALLOWAY, Edwin. Age 24 (CC). Mined on the Tuolumne River (Parcell letter AG:10/11/1850). Formed company with Keatts, Crease, Pennington, Thibault, and Lavenberg (Galloway letter AG:3/22/1850). Also mentioned by Woodruff and Thibault (AD:12/21/1849); Thibault (AG:4/19/1850); and CAC (AG:5/17/1850).

*GALLOWAY, James. Age 22 (CC). See Edwin, above.

*GARRITY, William. Native of St. Genevieve, Mo. Signed in at Rancho Santa Ana del Chino on September 29, 1849 (RB:24). Traveled with Brownlee and Clark to the Agua Fria Mines. See Brownlee.

*GRIGGS, Samuel P. From Clinton, Arkansas. Signed in at Rancho Santa Ana del Chino on October 16, 1849, "in Good Health" (RB:29).

GWYNN David L. Member of Captain Williams' Company of Fort Smith. From Lewisburg, Arkansas. Signed in at Rancho Santa Ana del Chino on October 5, 1849 (RB:27).

HACKNEY, Thos. G. Clarksville Company. Signed *Record Book* on October 26, 1849 (RB:31).

HAMILTON, H. A. Clarksville Company. Signed *Record Book* on October 25, 1849 (RB:31).

*HAMMOND, Wm. B. From Scott County. Signed in at Rancho Santa Ana del Chino on October 8, 1849 (RB:28).

*HARALSON, Major H. Signed in at Rancho Santa Ana del Chino on October 8, 1849 (RB:28). Mined on Rattlesnake Creek with Col. J. J. Joiner (Parsell letter AG: 10/11/1850). Also referred to in CAC letter (AG: 5/17/1850). See Brownlee.

HARRIS, John. Arrived at Rancho Santa Ana del Chino on August 17, 1849 (RB:7). One of the early arrivals; traveled with the Knickerbocker (NY) Company.

HARVICK. From Monroe County. Killed by Apache Indians near Albuquerque. See Sam W. Lewis.

*HAUGHTON, Edward William. From Little Rock. Signed in at Rancho Santa Ana del Chino on November 2, 1849, and wrote: "Arrived. A brother of his lives just across the marsh" (RB: 33).

HEIDER, Deidrick. Member of Captain Williams' Company from Fort Smith. From Lewisburg, Arkansas. Signed in at Rancho Santa Ana del Chino on October 4, 1849 (RB:28).

HICKEY, George. Member of Clarksville Company. "George Hickey of Johnson Co. Arkansas was shot on the Gila about 170 miles [east of the Colorado River] by order of a Court Martial of the Clarksville company to which he had belonged. He had stabbed a young man of the same company" (RB:25). This was one of the more dramatic incidents reported in the Record Book and the details of this example of frontier justice are contained in the A. D. King journal.

HOBSON, Hobson. From Arkansas. Signed in at Rancho Santa Ana del Chino on September 5, 1849 (RB:13).

HOGE, Hon. I. M. From Washington County, Arkansas. Signed *Record Book* on October 27, 1849 (RB:31). Said he was captain of a company of 130 men who had journeyed from Fort Smith to California by way of Salt Lake in Utah. Hoge's is the only signature in the *Record Book* that confirms travel by the long, hot and arid Salt Lake-Los Angeles Trail. Others who signed the *Record Book* on or about this date may also have been members of this large company.

HOLMAN, William T. From Arkansas. Signed in at Rancho Santa Ana del Chino on September 5, 1849 (RB:13).

HOOPER, James and Thomas. Members of Captain Williams' Company of Fort Smith. From Lewisburg, Arkansas. Signed in at Rancho Santa Ana del Chino on October 5, 1849 (RB:27–28).

HOWARD, N. Member of Capt. Davis' Washington Company. Signed *Record Book* on October 15, 1849, and wrote: "Left by Doct. Eaton a large Bay Horse to be recruited" (RB:30). (See Nathaniel Eaton above.)

*HOWELL, Philo. Age 40, native of New York (CC). Made $1000 the first week in Agua Fria (Wills letter AG:3/29/1850). Mentioned in Brownlee letter (AG:3/22/1850). Signed in at Rancho Santa Ana del Chino on October 17, 1849, from Little Rock (RB:30).

HOWEY, Jas. Member of Dr. Tucker's Company from Jefferson County. Signed in at Rancho Santa Ana del Chino on September 6, 1849 (RB:14).

*HUCHINGSON, John F. Native of Alabama, age 23 (CC). From Saline County,

Arkansas. Signed in at Rancho Santa Ana del Chino on October 15, 1849 (RB:29).
* HUGHES, John. Mined on the Tuolumne River then went into the trading business with Wm. Pennington (Woodruff letter, AG: 10/11/1850).
HUGHES, William. Traveled with Batesville Company. Arrived Rancho Santa Ana del Chino November 10, 1849 (RB:34).
* HUNT. Member of Henry Keatts' mess (Brownlee letter AG: 11/30/1849).
* HUTCHERSON (HUTCHESON), Thomas. Signed in at Rancho Santa Ana del Chino on October 8, 1849. Wrote the following: "some sick. Sold out our team & Waggon to Col. Williams" (RB:28). Worked with Calvin Dunahoo at Agua Fria (Wills letter AG: 3/29/1850).
JOBE, Leroy. See Cates. Signed *Record Book* on October 22, 1849 (RB:38)
JOHNSON, Burke. From Pope County. Constructed a boat at the Colorado River and charged new arrivals $1.25 to cross them (Woodruff letter, AG: 4/26/1850).
JOHNSON, J. G. From Washington, Arkansas. Signed in at Rancho Santa Ana del Chino on November 2, 1849 (RB:33). May have been a member of the Hoge Company and traveled via Salt Lake.
* JOINER (JOYNER), J. J. Signed in at Rancho Santa Ana del Chino on October 17, 1849 (RB:30). Went first to Agua Fria (Wills letter AG: 3/29/1850). Later worked on Rattlesnake Creek with Major Haralson (Parsell letter AG: 10/11/1850). Also mentioned in Brownlee letter (AG: 3/22/1850).
JOYCE, W. N. W. From Capten, Arkansas. Traveled with the Western Rovers. Signed *Record Book* on October 12, 1849 (RB:29).
* KAMY, John M. M. Signed *Record Book* on October 18, 1849 (RB:29).
* KEATTS, Henry. First Lt. of the Little Rock Company (AG: 2/9/1849). Mined at Hawkins Bar (Galloway letter AG: 3/22/1850). Told story of mining experiences on the Tuolumne River (AG: 10/11/1850). Also mentioned in Woodruff and Thibault letters (AD: 12/21/1849); Woodruff letters (AD: 1/25/1850 & AG: 4/26/1850); CAC letter (AG: 5/17/1850); and Parsell letter (AG: 10/11/1850). See Brownlee.
KERR, John C. Arrived at Rancho Santa Ana del Chino on August 17, 1849 (RB:7). Believed to have traveled with the Knickerbocker (NY) Company.
* KING, George B. Commissary of the Little Rock Company (AG: 2/9/1849). Signed in at Rancho Santa Ana del Chino on October 4, 1849 (RB:27).
* LAVENBERG. Mined at Hawkins bar on the Tuolumne River with Henry Crease (Woodruff Letter AG: 11/18/1849, AD: 1/25/1850). Also mentioned in Galloway letter (AG: 3/22/1850) and CAC letter (AG: 5/17/1850).
* LEWIS, Sam C. W. Stopped just beyond Albuquerque to prospect for gold, where Apache Indians killed his friends Harvick and Shaver. Lewis returned to Little Rock (AD: 10/26/1849).
LINSEICK, Oliver. Member of the Washington, Arkansas Company. A member of this company wrote that Linseick lost "his life at Warner's Camp the 12th of October" (RB:30).
LOCKRIDGE, William. Member of Clarksville Company. Signed *Record Book* on October 20, 1849 (RB:30).
LOGAN, David and James. Traveled with the Clarksville Company. Signed *Record*

Book on October 26, 1849 (RB: 31). James was 30 years old; David 20. Both went to mines in Tuolumne County (CC).

LOGAN, Jonathan and J. L. C. Clarksville Company members. "Arrived here on Oct. 8th/49. Left for pueblo [Los Angeles] Oct. 11th/49" (RB: 29).

*LOW (LOWE), Bun. On arrival in California, found a job that paid $12 a day (CAC letter AD: 12/21/1850). Later mined on the Tuolumne River (Parsell letter AG: 10/11/1850). Also mentioned in Robins letter (AD: 1/25/1850); Thibault letter (AG: 4/19/1850); and CAC letter (AG: 5/17/1850).

*McALLESTER. From Saline County (Brownlee letter AG: 3/23/1850).

*McHENRY, Jesup. Member of McVicar's mess. Mined on Tuolumne River (Parsell letter AG: 10/11/1850). Also mentioned in CAC letter (AG: 5/17/1850). See Brownlee.

*McVICAR, James. Captain of the Little Rock Company. See Brownlee. Also referred to by Anon from Fort Smith (AD: 3/26/1849); EWH letter from Cross Timbers (AD: 6/1/1849); Parsell and Woodruff letters (AG: 10/11/1850); and CAC letter (AG: 5/17/1850).

MAGRUDER, Floyd. Traveled with Batesville Company from Arkansas, and arrived at Rancho Santa Ana del Chino on November 10, 1849 (RB: 34).

MITCHELL, James W. Western Rovers. Arrived at Rancho Santa Ana del Chino on November 8, 1849 (RB: 34).

MUNROE, William I. Traveled with Dr. Tucker's Company from Jefferson County. Signed in at Rancho Santa Ana del Chino on September 6, 1849 (RB: 14).

MURPHY, Henry. A Clarksville Company member wrote: "Henry Murphy of Yell Co. Arkansas died on the Horhado [Jornado] this side of the Pimon [Pima] village August 30, and was buried on the Gila" (RB: 25).

*MURPHY, James. Second Lt. of the Little Rock Company (AD: 2/9/1849). Age 29, native state was Virginia (CC). Mined at Indian Bar on the Tuolumne River with McVicar and others (Parsell letter AG: 10/11/1850). Also mentioned in ANON letter (AB: 10/2/1849); Robins letter (AD: 1/25/1850); Thibault letter (AG: 4/19/1850); and CAC letter (AG: 5/17/1850). Returned to Little Rock to work as a clerk in the Post Office (POPE).

*PARSELL (PARCELL), Thomas. Helped to organize the Little Rock Company but traveled to California by way of Panama (AB: 10/2/1849). Wrote about experiences on the Merced River and advised all not to come to California (AG: 10/11/1850). Also mentioned in Robins letter (AD: 1/25/1850) and CAC letter (AG: 5/17/1850). Returned to Little Rock. For many years was a crier in the United States Court (POPE).

*PEARCE (PIERCE), James. Signed in at Rancho Santa Ana del Chino on October 8, 1849 (RB: 28). First went to Agua Fria mines (Brownlee letter AG: 3/22/1850). Also mentioned in CAC letter (AG: 5/17/1850).

PELHAM, J. E. Batesville, Arkansas Company. Signed *Record Book* on November 10, 1849 (RB: 34).

*PENNINGTON, William. Age 28, from Arkansas (CC). Worked at Indian Bar on the Tuolumne River (Thibault letter AG: 4/19/1850). Joined a John Hughes in trading business (Woodruff letter AG: 10/11/1850). Also mentioned in Thibault letter

(AG: 12/21/1849); Woodruff letter (AD: 1/25/1850); Galloway letter (AG: 3/22/1850); and CAC letter (AG: 5/17/1850).

*PENROSE, James W. Signed in at Rancho Santa Ana del Chino on October 4, 1849 (RB: 28).

PETERS, Chira. Batesville Company. Signed *Record Book* on November 10, 1849: "Chira Peters who lost his fiddle" (RB: 34).

PETTUS, R. W. From Sevier County. Signed in at Rancho Santa Ana del Chino on October 18, 1849 (RB: 29).

PHILLIPS, R. L. From Washington, Arkansas. Signed *Record Book* on November 2, 1849 (RB: 33). May have been a member of Hon. I. L. Hoge's Company.

*POOL, George Washington. From Charlestown, Franklin County. Signed in at Rancho Santa Ana del Chino on October 8, 1849 (RB: 28).

POOL, M. P. From Fort Smith, Arkansas. Signed in at Rancho Santa Ana del Chino on September 24, 1849 (RB: 24).

PREWITT (PREWETT), J. L. Clarksville Company. Signed *Record Book* on October 25, 1849 (RB: 31).

*QUIGLEY. Stopped in San Francisco (Robins letter AD: 1/25/1850) then went to the Agua Fria mines (Brownlee letter AD: 3/22/1850). Also mentioned in CAC letter (AD: 12/21/1850).

RICHARDSON, E. M. From Fort Smith, Arkansas. Signed in at Rancho Santa Ana del Chino on September 24, 1849 (RB: 24).

*ROBERTS, J. G. Taken ill on the prairies (Woodruff letter AD: 6/1/49). Died on the plains near Choteau's Fort (AD: 6/6/1849).

*ROBINS, Elijah. Left Little Rock in the last stages of consumption and arrived in California cured (POPE). Wrote from Santa Fe (AD: 8/17/1849) and described San Francisco (AD: 1/25/1850). Went to the Agua Fria mines (Brownlee letter AG: 3/22/1850). Also mentioned in Woodruff letter (AD: 6/1/1849).

ROGERS, Jacob. Clarksville Company. Signed *Record Book* on October 26, 1849 (RB: 31).

ROWLAND, W. A. Signed *Record Book* on September 10, 1849 (RB: 17).

ROWLAND, William Lee. From Union County. Signed in at Rancho Santa Ana del Chino on September 11, 1849 (RB: 17).

SAMSON, N. A. From Sevier County. Signed in at Rancho Santa Ana del Chino on October 3, 1849 (RB: 27).

SEARCY, James and W. B. Batesville Company. Arrived at Rancho Santa Ana del Chino on November 10, 1849 (RB: 34).

*SHAVER. From Hempstead County. Was killed by Indians near Albuquerque. See Sam C. W. Lewis.

SHELBY, George C. Clarksville, Company. Signed *Record Book* on October 25, 1849 (RB: 31).

SHIRMAN, Eli. From Arkansas. Traveled with Knickerbocker (NY) Company on the Gila Trail. Signed *Record Book* on August 17, 1849 (RB: 7).

SIMMONS, Jos. J. Clarksville Company. Arrived at Rancho Santa Ana del Chino October 11, 1849. Wrote that "All's well. Sold out to Col Williams" (RB: 30).

SPEARS, John. Clarksville, Arkansas. Signed in at Rancho Santa Ana del Chino on September 24, 1849 (RB:24).

*STEVENSON, J. C. From Little Rock. "Arrived at this place" on November 16, 1849 (RB:35).

STONE, John. Batesville Company. Signed *Record Book* on November 10, 1849 (RB:34).

STUART, James T., Samuel H., and W. M. From Washington, Hempstead County. Left a note for R. F. Sullivan: "Dear Sir: We leave the 24th after waiting 7 days. I have heard from some Gentlemen that you were about the Colorado . . . we had the misfortune of losing 15 head of our horses and mules crossing the River" (RB:23).

SULLIVAN, R. F. From Washington, Arkansas. (See Stuart above.) Arrived at Rancho Santa Ana del Chino with Brownlee and Clark on September 28, 1849. Wrote to an anonymous friend: "We arrived here today. Our mules are in bad plight and I think you had better sell your mules here and take water. We would wait for you, but for the uncertainty of your coming this way" (RB:24–25).

TAPPE, Dr. J. W. Traveled to California by way of the Horn and spent some time in San Francisco (ECG letter AD:3/21/1850). Also mentioned in Woodruff letter (AD:12/21/1850) and Robins letter (AD:1/25/1850).

*THIBAULT, F. J. See Brownlee. Mined on Tuolumne River (Parcell letter AG:10/11/1850). Mentioned by Woodruff (AD:1/21/1850 and 1/25/1850); Galloway (AG:3/22/1850); Woodruff (AG:4/26/1850); and CAC (AG:5/17/1850). Told of his experiences in the following letters: AD:12/21/1849; AG:4/18/1850; and AG:11/22/1850.

THOMAS, George. Dr. Tucker's Company. Arrived September 6, 1849. Wrote that he was from "Arkansaw Nation. A Chicksaw" (RB:14).

TUCKER, Dr. James. From Jefferson County. Age 27 (CC). Signed in at Rancho Santa Ana del Chino on September 6, 1849 (RB:14).

TUNIS, J. B. From Dardanelle, Arkansas, and traveled with Clarksville Company. He wrote: "Arrived on the 29 Sept. A.D. 1849. I advise the Citizens of the U.S. not to take their families this route for this reason. It is too dangerous a one" (RB:24).

*VANDERGRIEF (VANDERGRIFT), Leonard. Signed in at Rancho Santa Ana del Chino on October 15, 1849 (RB:29). First went to the Agua Fria mines (Brownlee letter AG:3/22/1850, Wills letter AG:3/29/1850).

WEBB, A. H. Clarksville Company. Arrived Rancho Santa Ana del Chino October 9, 1849 (RB:29).

*WEBB, Wm. C. H. From Little Rock. Signed in at Rancho Santa Ana del Chino on October 17, 1849 (RB:30). Mentioned by Woodruff (AG:10/11/1850).

WILLIAMS, R. L. and W. From Washington, Arkansas. Signed in at Rancho Santa Ana del Chino on November 2, 1849. Wrote they would sail to the mines from San Pedro (RB:33). Believed to be members of I. M. Hoge's Company who had traveled by way of Salt Lake.

*WILLS, Benjamin. From Saline County, age 26. Home state of Michigan (CC). Wrote to his wife from Agua Fria (AG:3/29/1850). Mentioned in Brownlee letter (AG:3/22/1850). Remained in California and became Cathey Valley Precinct Judge in 1863 (Mariposa County Supervisors' Minutes).

WILSON, A. D., A. M. and Dr. G. W. Wrote they were from Fort Gibson in the Cherokee Nation, and arrived on October 3, 1849 (RB:27). See Brownlee.

*WOODRUFF, Alden M. See Brownlee. Wrote of trip and California experiences: AD:6/1; 8/17 and 12/21/1849; 1/25/1850; AG:4/19, 4/26, 11/29; and 10/11/1850. Also mentioned in CAC letter (AG:5/17/1850). Returned to Arkansas.

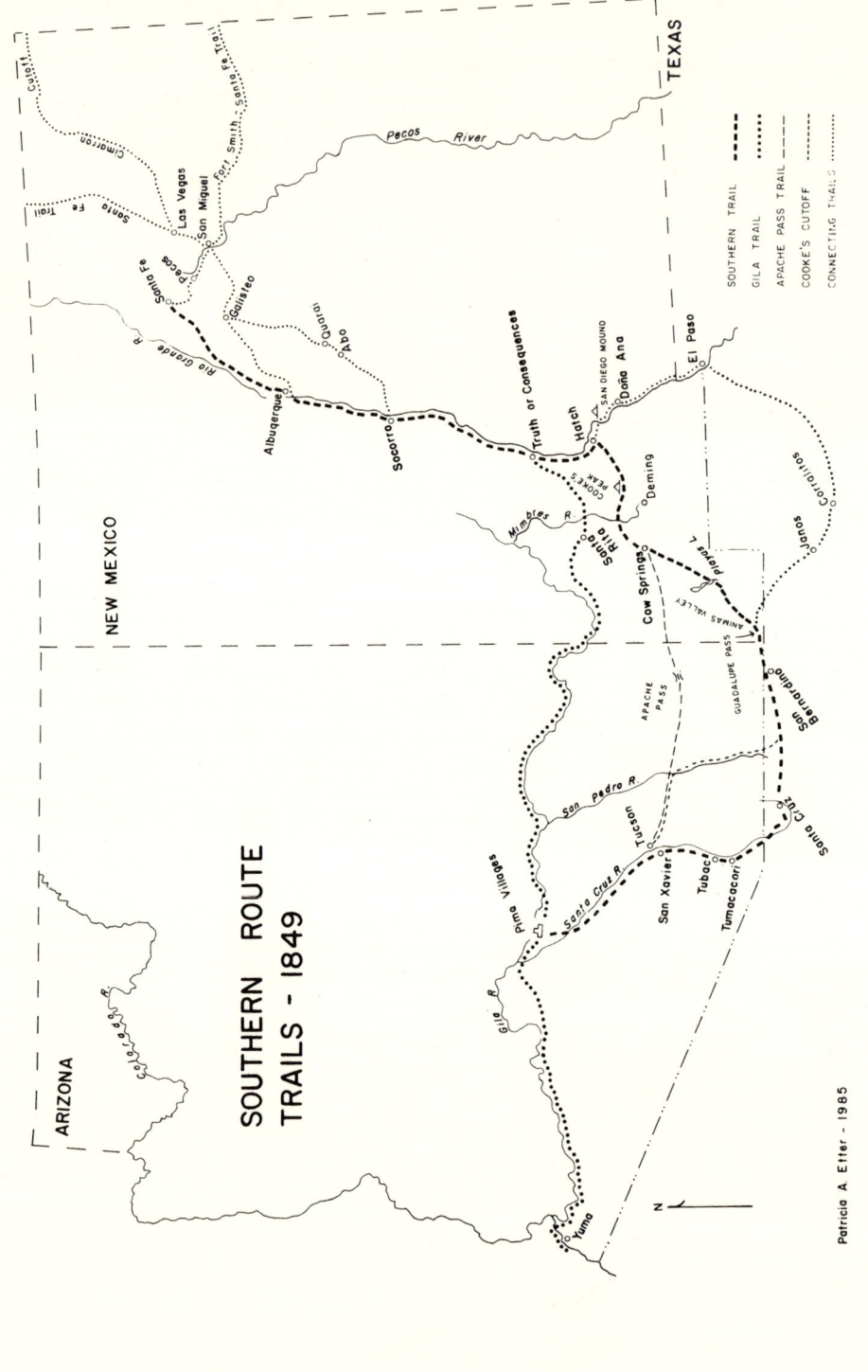

APPENDIX II

Southern Route Journals

Hundreds of published volumes present the story of travel to western goldfields by way of the California and Oregon trails. J. S. Holliday (1981:510) located 339 manuscript and letter collections, which documented travel to California by northern routes. Many of these stories have been repeated in various textbooks and have contributed to the study of the 1849 California gold rush and its historical significance in the Westward Movement. A discussion of southern trails to California is equally important. Hitherto, however, most histories have offered only a line or two about these alternate trails. Some do not mention them at all.

An estimated 12,000 Americans and 6,000 Mexicans chose to follow trails traversing the arid lands of the southwest, and their memoirs should receive more attention. Men and women on the southern trails suffered the same hardships as those who trod the northern roads and their '49 adventures are every bit as exciting. For added zest, their routes were partially on foreign soil, crossing the Mexican states of Sonora and Chihuahua.

Previous excellent studies of southern route trails include those written by Owen Coy in 1929; Ralph Bieber in 1937; and Grant Foreman in 1939. Ferol Egan published *The Eldorado Trail* in 1977, which discussed trails through Texas and Mexico. Harlan Hague's study, *The Road to California* (1978), covers trail history between 1540 and 1848. Two bibliographies, published in the 1960s, comprised 24 diaries and reminiscences written by men who traveled by southern trails. These were appended to the Lorenzo Aldrich Journal and E. I. Edwards' *Lost Oasis on the Carrizo*.

This study increases the list of journals and reminiscences to fifty-three (though many more may still be buried in archives or descendants' trunks). Twenty diaries remain in manuscript form. Of thirty-two published diaries, five are in old newspapers, nine are contained in historical quarterlies, and six were published in limited numbers and are found only in special collections libraries. The thirteen remaining volumes are in most libraries. Only six of these have been published since 1940.

The journals of Forty Niners have been a great help in reconstructing Robert Brownlee's excursion to California and in redefining two important segments of the trail which have been incorrectly reproduced on many published maps. These comprise the Guadalupe Pass area on the Arizona-New Mexico border, which is discussed in Chapter IV, note 30; and the trail from Yuma on the Colorado River to Warner's Ranch, California. This latter trail is discussed in Chapter V.

The writers of the diaries and reminiscences that follow took one of three trails, which were part of the southern route to California: the Southern Trail, the Gila Trail or the Apache Pass Trail. The men joined these trails at points near modern Hatch, Truth or Consequences, or Guadalupe Pass in New Mexico. Trails were reached from the Fort Smith-Santa Fe, or Santa Fe trails, or by trails out of Texas and Mexico (See map on page 206).

The Southern Trail was by far the most popular, with 74% of the emigrants following this wagon road. Forty-three diaries tell their stories. In the main, the westward migrants followed a wagon road opened by Philip St. George Cooke and his Mormon Battalion in 1846. However, the term "Southern Trail" is preferred rather than "Cooke's road" because Forty Niners diverged from the latter at several points. Emigrants traveled south out of Santa Fe to Albuquerque, followed the west bank of the Rio Grande, leaving the river in the vicinity of Hatch, then angled in a southwesterly direction to Guadalupe Pass. Their trail dipped into present-day Mexico before turning north to Tucson by way of the Santa Cruz Valley then on to the Pima Villages, where it joined the Gila Trail.

The Gila Trail was first negotiated by Stephen Watts Kearny and his Army of the West in 1846. The army marched south along the Rio Grande, left the river near Truth or Consequences, New Mexico, and followed the course of the Gila River (by way of the Pima Villages) to its junction with the Colorado. This was an extremely rugged trail suited only to pack animals. Twelve percent of the emigrants chose this route and left seven diaries to tell their story.

The Apache Pass Trail was the one least used in 1849. This road left the Southern Trail at Cow Springs, near Deming, New Mexico. In the main, it followed the route of modern highway 10, but at a point south of modern Willcox, Arizona, it meandered for several miles through a narrow pass. Robert Eccleston of the Fremont Company wrote the only extant diary of this trip. In later years, large groups of Apache Indians took advantage of the terrain to ambush and attack emigrant trains and the Butterfield stage. Thus it became known as Apache Pass, and one of the most dangerous roads in Arizona.

Sources have been intentionally annotated in the manuscript so the reader will have a complete bibliography of overland diaries and some personal information about their authors.

BIBLIOGRAPHY OF SOUTHERN ROUTE JOURNALS

ALDRICH, Lorenzo D.
> 1950 *A Journal of the Overland Route to California and the Gold Mines*. Glen Dawson, Ed. Los Angeles: Dawson's Book Shop.

Aldrich and a company of 32 men journeyed to Arkansas from Albany, New York, and headed West on May 11, 1849, by way of the Fort Smith-Santa Fe Trail. He kept a daily record of mileages, weather conditions and camping spots as he proceeded. After reaching New Mexico, the men decided to take the Southern Trail. They arrived in San Diego on December 3, 1849, and sailed to San Francisco and the mines. Aldrich returned home by way of Panama in November 1850.

ANONYMOUS
> 1849 *Diary of an Overland Journey from Albuquerque to Santa Cruz, New Mexico, 1849*. Formerly known as the journal of Caspar Ricks. MS in the Bancroft Library.

The author joined up with members of the Little Rock Company at Albuquerque on June 26, 1849, making daily entries in his diary and recording his adventures along the Southern Trail as far as Santa Cruz, Mexico, where the story ends abruptly. The journal complements the memoirs by R. Brownlee, F. J. Thibault, and A. M. Woodruff.

ANONYMOUS
> 1937 "From Texas to the Gold Mines." In *Southern Trails to California in 1849*, Volume V:260–280. Ralph P. Bieber, Ed. Glendale, California: The Arthur Clark Company.

A nameless pioneer left Austin, Texas, on April 8, 1849. He and his companions made their way to El Paso, Texas, where they turned south into the Mexican state of Chihuahua, continued on the trail to Janos, turning north to join the Southern Trail at Guadalupe Pass. The gold seekers arrived in the Mariposa diggings on September 5, 1849.

ANONYMOUS
> 1849 *Journal of a Journey to California*. MS in John Lewis RoBards Papers, 1832–1922; Joint Collection, University of Missouri Western Historical Manuscript Collection-Columbia and State Historical Society of Missouri Manuscripts.

This incomplete transcript of an emigrant's diary ends suddenly after a safe crossing of the Colorado River, on October 31, 1849. It is not known if the traveler succumbed to the rigors of crossing the California desert. His journal later made its way into the hands of John Lewis RoBards, a member of the train. The men started from Hannibal, Missouri, picked up the Santa Fe Trail to Santa Fe, then continued to California on the Southern Trail.

ANONYMOUS
    1849–1852 *Rough Abstract of a Forty-Niner's Diary.* MS in the Bancroft Library.

The author pulled out of Fort Smith on March 26, 1849, with the Knickerbocker Company from New York. The men followed the Fort Smith-Santa Fe Trail and then packed along the Gila Trail. The diarist arrived at Warner's Ranch, California, on September 7, 1849, and continued by foot to the Southern Mines. Though an abstract of a 322-page diary (location of original unknown), this emigrant's report is packed with details and dates.

AUDUBON, John Woodhouse
    1906 *Audubon's Western Journal: 1849–1850. Being the MS record of a trip from New York to Texas, and an overland journey through Mexico and Arizona to the gold-fields of California.* Frank Heywood Hodder, Ed. Cleveland: The Arthur H. Clark Company.

Audubon, son of the famous naturalist, left New York on February 8, 1849, and arrived in San Diego, California, on October 4, 1849. He and his fellow adventurers went first to Rio Grande City, Texas. In contrast to the majority of Forty Niners who turned north to take the Southern Trail from Guadalupe Pass, Audubon led his men across the Mexican States of Nueva Leon, Coahuila, Durango, Chihuahua and Sonora to Altar, where they turned north and traveled to the Pima Villages. Here they joined the Gila Trail. There are only two other published records by men who followed this route, one by companion J. H. Bachman; the other by a member of another company, Nicholas Dawson. In addition to making the observations of a naturalist, Audubon faithfully recorded day-to-day events of his memorable march; a story of suffering, deprivation and hardship. He also made hundreds of sketches. Thirty-four survive and are housed in Los Angeles' Southwest Museum.

BACHMAN, Jacob Henry
    1941 "Audubon's Ill-Fated Western Journey." Jeanne Skinner Van Nostrand, Ed. In *California Historical Society Quarterly.* Volume XXI: 289–310.

A cousin of J. W. Audubon, Bachman shared his adventures and left a diary that spelled out many of the reasons their journey to Eldorado was filled with more disasters than most.

    1943 "Diary of a 'Used-up' Miner." Jeanne Skinner Van Nostrand, Ed. In *California Historical Society Quarterly.* Volume XXII: 67–83.

Bachman's second diary discusses the sea voyage from San Diego to San Francisco. In addition, he continued to make sketchy entries about his mining experiences until January 1878.

BEECHING, R.

1849 *The Journal of R. Beeching.* MS in the Huntington Library.

Beeching was a member of the P. F. Smith Company of New York, and traveled the Southern Trail with D. D. Demarest and L. N. Weed as far as Tucson, where he decided to move on with the Carson Company (see Harvey Wood). He arrived in San Diego on October 20, 1849, and sailed to San Francisco. (Dr. Harlan Hague, Professor of History, San Joaquin Delta College, Stockton, California, is currently editing the manuscript.)

BLUNT, Phineas

1849–1852 *Notes of travel from New York to the Gold Region of California in the year Eighteen-hundred and forty-nine, February 5, 1849–January 14, 1852.* MS in the Bancroft Library.

Blunt came from New York with Capt. Ebbet's company of Knickerbockers and was embarked on the Fort Smith-Santa Fe Trail, by March 26, 1849. He arrived at Rancho Santa Ana del Chino on September 14, and continued by foot to the Southern Mines. Blunt made excellent observations during his cross-country trek and penned some rare descriptions of sites and people he encountered along the road.

BOYLES, John R.

1977 "None Dream but of Success." Sarah N. Shouse. In *Tennessee Historical Quarterly.* Volume XXVI: 512–523.

This article is based on letters written by John R. Boyles to his family describing his adventures on the Fort Smith-Santa Fe Trail and in California. Boyles was one of 34 members of Captain Robert Farquharson's company from Fayetteville, Tennessee. The men left on April 14, stopped briefly in Santa Fe, then moved along on the Southern Trail. Boyles arrived safely in San Diego and sailed to San Francisco. (The Boyles letters are contained in the Eliza H. Ball Gordon Boyles papers in the Perkins Library, Duke University.)

BRAINARD, David

1849 *David Brainard's Journal, Delaware, March 20, 1849–November 29, 1849.* MS in the Bancroft Library. Typescript copy held in State Historical Society of Wisconsin.

Another wayfarer took the Santa Fe Trail to New Mexico, bypassed Santa Fe to Galisteo, and followed a trail to Albuquerque. He headed west on the Southern Trail and crossed the Colorado River on November 29. This ends the first portion of his diary. Brainard traveled with Count Agostin Haraszthy, credited with initiating viticulture in California's Napa Valley. The second half of Brainard's diary tells about his return journey by way of Panama in 1850.

CHAMBERLIN, William H.
   1945 "From Lewisburg to California in 1849." Lansing C. Bloom, Ed. In *New Mexico Historical Review*. Volume XX: 14–57, 144–180, 239–268, 336–357.

Chamberlin departed from Fort Smith, Arkansas, on March 28, 1849, and followed Captain Marcy's road to Santa Fe. He left the Rio Grande River near modern Truth or Consequences, New Mexico and packed by way of the Gila River, the most rugged of the trails on the Southern Route. He arrived in Los Angeles on August 11, 1849.

CHATHAM, J. W.
   1849 *Overland Journal, February 27, 1849*. Holograph manuscript, Anderson Room, University of New Mexico, Albuquerque.

Chatham left Abbeville County, South Carolina, in February, 1849. He gives an interesting account of his journey across such southern states as Alabama, Mississippi, and Tennessee, as he moved toward Independence, Missouri, his departure point for California. His 182-page diary ends near Quarai, New Mexico. He has added some "reflections," which detail mileage to the gold fields, a recipe for malaria medicine, and a list of the stones he collected on his journey.

CLARKE, Asa Bennett
   1852 *Travels in Mexico and California: Comprising a Journal of a Tour from Bazos Santiago, through Central Mexico, by way of Monterey, Chihuahua, the country of the Apaches, and the River Gila to the Mining Districts of California*. Boston: Wright & Hasty's Steam Press.

With the Hampden Mining Company of New York, Clark sailed to Brazos Santiagos, an island near the mouth of the Rio Grande, on January 29, 1849. The men continued by way of Monterrey and Chihuahua to join the Southern Trail at Guadalupe Pass. After touching Los Angeles, Clarke proceeded to the Northern Mines by foot and was busy prospecting by July.

COLLIER, James
   1937 *The Adventures of James Collier, First Collector of the Port of San Francisco*. By Grant Foreman. Chicago: Black Cat Press.

Grant Foreman has compiled letters and documents relevant to Collier's trip to California. Collier left Fort Leavenworth, Kansas, on May 17, 1849, and, under the protection of a company of dragoons, followed the Santa Fe and Southern Trails. He arrived in San Diego on November 1, 1849, and continued north to San Francisco to assume his duties as Collector of the Port of San Francisco.

COX, Cornelius C.
   1925–1926 "From Texas to California in 1849." Mabelle Eppard Martin, Ed. In *Southwestern Historical Quarterly*. Volume XXIX: 36–50, 128–146, 201–223.

This adventurer left Harrisburg, Pennsylvania, on April 14, 1849, and reached Stockton, California on February 6, 1850. He traveled to El Paso, Texas, where he turned north to join the Southern Trail near Hatch, New Mexico. Cox's daily record tells of encounters with Col. Collier, J. W. Audubon, and Lt. Cave Couts. He arrived at Rancho Santa Ana del Chino on November 7, 1849.

CRUMPTON, H. J. & W. B.
    1912 *The Adventures of Two Alabama Boys.* Montgomery, Alabama: The Paragon Press.

Part I contains reminiscenses by Dr. H. J. Crumpton and recounts his trip to California via the Fort Smith-Santa Fe and Southern trails. He left Fort Smith on April 12, 1849. Parts II and III contain the memoirs of W. B. Crumpton, who recalls details of two visits to California, the first via Panama in 1849, and the second after a 40-year absence.

DAWSON, Nicholas "Cheyenne"
    1933 *Narrative.* San Francisco: Grabhorn Press.

"Cheyenne" left Sherman, Texas, on March 1, 1849. He and his party took the trail that J. W. Audubon followed across Mexico to Altar, then north to the Pima Villages, where they joined other emigrants on the California road. He arrived in the Mariposa diggings about the first of November. This was Dawson's second trip to California, having traveled across the northern plains in 1841 with the Bidwell Company.

DEMAREST, David Durie
    1849–1850 *Diary, March 8, 1849–May 1850 of a trip in a bark Norumbega to Galveston, Texas, then overland to California.* MS in the Bancroft Library.

Demarest and members of the P. F. Smith Company sailed from New York on March 8, 1849, for Galveston, Texas. They continued across Texas to El Paso, where they turned north to join the Southern Trail arriving at the Colorado River on November 29, 1849. Other versions are found in the diaries of L. N. Weed and R. Beeching.

DURIVAGE, John E.
    1937 "Through Mexico to California. Letters and Journals of John E. Durivage." In *Southern Trails to California in 1849.* Ralph P. Bieber, Ed. Volume V:159–255. Glendale, California: The Arthur H. Clark Company.

Durivage, a correspondent with the *Daily Picayune* (New Orleans), left for Rio Grande City, Texas, on March 4, 1849. He proceeded westward through Mexico to Chihuahua, where he turned north to join the Southern Trail near Guadalupe Pass, and arrived in San Diego, California, on July 1. He then sailed to San Francisco. O. M. Wozencraft was a traveling companion.

DUVAL, Isaac
    1977 "Overland to California." Gary C. Stein, Ed. In *American History Illustrated.* Volume XII:26–36.

Duval wrote his colorful memoirs in the 1890s, recalling a number of hostile encounters with Indians and Mexican troops as he led his company across Texas and through Mexico to Janos, where they joined the wagon road to Guadalupe Pass. B. B. Harris was one of Duval's traveling companions and said the company left Panola County Texas on March 25, and arrived at Rancho Santa Ana del Chino on August 26, 1849. Unfortunately, some material has been omitted from the published version. The original manuscript cannot be located.

ECCLESTON, Robert
> 1950 *Overland to California on the Southwestern Trail of 1849. Diary of Robert Eccleston.* George P. Hammond and Edward P. Howes, Eds. Los Angeles: University of California Press.

With the Fremont Association, Eccleston left New York for Port Lavaca, Texas, on September 8, 1849. The party continued overland to El Paso and followed the Southern Trail as far as Cow Springs, New Mexico. Here they left the popular emigrant trail and charted a new cutoff for Tucson, which became known as the Apache Pass Trail. They continued on the regular emigrant trail out of Tucson, traveling in convoy with Col. J. C. Hayes, a Texas Ranger, who had been appointed Indian Agent for the Gila River Valley. The diary ends with the party's arrival at New River, California, on December 22, 1849. Eccleston's diary is the only one that has come to light describing 1849 travel on the trail. (The original manuscript is in the Bancroft Library.) Eccleston kept a number of diaries describing his sojourn in the mines, which were published in 1974 under the title, *The Mariposa Indian War of 1850–1851*, C. Gregory Crampton, Ed.

ELIOT, Robert
> 1899 "Account of Journey." In *Essex County Republican* (Port Henry, New York), March 16, 23 and 30, 1899. Typescript copy in Wisconsin Historical Society Collections, File #700.

Eliot and the members of his company started out on the Fort Smith-Santa Fe Trail on April 18. After leaving Albuquerque, the men decided to pack along the Gila Trail, reaching the Colorado River on August 15, about six weeks in advance of companies which had chosen to travel the Southern Trail. Eliot's reports also describe a year's stay in California. Robert and six of his friends signed the *Record Book* at the Rancho Santa Ana del Chino on September 2, 1849.

EVANS, George W. B.
> 1945 *Mexican Gold Trail, the Journal of a Forty-Niner.* Glenn S. Dumke, Ed. San Marino, California: The Huntington Library.

Evans started for California on February 20, 1849, with the Defiance (Ohio) Gold Hunters' Expedition. Dr. Lafayette Bunnell, who later reported on the discovery of the Yosemite Valley, was also a member of this group. These California-bound emigrants sailed to Port Lavaca, Texas, then traveled overland to San Antonio. After arriving at Eagle Pass on the Rio Grande, the party hired a guide to lead them west over the barren uplands of the Serranía del Burro. They rejoined the established road at Chihuahua and came upon the Southern Trail near Guadalupe Pass in early August. Evans arrived in the southern mining camp of Agua Fria on October 29, 1849. (The original can be found in the Huntington Library.)

FORSYTHE, John Robert
    1849 *Diary.* MS in the Peoria, Illinois, Public Library. Microfilm copy at the Bancroft Library.

Forsythe started from Peoria on April 5, 1849. He and members of the Peoria Company traveled the Santa Fe Trail out of Fort Leavenworth, Kansas, and after a brief stop at Santa Fe, continued on the Southern Trail to California, arriving on December 3, 1849. C. E. Pancoast writes another version of the company's travels.

GOULDING, William R.
    1849 *Journal, March 10–September 18, 1849.* MS in the Coe Collection, Yale University Library.

Goulding and the Knickerbocker Company of New York, set out on the Fort Smith-Santa Fe Trail on March 26, 1849. Goulding split from the Knickerbocker train and completed his trip to California on the Southern Trail, while many of his companions packed along the Gila Trail. He has achieved distinction by making the first entry in the register at the Rancho Santa Ana del Chino on August 12, 1849. Goulding noted that Isaac Duval and his sixty men joined up with him at Tucson.

GREEN, Robert B.
    1955 *On the Arkansas Route to California in 1849. The Journal of Robert B. Green of Lewisburg, Pennsylvania.* J. Orin Oliphant, Ed. Lewisburg, Pennsylvania: Bucknell University Press.

Green traveled in company with William H. Chamberlin. His colorful daily opinions make a good supplement to Chamberlin's journal. He died on December 29, 1849, just a few months after his arrival in the golden land. (The original and typed transcripts are in the Ellen Clarke Bertrand Library, Bucknell University.)

HARRIS, Benjamin Butler
    1960 *The Gila Trail. The Texas Argonauts and the California Gold Rush.* Richard H. Dillon, Ed. Norman: University of Oklahoma Press.

This prospector left Panola County, Texas, on March 25, 1849, bound for El Paso. He turned south here, and took a trail through Corralitos and Janos in Mexico before joining the Southern Trail near Guadalupe Pass. Although the book's name suggests differently, Harris did not join the Gila Trail until he arrived at the Pima Villages. He signed in at Rancho Santa Ana del Chino on August 26, 1849. Refer to the Duval memoirs for another version of this trip.

HARRIS, Lewis Birdsall
   1926 "Letters to Brother." In *Southwestern Historical Quarterly*. Volume XXIX: 215–223.
   1949 "Overland by Boat to California." Aurora Hunt, Ed. In *The Historical Society of Southern California Quarterly*. Volume XXI: 212–218.

Lewis B. Harris made his California trip in a green "Boat-wagon" as a member of Cornelius Cox' company. He signed in at the Rancho Santa Ana del Chino on November 7, 1849. (Copies of the Harris letters are in California State Library, Sacramento.)

HAYES, Judge Benjamin
   1929 *Pioneer Notes from the Diaries of Judge Benjamin Hayes*. Marjorie Tisdale Wolcott, Ed. Los Angeles: Marjorie Tisdale Wolcott.

Hayes left Independence, Missouri, on September 10, 1849, and started out on the Santa Fe Trail. His party bypassed Santa Fe and Albuquerque and went to Socorro by way of Abo and Galisteo. After leaving Socorro, the Hayes expedition proceeded to California on the Southern Trail and arrived in Los Angeles on February 26, 1850. Hayes' *Pioneer Notes* are in the Bancroft Library.

HESLEP, Augustus M.
   1937 "The Santa Fe Trail. Journal and Letters of Augustus M. Heslep." In *Southern Trails to California in 1849*. Ralph P. Bieber, Ed. Volume V: 353–386. Glendale, California: The Arthur H. Clark Company.

Heslep came from Illinois to Independence, Missouri, and started for California on May 15, 1849. He and his men traveled by way of the Santa Fe and Southern trails. The Heslep letters were first printed in issues of the *Daily Missouri Republican*. His last letter was written from the pueblo of San Jose on January 24, 1850.

HOWARD, David "Deacon"
   1849 *Journal of David Howard*. Transcript (1849) in the Ellen Clark Bertrand Library of Bucknell University.

Howard's journal complements those of Robert Green and William H. Chamberlin.

HUDGINS, John
   1970 "California in 1849." In *Westport Historical Quarterly*. Volume VI: 3–16.

Hudgins left Livingston County, Missouri, on May 6, 1849, and followed the Santa Fe Trail as far as Pecos, New Mexico. Here, he turned south (passing through Galisteo) and joined the Southern Trail near the village of La Joya on the Rio Grande in New Mexico. The company continued along the Southern Trail to Los Angeles, then overland through the San Fernando Valley to the mines. The Hudgins memoirs were written about 1905.

HUNTER, William W.
  1849 *Diary-Journal of Events on a Journey from Missouri to California*. MS in the University of Arizona Special Collections Library.
Hunter joined the Callaway County Missouri Pioneers and traveled to California by way of the Santa Fe and Southern trails. The party rode out of Montgomery County, Missouri, on April 23, and arrived in San Diego on December 13, 1849. Hunter left an extensive account of his travels and included a table that listed all the camping spots and distances covered. (David P. Robrock, Special Collections Librarian, University of Arizona, is currently editing this manuscript.)

KING, A. D.
  1941 "Trip to the Gold Fields." In Sunday Magazine Section, *Arkansas Gazette* (Little Rock). Twenty-four weekly installments starting January 19.
A. D. King was Co-Captain of the Clarksville (Arkansas) & California Mining Association and departed Fort Smith on April 11, 1849. Once in New Mexico, the company picked up the Southern Trail. This is an exhaustive but colorful and interesting account of the group's trip to California. However, by King's own admission, several people wrote in the journal and all wanted to make it interesting for the folks back home. One of these correspondents, perhaps a little overzealously, copied some of Josiah Gregg's (*Commerce of the Prairies*) descriptive material into the New Mexican portion of the journey. The second half of the Journal, July 6–December 22, 1849, is located at the University of Arkansas Library, Fayetteville.

LASSELLE, Stanislaus
  1937 "Diary." In *A History of Travel in America*. Seymour Dunbar, Ed. New York: Tudor Publishing Co.
Lasselle left Logansport, Indiana, on February 6, 1849, for his departure point at Fort Smith, Arkansas. He recalls meeting young J. W. Audubon who was setting out on his own memorable journey, aboard the steamboat *South America*. At Santa Fe, Lasselle and his companions decided to pack by way of the Gila Trail. They stayed close to the Knickerbocker Company, and Laselle often comments on the dissension within that group. He signed in at the Rancho Santa Ana del Chino on August 21, 1849. There are many gaps in the published version. The original and complete transcript can be found in the Charles B. Lasselle Papers, Indiana State Library.

NOBLE, Robert Watson
  1849 *Diary of a Journey from Chihuahua, Mexico to the Pueblo of San Jose, California, April 10–August 1, 1849*. MS in Parkman Family Papers, Bancroft Library.
Noble departed Chihuahua, Mexico on April 10, 1849, traveled north to Janos and came on the Southern Trail at Guadalupe Pass. Noble and fourteen trail hands were taking a large number of mules to California for sale to

miners. These men completed their journey with a minimum of trouble and in record time.

PANCOAST, Charles Edward
>1930 *A Quaker Forty-Niner.* Anna Paschall Hannum, Ed. Philadelphia: University of Pennsylvania Press.

Pancoast joined the Peoria, Illinois Company. His reminiscences tell us he started out upon the Santa Fe Trail out of Fort Leavenworth, Kansas, on April 29, 1849. After visiting Santa Fe, Pancoast followed the Southern Trail and arrived at the Mariposa mines on February 15, 1850. The author additionally details four years of wanderings in California before returning to his home in Philadelphia.

PATTISON, George K.
>1849 "Journal." In *Newark* (NJ) *Morning Eagle*: April 3 & 23, May 17 & 23, June 2 & 27, November 20 & 21, 1849.

Pattison was a member of the Havilah Mining Company of New York and traveled with George Sniffen and Woolsey Teller. His views of life on the trail complement other stories of this group's adventures.

POWELL, H. M. T.
>1931 *The Santa Fe Trail to California, 1849–1852. The Journal and drawings of H. M. T. Powell.* Douglas S. Watson, Ed. San Francisco: The Grabhorn Press.

Powell left Greenville, Illinois, on April 3, 1849, to follow the Santa Fe Trail. They picked up the Southern Trail at Socorro, arriving in San Diego on December 3. One of the best overland journals, Powell's daily entries give vivid accounts of his adventures. He also leaves some remarkable sketches of early landmarks. The original manuscript is located in the Bancroft Library.

POWNALL, Joseph
>1949 "From Louisiana to Mariposa." Robert Glass Cleland, Ed. In *Pacific Historical Review*. February: 24–32.

Pownall departed Keachie, Louisiana, on March 28, 1849, and arrived in Mariposa, California, on September 7, 1849. His travels took him through Texas to El Paso, where he turned southwest through Mexico toward Janos before joining the Southern Trail at Guadalupe Pass. After arriving at Warner's Ranch, Pownall and his companions walked to the mines by way of Santa Barbara, San Luis Obispo, and San Jose. Pownall's journal and letterbook can be found in the Huntington Library.

SIMMONS, Joseph R.
>1849 *Across the Plains from Misouri to California AD 1849.* MS in the Joint Collection, University of Missouri Western Historical Manuscript Collection-Columbia and State Historical Society of Missouri Manuscripts.

Simmons and thirty-two companions under the direction of former Governor John C. Edwards of Missouri, left Jefferson City on April 20, 1849, and followed the Santa Fe Trail into Las Vegas, New Mexico. They picked up the

Southern Trail and arrived in Agua Fria, California, on February 27, 1850. Simmons and Company were one group of emigrants who built a boat to carry their supplies down the Gila River. Simmons left an original diary and a 1902 rewritten version with notes.

SNIFFEN, George S.
> 1849 *Notes by the Camp-Fire; being a Narrative of an overland journey from the United States to California in the year 1849.* MS in a private collection.

George Sniffen's daily journal recounts his experiences as a member of the Havilah Mining Company of New York. His trip took some 260 days and covered 4,497 miles. The men started out on the Fort Smith-Santa Fe Trail on April 23, 1849, and joined the Southern Trail out of Santa Fe. They arrived in San Diego, California, on December 2. Woolsey Teller and George Pattison were also members of this association.

STRENTZEL, John Theophil
> 1890 *Autobiography.* MS in the Bancroft Library.

Strentzel and a company of 135 men left Dallas, Texas, on March 29, 1849, bound for El Paso. This group went through northern Mexico to pick up the Southern Trail at Guadalupe Pass. The company arrived in San Diego after a trip occupying eight months, in December 1849. Strentzel later established the Alhambra Orchards near Martinez. A daughter was married to John Muir, the naturalist.

STUART, Jacob
> 1849–1850 "Letters from the California Adventurers." In *Knoxville Register.* August 18 & 25, September 22, December 29, 1849; January 5, June 6, 1850.

Taking the Santa Fe Trail out of St. Joseph, Missouri, on July 20, 1849, a group went west under the leadership of General Alexander Outlaw Anderson, who was later elected to California's first Senate. The Stuart letters give a good report of the group's adventures on the road to California. The men arrived at the Santa Ana Rancho del Chino on March 26, 1850.

TELLER, Woolsey
> 1849–1850 *Letters from Woolsey Teller to his brother, Daniel W. Teller, in New York, written on the trail to California and from San Francisco, March 22, 1849, to May 31, 1850.* MS in the Coe Collection, Yale University Library.

Teller left New York on March 19, 1849, with the Havilah Mining Association, enroute for Fort Smith, Arkansas, the departure point for his overland journey. Teller's letters describe the journey as far as Santa Fe. Traveling companions, George Sniffen and George Pattison wrote other versions of the same trip.

THIBAULT, F. J.
> 1851 "Excerpts from the Journal of F. J. Thibault." In *Arkansas State Gazette and Democrat* (Little Rock). January 31, July 11, and May 9.

The complete journal has not come to light. However, Thibault, one of Robert

Brownlee's traveling companions, gives colorful descriptions of the Little Rock Company's adventures at Guadalupe Pass and on the Colorado River. He also left an excellent description of his return trip by way of Nicaragua.

WEED, L. N.
    1859 *Narrative of a journey to California in 1849*. MS in the Coe Collection, Yale University Library.

Weed sailed from New York on the *Norumbega* on March 8, 1849, and began the overland part of his journey in Texas. Upon arrival in El Paso, he turned north to intersect the Southern Trail near Hatch, New Mexico. Weed arrived in Stockton, California on October 26, 1849. Traveling companions D. D. Demarest and R. Beeching of the P. F. Smith Company also left diaries of the march.

WOOD, Harvey
    1955 *Personal Recollections*. John B. Goodman, Ed. Pasadena: Grant Dahlstrom. Reprinted from a pamphlet printed in 1896 by the Echo Job Printing Office at Angel's Camp, California.

Harvey Wood sailed from New York with the Kit Carson Association on February 13, 1849. After arriving in Corpus Christi, Texas, Wood and his companions chose to travel through Mexico, and sought a 500-mile shortcut through a barren area near Monclova in the state of Coahuila. They came on the Southern Trail near Guadalupe Pass, continued to California, and reached the Southern Mines on July 30, 1849.

WOODRUFF, Alden B.
    1849–1850 "Letters." In *Arkansas Democrat*, June 1, August 17 & December 21, 1849; January 25, 1850. In *Arkansas Gazette*, April 19 & 26, October 11, & November 29, 1850.

Woodruff wrote lengthy and colorful reports of his journey with the Little Rock Company and subsequent sojourn in the southern mines near Indian Bar on the Tuolumne River.

WOZENCRAFT, O. M.
    1882 "Through Northern Mexico in '49." In *California and Overland Monthly*. Volume VI:421–428. San Francisco.

The author sailed from New Orleans in February 1849, and embarked at Brownsville, Texas, to start his overland trek. This overlander joined the Southern Trail near Guadalupe Pass after coming north through Mexico. His story ends near Yuma, California. Dr. Wozencraft was one of three commissioners appointed by the Federal government to study California's Indian problem, determine policy and a course of action, and to negotiate treaties.

References Cited

The following code has been used for some frequently cited sources:

    DOJ   *Diary of an Overland Journey from Albuquerque to Santa Cruz, New Mexico, 1849.*
    MBH   *Memorial & Biographical History of Northern California.*
    DAR   D.A.R. of California.

Abbott, John Stevens Cabot
    1859   *South and North; or, Impressions Received During a Trip to Cuba and the South.* New York: Abbey & Abbot.

Aldrich, Lorenzo D.
    1950   *A Journal of the Overland Route to California and the Gold Mines.* Los Angeles: Dawson's Book Shop.

Archibald, Mr. & Mrs. Henry
    1981   Residents of Bonkle, Scotland. Personal interview.

Arkansas. A Guide to the State
    1941   Arkansas Writers' Project. New York: Hastings House.

Arkansas History Commission
    1913   *Bulletin of Information #6.*

Arkansas *House Journal*, 1843.

Audubon, John Woodhouse
    1906   *Audubon's Western Journal: 1849–1850. Being the MS record of a trip from New York to Texas, and an overland journey through New Mexico and the gold-fields of California.* Frank Heywood Hodder, Ed. Cleveland: The Arthur H. Clark Company.

Bachelor, Mrs. Thelma Halterman
    1981   Personal Recollections.

Bancroft, Hubert Howe
    1886   *History of California.* Volumes III, IV, V. San Francisco: A. L. Bancroft & Company, Publishers.

Bartlett, John Russell
- 1854   *Personal Narrative of Explorations and Incidents in Texas, New Mexico, California, Sonora, and Chihuahua, etc.* Two volumes. New York: Appleton & Company.

Beck, Warren A., and Inez D. Haase
- 1974   *Historical Atlas of California.* Norman: University of Oklahoma Press.

Bennett, Swannee
- 1982   Research Curator, Arkansas Territorial Restoration. Personal interview.

Bieber, Ralph P., Ed.
- 1937   *Southern Trails to California in 1849.* Volume V. Glendale, California: The Arthur H. Clark Company.
- 1938   *Exploring Southwestern Trails 1846–1854.* Volume VII. Glendale, California: The Arthur H. Clark Company.

Blunt, Phineas
- 1849–1852   *Notes of travel from New York to the Gold Region California in the year Eighteen hundred and forty-nine, February 5, 1849–January 1852.* MS in the Bancroft Library.

Book of British Birds
- 1973   London: Drive Publications Limited.

Botkin, B. A.
- 1944   *A Treasury of American Folklore.* New York: Crown Publishers.

Branch, L. C.
- 1881   *History of Stanislaus County, California.* San Francisco: Elliott & Moore.

Brotherton, I. N. "Jack"
- 1982   *River Towns & Ferries.* Santa Cruz: Western Tanager Press.

Brown, Rev. Peter
- 1859   *Historical Sketches of the Parish of Cambusnethan.* Wishaw, Scotland: David Johnson.

Browne, J. Ross
- 1972   *A Dangerous Journey.* Ferol Egan, Ed. Ashland: Lewis Osborne.

Brownlee Clark & Company
- 1851a   *General Ledger for Store.*
- 1851b   *Ledger for Mariposa Battalion.* Originals in Sacramento Area State Parks Collections. Microfilm CF 77 in the Bancroft Library.

Brownlee, Robert
- 1849   September 16 letter from San Felipe, California. In *Arkansas State Gazette & Democrat*. November 30, 1849.
- 1849   December 1 letter from Agua Fria, California. In *Arkansas State Gazette & Democrat*, February 22, 1850.
- 1850   January 4 letter from Stockton, California. In *Arkansas State Gazette & Democrat*, March 22, 1850.
- 1850   January 27 letter from Stockton, California. In *Arkansas State Gazette & Democrat*, March 29, 1850.
- 1850   Advertisement. In *Arkansas State Gazette & Democrat*, April 12, 1850.
- 1889   Interview in the *Los Angeles Herald*, January 4.

Bunnell, Lafayette Houghton
- 1911   *Discovery of the Yosemite and the Indian War of 1851 which led to that event.* Los Angeles: G. W. Gerlicher.

Burleigh, J. H. S.
- 1960   *A Church History of Scotland.* Toronto: Oxford University Press.

Burney, James
- 1851   James Burney to Peter H. Burnett, Agua Fria, January 13. In *California Legislature, Senate Journal*, Second session, 603–605.
- 1853   Memorial of James Burney. In *California Legislature, Senate Journal*, Document 43, dated March 3, 1853.

Bynum, Linley
- 1934   "The Record Book of the Rancho Santa Ana del Chino." In *Historical Society of California*. Volume XVI: 1–55.

California Census
- 1870   Mariposa County.
- 1972   *Index to the 1850 Census of the State of California.* Alan P. Bowman, Ed. Baltimore: The Genealogical Publishing Co., Inc.

Cambusnethan Parish (Scotland) Census, 1841–1891.

Cambusnethan Parish Records. Parochial Registers, County of Lanark, Scotland: 1634–1854 births; 1634–1819 marriages; 1649–1652 and 1742–1750 deaths.

Caulfield, S. F. A.
- 1972   *Encyclopedia of Victorian Needlework.* Volume II. New York: Dover Publication, Inc.

Chamberlin, Newell D.
- 1936   *The Call of Gold: True Tales on the Gold Road to Yosemite.* Mariposa: Gazette Press.

Chamberlin, William H.
 1945 "From Lewisburg (PA) to California in 1849. Notes from the Diary of William H. Chamberlin." Lansing B. Bloom, Ed. In *New Mexico Historical Review*. Volume XX:24–57, 144–180, 239–278, 336–357.

Clark, Arthur H.
 1911 *The Clipper Ship Era 1843–1869*. New York: G. P. Putnam Sons, 1911.

Clarke, Asa Bennett
 1852 *Travels in Mexico and California: Comprising a Journal of a Tour from Brazos Santiago, through Central Mexico, by way of Monterey, Chihuahua, the country of the Apaches, and the River Gila to the Mining Districts of California*. Boston: Wright & Hasty's Steam Press.

Clemens, Samuel Langhorne
 1957 *Life on the Mississippi*. New York: Hill & Wang.

Coffey, Jesse, and George Hooper
 1972 *Bacon and Beans from a Gold Pan*. New York: Doubleday & Company, Inc.

Collins, Carvell
 1949 *Sam Ward in the Gold Rush*. Stanford University Press.

Cooke, Lt. Col. P. St. George, U.S. Army Corps of Engineers
 1848 *Report of Lieutenant Colonel P. St. George Cooke of his March from Santa Fe, New Mexico to San Diego, Upper California*. Thirtieth Congress, First Session. Ex. Doc. No. 41.

Corcoran, May Stanislaus
 The Land of Hidden Gold. Undated MS in the Mariposa County History Center.

Couts, Cave J.
 1932 *From San Diego to the Colorado in 1849. The Journal and Maps of Cave J. Couts*. William McPherson, Ed. Los Angeles: Arthur M. Ellis.
 1961 *Hepah, California! The Journal of Cave Johnson Couts from Monterey, Nuevo Leon, Mexico to Los Angeles, California During the Years 1848–1849*. Henry F. Dobyns, Ed. Tucson: Arizona Pioneers' Historical Society.

Coy, Owen Cochran
 1929 *The Great Trek*. Los Angeles: The Powell Publishing Company.

Crampton, C. Gregory
    1941   *The Opening of the Mariposa Mining Region, 1849–1859, with Particular Reference to the Mexican Land Grant of John Charles Fremont.* Ph.D. dissertation, University of California, Berkeley.
    1975   *The Mariposa Indian War 1850–1851. The Diaries of Robert Eccleston: The California Gold Rush, Yosemite, and the High Sierra.* Salt Lake City: University of Utah Press.

Cringean, Margaret
    1982   Resident of Bonkle, Scotland. Personal interview.

Dana, Richard Henry, Jr.
    1966   *To Cuba and Back.* Carbondale and Edwardsville: Southern Illinois University Press.

D.A.R. of California
    1936   *Records of the Families of California Pioneers.* Volume IV: 73–76, 271–274.

Davis, Charles
    1853   *Letters from Quartzburg, California.* January 5 and 6, June 6. In the Charles Davis Collection. Beinecke Rare Book and Manuscript Library, Yale University.
    1854   *Letter from Mariposa County, 2-1/2 miles from Quartzburg.* In the Charles Davis Collection.

Delgado, James P.
    1979/80   "No Longer a Buoyant Ship." In *California History.* Volume LVIII: 316–325. California Historical Society.

Derbec, Etienne
    1964   *A French Journalist in the Gold Rush.* A. P. Nasatir, Ed. Georgetown, California: Talisman Press.

Diary of an Overland Journey from Albuquerque to Santa Cruz, New Mexico.
    1849   MS in the Bancroft Library. Formerly known as the Diary of Caspar Ricks.

Donaldson, Gordon
    1976   *The Scots Overseas.* Westport, Conn.: Greenwood Press Publishers.

Dumke, Glenn S. Ed.
    1945   *Mexican Gold Trail: The Journal of a Forty-Niner.* San Marino: The Huntington Library.
    1980   Personal Interview.

Dunbar, John G.
    1966   *The Historic Architecture of Scotland.* London: B. T. Batsford, Ltd.

Dunbar, Seymour
    1937   *A History of Travel in America*. New York: Tudor Publishing Company.

Durivage, John
    1937   "Through Mexico to California, Letters and Journals of John E. Durivage." In *Southern Trails to California in 1849*. Ralph P. Bieber, Ed. Volume V:159–255. Glendale, California: The Arthur H. Clark Company.

Easterby, A. Y.
    1875   *Indenture. A. Y. Easterby/Robert Brownlee*. October 18, 1875–October 1876. California State Library, Sacramento.

Eccleston, Robert
    1849–1854   *Diaries*. Ten volumes. Bancroft Library.

Edgar, Wm. F., M.D.
    1893   "Old Fort Miller." In *Southern California Quarterly*. Volume III:25–26.

Edwards, E. I.
    1961   *Lost Oases Along the Carrizo*. Los Angeles: The Westernlore Press.

Eldredge, Zoeth Skinner.
    c. 1915.   *History of California*. Volume III. New York: The Century History Co.

Elias, Solomon Philip
    1924   *Stories of Stanislaus. A Collection of Stories on the History and Achievements of Stanislaus County*. Modesto, California.

Elliott, Wallace W.
    1882   *History of Fresno County, California*. San Francisco.
    1883   *History of San Bernardino and San Diego Counties, California*. Riverside, California: Riverside Museum Press. 1965 reprint of the 1883 edition.

Emory, Lt. Col. W. H.
    1848   *Notes of a Military Reconnaissance from Fort Leavenworth, in Missouri, to San Diego, in California*. Thirtieth Congress. First Session. Ex. Doc. 41.
    1857   *Report of William H. Emory*. Volume I. Thirty-fourth Congress, First Session. Ex. Doc. 135.

Emparan, Madie Brown
    1968   *The Vallejos of California*. The Gleeson Library Associates of San Francisco.

Evans, George W. B.
   1945   *Mexican Gold Trail, The Journal of a Forty-Niner*. Glenn S. Dumke, Ed. San Marino, California: The Huntington Library.

Fagan, Dr. James
   1849   Letter, 20 miles from Santa Fe. In the *Arkansas State Democrat*, August 17, 1849.

Ferguson, John L., and J. H. Atkinson
   1966   *Historic Arkansas*. Little Rock: Arkansas History Commission.

Fletcher, John Gould
   1947   *Arkansas*. Chapel Hill: The University of North Carolina Press.

Foote, H. S., Ed.
   1888   *Pen Pictures from the Garden of the World or Santa Clara County, California*. Chicago: The Lewis Publishing Company.

Foreman, Grant
   1934   *The Five Civilized Tribes*. Norman: University of Oklahoma Press.
   1968   *Marcy and the Gold Seekers; the Journal of Captain R. B. Marcy, with an Account of the Gold Rush over the Southern Route*. Norman: University of Oklahoma Press. First Printing, 1939.

Galloway, Edwin (C. E. G.)
   1849   June 20 letter from Santa Fe. In *Arkansas State Democrat*, August 31, 1849.

Gates, Paul W.
   1958   "Adjudication of Spanish-Mexican Land Claims in California." In *Huntington Library Quarterly*. May: 213–236.

Gerstäcker, Friedrich
   1845   *The Regulators in Arkansas*. Translation by Leroy Higgins.
   1854   *Wild Sports in the Far West. The Narrative of a German Wanderer beyond the Mississippi, 1837–1843*. Edna Steeves and Harrison R. Steeves, Eds. Reprinted from the English translation of 1854. Durham: Duke University Press.

Gilbert, Bil
   1983   *Westering Man: The Life of Joseph Walker*. Norman: University of Oklahoma Press.

Givens, Robert R.
   1849–1859   *Letters to Family*. MS in the Bancroft Library.

Green, Robert B.
    1955   *On the Arkansas Route to California in 1849. The Journal of Robert B. Green of Lewisburg, Pennsylvania.* J. Orin Oliphant, Ed. Lewisburg, Pennsylvania: Bucknell University Press.

Gregg, Josiah
    1844   *Commerce of the Prairies or the journal of a Santa Fe trader during eight expeditions across the great western prairies, and residence of nearly nine years in northern Mexico.* Volumes I & II. New York: Henry G. Langley.

Gregory, Jack, and Rennard Strickland
    1967   *Sam Houston with the Cherokees 1829–1833.* Austin: University of Texas Press.

Gregory, Tom
    1912   *History of Solano and Napa Counties California.* Los Angeles: Historic Record Company.

Gudde, Irwin G.
    1969   *California Place Names.* Berkeley: University of California Press.

Guinn, James Miller
    1909–1910   "The Sonoran Immigration." In *Historical Society of Southern California.* Volume VIII: 31–36.

Hall, Dr. Thomas B.
    1971   *Medicine on the Santa Fe Trail.* Dayton, Ohio: Morningside Book Shop.

Hamlin, Talbot
    1964   *Greek Revival Architecture in America.* New York: Dover Publications.

Harris, Benjamin Butler
    1960   *The Gila Trail: The Texas Argonauts and the California Gold Rush.* Edited and annotated by Richard H. Dillon. Norman: University of Oklahoma Press.

Hayes, Judge Benjamin
    1849–1850   *Journey overland from Socorro to Warner's Ranch from October 31, 1849–January 14, 1850.* MS in the Bancroft Library.
    1929   *Pioneer Notes from the Diaries of Judge Benjamin Hayes.* Marjorie Tisdale Wolcott, Ed. Los Angeles: Privately printed by Marjorie Tisdale Wolcott.

Hazard, Samuel
    1871   *Cuba with Pen and Pencil.* Hartford, Conn: Hartford Publishing Company.

Heizer, Robert
  1978 *Handbook of the North American Indians*. California, Volume VIII. Washington, Smithsonian Institution.
Holliday, J. S.
  1981 *The World Rushed In*. New York: Simon and Schuster.
Hollon, W. Eugene
  1955 *Beyond the Cross Timbers: The Travels of Randolph B. Marcy, 1812–1887*. Norman: University of Oklahoma Press.
Hoover, Mildren Brooke, Hero Eugene Rensch, Ethel Grace Rensch
  1962 *Historic Spots in California*. Stanford University Press.
Houston, J. M.
  1948 "Village Planning in Scotland, 1745–1845." In *Advancement of Science*, 129–132.
Hunt, Marguerite
  1926 *History of Solano County, California*. Chicago: J. W. Clark Publishing Co.
Hurd, Henry M., et al.
  1916 *The Institutional Care of the Insane in the United States and Canada*. Four volumes. Baltimore: The John Hopkins Press.
Hussman, George C., M. Ag.S.
  1912 "Viticulture of Napa County." In *History of Solano and Napa Counties*, 147–149.
Hutchings, J. M.
  1888 *In the Heart of the Sierras: The Yosemite Valley, Both Historical and Descriptive: And Scenes by the Way*. Oakland: Pacific Press Publishing House.
Invitation to National Ball
  1855 From the archives of the California Historical Society. State House, Vallejo.
Irvine, Leigh H.
  1915 *History of Humboldt County, California*. Los Angeles: Historic Record Co.
Jaeger, Edmund C.
  1967 *The North American Deserts*. Stanford University Press.
Johnson, J. Neely
  1851 "J. Neely Johnson to J. G. Marvin." In *California House Journal*, 375. Exhibit A.
Jones, Dallas L.
  1970 *The Background and Motives of Scottish Emigration to the United States of America in the period 1815–1861, with special*

reference to emigrant correspondence. Ph.D. Thesis. University of Edinburgh.

Journals of the Legislature, State of California, 1851–1854.

Kanaga, Mrs. Tillie
    1901   *History of Napa County California.* Oakland.

Kennan, Clara
    1950   "Arkansas's Old State House." In *Arkansas Historical Quarterly.* Volume IX: 33–42.

Kidder, Alfred Vincent
    1962   *An Introduction to the Study of Southwestern Archaeology with a Preliminary Account of the Excavation at Pecos.* New Haven: Yale University Press. First Printing, 1924.

King, A. D.
    1941   "Trip to the Gold Fields." In *Arkansas Gazette,* Sunday Magazine Section. Twenty-four weekly installments, starting January 19, 1941.

Kroeber, A. L.
    1953   *Handbook of the Indians of California.* Berkeley: California Book Company, Ltd.

Lamont, Annie (Brownlee)
    1849   *Copy Book.* Little Rock, Pulaski County. MS in the Sutter's Fort Pioneer Collection, Box 345, Folder 18. California State Library, Sacramento.

Lapp, Rudolph M.
    1977   *Blacks in Gold Rush California.* Yale University Press.

Lasselle, Stanislaus
    1851   *Letter from Jacksonville, California.* Manuscript in the Charles B. Lasselle papers. Indiana State Library.

Lavicka, William L., Ed.
    1977   *The Art of Architecture, Engineering and Construction in 1889, Masonry, Carpentry, Joinery.* Chicago: Chicago Review Press.

Leach, Frank A.
    1918   *Recollections of a Newspaperman.* San Francisco: Samuel Levinson.

Levitt, Ian, and Christopher Smout
    1979   *The State of the Scottish Working-class in 1843. A statistical and spatial enquiry based on data from the Poor Law Commission Report of 1844.* Edinburgh: Scottish Academic Press, Inc.

Lindsay, Diana Elaine
    1973   *Our Historic Desert*. San Diego, California: Copley Press, Inc.

Lockhart, D. G.
    1980   "The Planned Villages." In *The Making of the Scottish Countryside*. Montreal: McGill-Queens University Press. M. L. Parry and T. R. Slater, eds.

Lyons, W. H.
    1852   Report by W. H. Lyons. In *California Assembly Journal*. Third Session, 372–374.

McCullough, David
    1975   "Steam Road to Eldorado." In *American Heritage*. June: 58–59, 94–95.

McKittrick, Myrtle
    1944   *Vallejo Son of California*. Portland, Oregon: Binford and Mort.

McReynolds, Edwin C.
    1957   *The Seminoles*. Norman: University of Oklahoma Press.

Marcy, Randolph B.
    1863.   *The Prairie Traveler, A Hand-book for Overland Expeditions*. London: Trübner and Co.

Mariposa County (California) Records: Court of Sessions Minutes, Volume I; Deeds Book Y; District Court Minutes, Book I; Judgments, District Court; Records Books I & II; Supervisors' Minutes Book A.

Mariposa Quartz Convention
    1851   Document dated June 25, 1851. In the collection of the California Historical Society.

Marryat, Frank
    1952   *Mountains and Molehills or Recollections of a Burnt Journal*. Reprinted in facsimile from the first American edition of 1855. Stanford University Press.

Menefee, Campbell Augustus
    1873   *Historical and Descriptive Sketch Book of Napa, Sonoma, Lake and Mendocino Counties*. Napa City: Reporter Publishing House.

Memorial and Biographical History of the Counties of Fresno, Tulare, and Kern, California
    1891   Chicago: The Lewis Publishing Company.

Memorial and Biographical History of Northern California
    1891   Chicago: The Lewis Publishing Company.

Middleton, J. W.
 1883   *History of the Regulators and Moderators and the Shelby County war in 1841 & 1842, in the Republic of Texas*. Fort Worth, Texas: Loving Publishing Company.

Miller, Donald C.
 1978   *Ghost Towns of California*. Boulder, Colorado: Pruett Publishing Company.

Mitchell, Annie R.
 1941   *King of the Tulares and other Tales from the San Joaquin Valley, 1772–1852*. Visalia, California: Times-Delta Press.

Monoghan, Jay
 1966   *Australians and the Gold Rush*. Berkeley: University of California Press.

Muñoz, Jeanne
 1980   *Political Middlemanship and the Double Bind: James D. Savage and the Fresno River Reservation*. Ph.D. dissertation, University of California, Riverside.

Munro Fraser, J. P.
 1879   *History of Solano County*. San Francisco: Wood, Alley & Co.

Napa County (California) Records: Deed Books D, K, 34, and 231.

Napa and Solano County (California) Directory, 1871–1872.

Nash, Gerald D.
 1964   *State Government and Economic Development*. Berkeley: University of California.

Neimeier, Jean Gilbreath
 1968   *The Panama Story*. Portland, Oregon: Metropolitan Press.

Oakley, Francile Battenburg
 1947   "Arkansas' Golden Army of '49." In *Arkansas Historical Quarterly*. Volume VI: 1–85.

Owen, Wilfred, and Ezra Brown
 1967   *Wheels*. New York: Time, Inc.

Palmer, Lyman L.
 1881   *History of Napa and Lake Counties, California*. San Francisco: Slocum, Bowen & Co., Publishers.

Palmer, T. G.
 1851   "T. G. Palmer to his Father, Hart's Ranch, California. January 16, 1851." In *Discovery of Yosemite*, L. H. Bunnell, 1911:30–33.

Pancoast, Charles Edward
 1930   *A Quaker Forty-niner: The Adventures of Charles Edward Pancoast on the American Frontier*. Anna Paschall Hannum, Ed. Philadelphia: University of Pennsylvania Press.

Pattison, George
 1849   "En Route to California." In *Newark* (NJ) *Morning Eagle*, April 23, 1849.

Peterson, Charles S.
 1982   Personal Communication.

Pope, William F.
 1895   *Early Days in Arkansas*. Arranged and edited by his son, Dunbar H. Pope.

Powell, H. M. T.
 1931   *The Santa Fe Trail to California, 1849–1852. The Journal and Drawings of H. M. T. Powell*. Douglas S. Watson, Ed. San Francisco: The Book Club of California.

Pulaski County (Arkansas) Records: Deed Books B, D, N, O, W, 263; Tax Records 1848–1852; Census 1840 & 1850.

Rasmussen, Louis J.
 1965   *San Francisco Passenger Lists*. Four volumes. San Francisco: Historical Records.

Robinson, Lucy K.
 1980   Director, Old State House, Arkansas. Personal Communication.

Ross, Margaret Smith
 1955   "The McHenry Family, Pulaski County Pioneers." In *Pulaski County Historical Review*. Volume III: 3–9.

Rothman, David J.
 1971   *The Discovery of the Asylum*. Boston: Little Brown and Company.

Russell, Carl P.
 1968   *One Hundred Years in Yosemite*. Reprint of the 1931 edition with added chronology by the Yosemite Natural History Association. Berkeley: University of California Press.

Sargent, Shirley
 1980   *Seeking the Elephant, 1849. James Mason Hutchings' Journal of his Overland Trek to California*. Glendale, California: The Arthur H. Clark Company.

Sawyer, Eugene T.
 1922   *History of Santa Clara County, California*. Los Angeles: Historic Record Co.

Schroeder, Bertha
    1979   Historian in Mariposa County. Personal interview.

Shouse, Sarah N.
    1977   "None Dream But of Success. The Story of a Young Tennessean's Journey to the Gold Fields of California." In *Tennessee Historical Quarterly*. Volume XXXVI: 512–523.

Sinclair, Sir John
    1792   *The Statistical Account of Scotland. Drawn up from the Communications of the Ministers of the Different Parishes*. Volume XII: 568–574. Edinburgh: William Creech.

Slater, T. R.
    1980   "The Mansion and Policy." In *The Making of the Scottish Countryside*. Montreal: McGill-Queen's University Press.

Slaven, Anthony
    1975   *The Development of the West of Scotland*. London: Routledge & Kegan Paul.

Smith, Frank Merriweather
    1883   *San Francisco Vigilance Committee of '56 with some interesting sketches of events succeeding 1846*. San Francisco: Barry, Baird & Co., Printers and Publishers.

Smout, T. Christopher
    1969   *A History of the Scottish People 1560–1830*. London: Collins.
    1970   "The Landowner and the Planned Village in Scotland, 1730–1830." In *Scotland in the Age of Improvement*. N. T. Phillipson and Rosalind Mitchison, Eds. Edinburgh: Edinburgh University Press.
    1981   Personal Communication.

Sniffen, George S.
    1849   *Notes by the Campfire; being a Narrative of an overland journey from the United States to California in the year 1849*. MS in a private collection.

Solano County (California) Records: Deed Books F, G, H, I, J, K, L.

Steuart, Sir Henry Seton
    1785   *Tack between Henry Seton Steuart Esq. of Allanton and William Brownlie for 999 years from Whitsunday*.
    1792   *Tack between Henry Steuart Esq. of Allanton and Alexander Brounlee in Bonkyll for 999 years from Whitsunday*.
    1828   *The Planter's Guide*. London: T. Cadell Strand.

Stevenson, W. W.
    1849   November 27 letter from Los Angeles. In *Arkansas State Gazette & Democrat*, March 15, 1850.

Stokes, I. N. Phelps
  1915 *Iconography of Manhattan Island, 1498–1909.* Volume V: 1737. New York: Arno Press.

Strong, William
  1929 *Aboriginal Society in Southern California.* Berkeley: University of California Publications in American Archaeology and Ethnology.

Summerfield, Charles (pseud. Alfred Arrington)
  1847 *The Desperadoes of the South-West: containing an account of the Cane-Hill Murders, together with the Lives of Several of the Most Notorious Regulators and Moderators of that Region.* New York: George P. Putnam & Co.

Taylor, Bayard
  1857 *Eldorado, or, Adventures in the Path of an Empire.* New York: George P. Putnam & Co.

Taylor, Orville W.
  1958 *Negro Slavery in Arkansas.* Durham: Duke University Press.

Thibault, F. J.
  1850 September 30 letter from Indian Bar, California. In *Arkansas State Gazette & Democrat*, November 22, 1850.
  1851 "Excerpts from the journal of H. J. Thibault." In *Arkansas State Gazette & Democrat*, January 31, July 11, May 9.

Thompson & West
  1880 *History of Los Angeles County.* Oakland.

Tinling, Marion
  1982 "Bloomerism Comes to California." In *California History*. Volume LXI: 18–25.

Tomes, Robert
  1855 *Panama in 1855.* New York: Harper & Brothers.

United States State Department
  1820–1897 *Passenger lists at New York.* ZI–131, Reel 29. January 20–May 17, 1836.

Vallejo, M. G.
  1851 "Bond of M. G. Vallejo, John B. Frisbie, Salvador Vallejo, J. M. Estill, and Robert Allen, together with their Affidavits to the amount each is worth." In *California Senate Journal*, 709–712.

Vandor, Paul E.
  1919 *History of Fresno County, California with Biographical Sketches of the Leading Men and Women of the County Who Have Been*

Identified with its Growth and Development from the Early Days to the Present. Two volumes. Los Angeles: Historic Record Co.

Walker and Stanton
1865   *In the Case of the Settlers on the "Soscol Ranche," in the State of California, as against the Purchasers under the Vallejo Claim.* Washington, D.C.: Gibson Brothers. Document in the Bancroft Library.

Wallace, William J.
1978   "Northern Valley Yokuts." In *Handbook of North American Indians*. Volume 8. Washington: Smithsonian Institution.

Waugh, Elizabeth Culbertson
1967   *North Carolina's Capital*. Chapel Hill: University of North Carolina Press.

West, Virginia
1941   *Writers' Program*. New York: Oxford University Press.

Whipple, Lt. Amiel Weeks
1961   *The Whipple Report, Journal of an Expedition from San Diego, California, to the Rio Colorado, from September 11 to December 11, 1849*. E. I. Edwards, Ed. Los Angeles: Westernlore Press. Reprint of 1851 Senate Ex. Doc. 19.

Winchester, Rev. James
1937   "The Muirkirk of Cambusnethan." In the *Wishaw Press and Advertizer*, August 20 and 27.
1937   "Bonkle Church from 1800." In the *Wishaw Press and Advertizer*, September 3.

Wood, Raymund F.
1954   *California's Agua Fria, the Early History of Mariposa County*. Fresno: Academy Library Guild.

Woodruff, Alden M.
1849   May 3 letter from camp near Cross Timbers. In *Arkansas State Democrat*, June 1, 1849.
1849   November 18 letter from Curtis Creek, California. In *Arkansas State Democrat*, January 25, 1850.
1850   February 6 letter from Curtis Creek, California. In *Arkansas State Gazette & Democrat*, April 19, 26, 1850.
1850   August 6 letter from Indian Bar, California. In *Arkansas State Gazette & Democrat*, October 11, 1850.

References Cited   237

The following newspapers are referenced:

Arkansas Banner (Little Rock) 1849
Arkansas Gazette (Little Rock) 1849, 1850, 1940, 1941
Arkansas State Democrat (Little Rock) 1848, 1849
Arkansas State Gazette & Democrat (Little Rock) 1850, 1851
Los Angeles Herald 1889
Los Angeles Times 1905
Mariposa Democrat (California) 1857
Mariposa Gazette (California) 1866
Napa County Recorder (California) 1882, 1886, 1887, 1888
Napa County Reporter (California) 1869, 1870, 1872, 1882
Napa Register (California) 1864–1866, 1873–1880, 1897
Newark Morning Eagle (New Jersey) 1849
Pennsylvania Freeman (Philadelphia) 1850
Solano Republican (California) 1909
Wishaw Press and Advertizer (Wishaw, Scotland) 1937

Index

Agua Fria, California: description and history, 109–110, 133–134; international character of, 119, 140; law and order in, 119–122, 141–142; gambling at, 118–119, 134, 139, 140
Anza Borrego Desert State Park: emigrant trail in, 100
Apache Indians: trade with, 61–62, 79; raid on Santa Cruz, 65, 85
Apache Pass Trail, Arizona, 208
Arkansas Territorial Restoration, Little Rock, 45–47

Blacks: Arkansas, 32, 44; California, 136–138
Brownlee, Annie Lamont (1834–1901): wedding of, 163; visits Yosemite, 174, 190; in Panama, 159, 163; mentioned, 39, 50, 152, 161, 184
Brownlee Clark & Company: established, 117, 118, 134; evening at, 118–119; sales and supplies, 118, 139–140, 145; sutler to Mariposa Battalion, 125, 144–145; sold, 128, 147

Clarksville Company, 63, 78, 79, 80
Cooke's Peak, New Mexico, 79–80

Farragut, Admiral David G., 184, 185
Fort Smith–Santa Fe Trail, 52, 70, 72

Frémont, John Charles, 124, 133, 142
Frontier life, Arkansas, 28, 37–38, 47–49

Gila Trail, 70, 208
Glorieta Pass, New Mexico, 59, 75–76
Gold discovery, California, 51, 53, 70
Gold mining: described, 109–110; types of, 132–133
Guadalupe Pass, New Mexico, 64, 81–84

Kearny, Gen. Stephen Watts: at Glorietta Pass, 60, 75; and Gila Trail, 70, 208

Land grants, California, 188–189
Law and order: Agua Fria, California, 119–122, 141–142; Arkansas, 29–30, 38, 39–40
Los Angeles, California: arrival at, 94, 103; blacks in, 137
Little Rock Company: departure, 52, 53, 72; articles of association, 70–71; route of, 72–73, 208

Mariposa and Indian War, 124–126, 142–145
Mariposa and Indian War Scrip: value of, 125, 160, 167; bonding of, 129, 130

McVicar & Company, Little Rock, Arkansas, 40, 41
McVicar, James: appointed warden, 32; biography, 43–44; mining interests, 106; Captain of Little Rock Company, 54, 70, 85; storekeeper, 132; 22–45, 67–114 *passim*
Miners' Code, 119, 140–141
Miners: success, 110, 132–133; generosity, 122, 140; health of, 122, 134, 140
Mining. *See* gold mining
Mount Holly Cemetery, Little Rock: burials, 41, 43, 161; described, 44

Old State House, Arkansas. *See* State House, Arkansas

Pacheco Pass, California: travel over, 96–97
Panama crossing: 141, 150–151, 159–160, 163–164

Quartz mining, 119, 124, 133, 134

Railroads: Petersburg & Roanoke, 26; Wishaw-Coltness, 25–26; California Pacific, 177, 192–193
Rancho Bolsa Nueva y Moro Cojo, California, 104
Rancho San Bernardino, Arizona and Sonora, 84
Rancho San Ysidro, California, 104
Rancho Santa Ana del Chino, California, 101; *Record Book:* statistics on, 102–103, 197; mentioned, 93
Rancho period, California, 90–91, 183

San Juan Bautista Mission, California, 95
San Miguel Archangel Mission, California: murder at, 94–95, 104
San Miguel del Bado, New Mexico, 76
San Xavier del Bac, Arizona, 65, 85
Santa Cruz, Sonora, 65, 84–85
Santa Fe, New Mexico, 60–61, 76–77
Slavery: Arkansas, 32, 44; California, 136–137
Southern Trail, 71, 207–208
State House, Arkansas, 22, 40–41
State House, North Carolina, 20, 21–22, 26

Tennessee Company, 61–80 *passim*
Tin mining, California, 92, 101

Vigilance Committee: hangings, 120, 141